Obligation and the Fact
of Sense

Obligation and the Fact of Sense

Bryan Lueck

EDINBURGH
University Press

Edinburgh University Press is one of the leading university presses in the UK. We publish academic books and journals in our selected subject areas across the humanities and social sciences, combining cutting-edge scholarship with high editorial and production values to produce academic works of lasting importance. For more information visit our website: edinburghuniversitypress.com

Edinburgh University Press Ltd
The Tun – Holyrood Road
12(2f) Jackson's Entry
Edinburgh EH8 8PJ

Typeset in 10/13 Meridien by
IDSUK (DataConnection) Ltd, and
printed and bound in Great Britain.

A CIP record for this book is available from the British Library

ISBN 978 1 4744 4272 5 (hardback)
ISBN 978 1 4744 4275 6 (webready PDF)
ISBN 978 1 4744 4274 9 (epub)

Contents

Acknowledgements

During the writing of this book I have benefited from the intellectual inspiration and encouragement of many people. I cannot even imagine having written this book without the help of Al Lingis and Charles Scott, both of whom, in their very different ways, forced me to rethink everything I thought I knew about ethics. My good friend Michael Deere helped to sharpen my understanding of the work of Jean-Luc Nancy over the course of years of conversations. My colleagues and friends in the wonderfully diverse Philosophy Department at Southern Illinois University Edwardsville have broadened my philosophical horizons, and I am certain that this book is better for it. Carol Macdonald at Edinburgh University Press provided me with so much helpful advice as she guided this project to completion. And Lucian Stone's support has been indispensable; it was he more than anyone else who convinced me that my approach to the question of obligation was important and that it deserved a book-length treatment. I also benefited from the constant encouragement of my brother Ryan Lueck and my mother Mary Lueck, both of whom inquired into the status of my book nearly every time we spoke. And of course I cannot neglect to mention the contributions of Wheatie, Geneviève, Diderik and João-Estêvão (my cats) and Oskar (my dog), all of whom gave me much to smile about as I struggled to give expression to the ideas in this book. Finally, I am grateful beyond words to my partner Jessa Farquhar, who has made my life better in every way.

Dedicated to the memory of Juliana Eimer

Introduction: Ethics in the Sheep's Shop

'"What is it you want to buy?" the Sheep said at last, looking up for a moment from her knitting.' Needless to say, Alice had not expected this question: only a few moments earlier, she had been in the wood helping the White Queen straighten her shawl. All of a sudden a gust of wind blew the shawl across a little brook. As soon as they retrieved it on the other side, the White Queen began bleating, and before Alice knew what had happened, she found herself in a shop responding to the sheep's question. 'I don't *quite* know yet,' Alice replied. She decided to have a look around the shop to see if there was anything she might want to buy. But this task turned out to be much more difficult than she had imagined, for 'whenever she looked hard at any shelf, to make out exactly what it had on it, that particular shelf was always quite empty, though the others round it were crowded as full as they could hold'. There was one thing in particular that had caught Alice's attention and that she wanted to get a better look at. She could not make out exactly what the thing was, though, as it seemed always to be changing its form, looking at one point like a doll and at another like a workbox. Whenever she tried to get a closer look, the 'large bright thing' always appeared on the shelf above the one she was looking at. 'Things flow about here so!' Alice exclaimed.[1] The thing she wanted to grasp was always outside its place, no matter what place that was. And the place where the thing was supposed to be was always empty.[2] Undeterred, Alice formulated what seemed to her a foolproof plan:

'I'll follow it up to the very top shelf of all. It'll puzzle it to go through the ceiling, I expect!'

But even this plan failed: the 'thing' went through the ceiling as quietly as possible, as if it were quite used to it.[3]

Philosophical Reflection on Obligation

Alice's adventure in the Sheep's Shop is in many ways the adventure of philosophical reflection on obligation. The history of this reflection begins in earnest with the natural law theorists of the early seventeenth century, and especially with Francisco Suarez and Hugo Grotius, who articulated a conception of ethical experience and of practical reasoning that was sharply at odds with the older natural law tradition associated most closely with the work of Thomas Aquinas. For the older tradition, practical deliberation was oriented entirely by a perfectionist conception of the good. Each being, in accordance with God's eternal law, had its own distinctive end, which constituted its ideal state or perfection. To reason well about practical matters, on this account, was simply to reason in accordance with the eternal law, or what amounts to the same thing, to reason in ways that contributed to realising one's own good. Because the good for human beings, both individually and collectively, was established by God's eternal law, there was no need to worry about any conflict that might arise from people's pursuing their own rightly conceived goods. The harmony of these goods was guaranteed in advance. It was this assumption, grounded in a teleological metaphysics that was no longer compatible with the most recent advances in the natural sciences, that began to seem dubious to the natural law theorists of the early modern period. The transition from the medieval to the modern conception of natural law was signalled especially clearly in the Prolegomena to *The Rights of War and Peace*, where Hugo Grotius put forward a potentially fatal objection to the very the idea of natural law:

Men have established *jura* according to their own interests [*pro utilitate*], which vary with different customs, and often at different times with the same people. So there is no natural *jus*: all men and the other animals are impelled by nature to seek their own interests. Consequently, either there is no justice, or if there is such a thing, it is completely irrational, since pursuing the good of others harms oneself.[4]

As Stephen Darwall notes, this objection simply does not arise from within the framework of Thomistic natural law theory.[5] Grotius, unlike Thomas, takes seriously the possibility that acting in accordance with natural law might not be conducive to one's good, and indeed might even entail genuine sacrifices. It might be the case, in other words, that the law does not point us in the direction of our best interest like a loving and wise parent, but rather *obligates* us, binding our wills without regard to our perceived or actual well-being. If this is right, then we are faced with some very difficult questions: by what means can the law obligate us to perform acts that harm us? And by what authority? What could possibly motivate us to act in accordance with the natural law once we stop thinking of it as standing in a necessary relation to our well-being? Why should we not simply disregard the law when it benefits us to do so? How, in sum, can we make sense of the bindingness of moral obligation?

It is the history of early modern reflection on these sorts of questions, from Francisco Suarez to Immanuel Kant, that resembles Alice's adventure in the Sheep's Shop. Those who adopted a voluntarist position on these questions conceived of obligation's bindingness juridically, as having its origin in the will of someone with the authority to issue commands and the power to enforce them by means of sanctions. But when they tried to get hold of the phenomenon at the level of command, it slipped away from them: on the voluntarist account, obligation turned out to be indistinguishable from mere coercion. Those who adopted a rationalist position, then, were sure that they had located obligation's bindingness at the level of the intellect: just as we cannot help assenting to speculative truths that we conceive clearly and distinctly, such as that triangles have three sides or that $2 + 3 = 5$, so we cannot help assenting to clearly and distinctly conceived moral truths. But while looking for obligation at the level of the understanding, the rationalists let its characteristic 'must' slip away: as the voluntarist Jean Barbeyrac argued, to recognise something as having the property of goodness is distinct from being actually bound to do it. Egoist moral philosophers such as Baron d'Holbach looked for the bindingness of obligation at the level of self-interest, but this entailed a deeply implausible view of the process of moral reasoning. Sentimentalists responded to the problems in the egoist position by trying to locate obligation's bindingness not in our self-regarding feelings, but rather in our feeling of benevolence. What slipped away from the sentimentalists' grasp, though, was obligation's normativity: as John Balguy argued, it does not follow from the fact that we *do* approve of benevolent acts that we *ought* to do so. And finally, over the course of his philosophical career Immanuel Kant offered three different accounts of the source of normativity. His final position was that the genuine bindingness of obligation is simply a fact for which no rational justification can be given. Readers of Kant, not surprisingly, have been strongly critical of this strategy, arguing that it amounts to little more than a cutting of the Gordian knot. With the doctrine of the fact of reason, Kant seems to have definitively renounced the modern project of accounting for the legitimacy and the bindingness of obligation.

If the moral philosophers of the early modern period all failed to find the source of obligation on the shelves where it seemed to them to be, perhaps that is because there was never really anything to find. Perhaps obligation, in the sense of an authoritative prescription, is something like an optical illusion. The afterimages we have after looking at a bright light, for example, seem to have a place in objective space, but of course they are not really there where we see them. Perhaps obligation is like that. This is the position advanced by emotivist metaethicists in the twentieth century. Among the most important and influential of these is A. J. Ayer, who argued in *Language, Truth and Logic* that fundamental ethical concepts are in fact pseudo-concepts.[6] Judgements of ethical value, according to Ayer, are not meaningful statements at all, since they are neither analytic nor empirically verifiable. There remains nothing for ethical philosophers to do, then, except to clarify the meanings of moral terms. According to emotivists like Ayer, these terms function simply as expressions of the speaker's feelings. C. L. Stevenson, another important emotivist, argued that the sentence 'This is good' means roughly the same thing as 'I approve of this; do so as well'.[7] And more specifically, sentences containing the word 'obligation', or similarly, the words 'duty' and 'ought', function to express the speaker's disapproval of the omission of some act that a person is typically disinclined to perform.[8] If a professor tells her students that they ought to study for their exams, what she is really doing, according to Stevenson, is expressing her disapproval of their neglecting to study. On this account, the students do not 'really' have an obligation to study for their exams; the purported obligation is merely the disguised form of the professor's feeling of disapproval.

But this is unconvincing. If it seemed that the emotivists had finally succeeded in fixing the true sense of obligation, this was primarily a function of their having adopted a point of view entirely incommensurable with that of the moral agent. Against her will, or at least without regard to her will, Alice finds herself all of a sudden inside the Sheep's Shop. Before she knows what has happened and what it all means, she is faced with a pressing practical demand. The emotivists are not inside the Sheep's Shop at all; they are standing outside looking in, trying to make sense of what Alice is doing in there. What the moral agent is looking for from her first-person point of view is not the same thing as what the emotivist is looking for from the third-person, objectivating point of view. The emotivist is looking for a way to make consistent sense of how the term 'obligation' functions when people use it in moral judgements. But a moral agent, for example a mother who must choose whether or not to remove her son from life support after he has been badly injured in a car accident, is looking for something entirely different: she wants to know what she ought to do. And since the answer is not at all obvious, she might also be interested in the more abstract question of how she can go about solving the problem she faces. The emotivist theory has nothing to offer her in that regard. Of course one could argue that the moral agent's conception of her problem is simply confused in much the same way that the project of trying to locate one's afterimages in objective space is confused. But this seems like the kind of conclusion one could accept only, as Aristotle says, if one were 'maintaining a thesis at all costs'.[9] Clearly, the mother who must choose about her son's life support is faced with as real a question as one can face. And so once again, the phenomenon of obligation has slipped away.

Since the middle of the twentieth century, moral philosophers have intensified their efforts, proposing an extraordinary variety of solutions to the question concerning the bindingness of obligation. Jean-Paul Sartre has argued, most explicitly in 'The Humanism of Existentialism', that no moral theory can tell us what our obligations are. When we are faced with what seem to be incompatible obligations, we can only determine our obligation by an act of free choice. (This may well have been Humpty Dumpty's position as well had he concerned himself with moral philosophy and not just with philosophy of language.) Jürgen Habermas has attempted to show how obligation has its locus in communicative rationality. For Emmanuel Levinas, obligation arises in our subjection to the absolute Other who approaches from on high, while for Jean-François Lyotard, our obligation comes from our being the addressees of obligatory phrases. In the analytic tradition, Christine M. Korsgaard has argued that obligation is grounded in practical identity, and specifically in the practical identity 'human being', which is presupposed in all rational practical activity. Stephen Darwall has attempted to isolate the source of obligation in reactive attitudes that arise within what he calls the second-person standpoint. And in very different ways, David Gauthier and T. M. Scanlon have tried to locate the source of obligation in an idealised interpersonal agreement conceived on the model of a contract.

This proliferation of theories trying to fix obligation in its proper place testifies to the extraordinary slipperiness of the phenomenon. Given the pervasiveness and the remarkably wide range of disagreement on the issue, do we have any good reason to believe that we will eventually find that ceiling through which obligation cannot pass? Is there any prospect of our making obligation stand still so that we can get a good look at it and examine it from all angles? My project in this book is to propose a fundamentally new way of approaching the problem of obligation and its normativity in response to questions like these. Most basically, I believe that we ought to give up the task of trying to fix the bindingness of obligation in place. No matter where we look for it, whether in command, intellect, feeling or anywhere else, the source of normativity will continue to slip away from us. Importantly, though, we ought not to conclude from this that obligation is just a hopelessly imprecise pseudo-concept. An adequate account of obligation, I will argue, must begin by recognising that the slippage we noted throughout the history of modern reflection on obligation is not simply the result of insufficient conceptual and theoretical rigour. There is no source of normativity, in other words, that would stand still for us if only we had a better theory. Rather, it is an essential and ineliminable feature of the phenomenon of obligation itself that the source of its bindingness should constantly slip away from us wherever we try to grab hold of it. To be obligated is to be given over to that slippage.

The primary thesis of this book is that obligation, understood in this way, has its origin in sense. More specifically, I will argue that we can gain some insight into the phenomenon of obligation – what it means, what it requires of us, how it has normative force, and even why it perpetually slips away – on the basis of the fact that we find ourselves in the midst of sense and responsive to it always already. This argumentative strategy, of course, forces us to address another big philosophical question: what, precisely, is sense? If the phenomenon of obligation really does originate in sense, then it seems that a rigorous determination of the sense of sense should yield clear answers to the kinds of questions that arise in moral reflection. Unfortunately, matters are not quite so simple. As it turns out, we discover in our reflection on sense exactly the same difficulty we discovered in our reflection on obligation, namely that it constantly slips away whenever we seem to have fixed it in place. Sense, in short, does not have a single, determinate sense. This is not to say that sense is nonsensical or senseless. It is to say, rather, that sense is always in excess of itself: we can never hope to produce a signification that would definitively fix its sense. This is the point that Hegel expressed so perspicuously in his *Aesthetics*:

'Sense' is this wonderful word that is used in two opposite meanings. On the one hand it means the organ of immediate apprehension, but on the other hand we mean by it the sense, the meaning, the thought, the universal underlying the thing.[10]

Hegel is referring here to the German word *Sinn*, but his point applies equally well to the English 'sense'. The intelligible sense of the given particular – its meaning – is not given with the particular as one of its sensible properties. 'Coffee', for example, is not given right there with the dark brown colour that I see, the heat that I feel, and the bitterness that I taste. The sense 'coffee' is elsewhere, missing from its place. Likewise, the sense 'coffee' is not present in the sensibly given black marks on this page; one encounters the sense, rather, by seeing through and beyond those marks. And indeed, the sense of the previous sentence is not present right there in the sentence itself. It would require another sentence to state its sense, and another sentence to state the sense of that sentence, and so on. To find ourselves engaged with sense is to find ourselves given over to this kind of slippage always already.

In the chapters that follow, I will attempt to show how we can understand moral phenomena, and especially the phenomenon of obligation, in terms of this kind of slippage. In Chapter 1 I will examine in close detail the voluntarist, rationalist, egoist and sentimentalist strategies for determining the source of normativity, showing in each case precisely how the phenomenon of obligation slips away. In Chapter 2 I will describe the three different accounts of the bindingness of obligation that Immanuel Kant advances in the Collins lectures, the *Groundwork of the Metaphysics of Morals* and the *Critique of Practical Reason*, showing how each of these also fails. I will argue, though, that Kant's third account, based on the doctrine of the fact of reason, provides the key to a more adequate account of obligation. More specifically, I will argue that the fact of reason can play the role that Kant clearly meant it to play only if it is reconceived as what I will call the fact of sense. In the remaining chapters, then, I will develop what I take to be a progressively more adequate conception of the fact of sense, and thus of obligation. In doing so, I will make extensive reference to twentieth-century and contemporary Continental philosophers who are not known primarily for their work in ethics, but rather for their accounts of sense. In Chapter 3, I will develop Maurice Merleau-Ponty's idea that 'because we are in the world, we are condemned to sense'.[11] I will argue that we can discover a kind of normativity inherent in the perceptual and expressive sense to which we find ourselves given over always already. In Chapter 4 I will make use of the work of Michel Serres to show that Merleau-Ponty's phenomenologies of perception and expression do not quite account for the dimension of sense that information theorists refer to as noise. I will attempt to show how our account of obligation is improved with the inclusion of this dimension. Chapter 5 will focus on Jean-Luc Nancy's conception of abandoned sense, arguing that this notion is essential for understanding the experience of unconditional necessitation that seems essential to the phenomenon of obligation. But then in Chapter 6 I will make use of the idea of indifference that Charles E. Scott develops in *The Lives of Things* and *Living with Indifference* in order to begin to problematise this strongly Kantian conception of obligation as an unconditionally binding prescription. Finally, in Chapter 7 I will examine the question whether the moral phenomenon that I have attempted to ground in the fact of sense is still recognisable as obligation.

Elements of a General Conception of Obligation

In order to judge whether the account I propose in this book is successful, it will be necessary at the beginning to spell out more precisely what moral philosophers, and especially moral philosophers of the early modern period, had in mind when they wrote about obligation. At minimum, a successful account must be able to make sense of the elements that the early modern moral philosophers considered essential to the phenomenon. Unfortunately, it is not as easy as it might seem to isolate those essential elements. As it turns out, from the very beginning obligation has been a kind of patchwork concept, stitched from heterogeneous parts that do not fit neatly together. It is this heterogeneity that accounts for much of the difficulty that early modern philosophers had in making consistent sense of the concept. As different moral philosophers articulated their own conceptions of obligation, they emphasised some elements and de-emphasised, or even omitted, others. Despite these differences in emphasis, though, we can isolate eight different elements that have been commonly understood to belong to the concept of obligation.

1. *Necessitation.* To be obligated to perform a particular act is to be in some sense necessitated or constrained to perform it. Thomas Hobbes captures this insight in a well-known passage from *De Cive*, asserting that 'where Liberty ceaseth, there beginneth Obligation'.[12] Samuel Pufendorf, in many ways a critic of Hobbes, expresses a similar idea in his *On the Duty of Man and Citizen According to Natural Law*: 'Obligation is commonly defined as a bond of right by which we are constrained by the necessity of making some performance. That is, obligation places a kind of bridle on our liberty.'[13] And Immanuel Kant defines obligation as a 'necessitation . . . to an action'.[14] Different philosophers have conceived the nature of this necessitation of the will in very different ways, but all have agreed at minimum that obligation entails some sort of restriction on moral agents' capacity to do as they please.

2. *Law.* Obligation is given in the form of a law that commands obedience. This view, of course, is closely associated with Kant:

A categorical imperative, because it asserts an obligation with respect to certain actions, is a morally practical *law*. But since obligation involves not merely practical necessity (such as a law in general asserts), but also *necessitation*, a categorical imperative is a law that either commands or prohibits.[15]

But Kant was by no means the first to link obligation and law in this way. In his *Treatise on Laws and God the Lawgiver*, Francisco Suarez gives precise expression to this point by means of a distinction between law, counsel and petition, a distinction that has shaped modern conceptions of obligation perhaps more than any other. Law, according to Thomas Aquinas, can be defined as 'a rule and measure of acts, whereby man is induced to act or is restrained from acting'.[16] Suarez argues that this definition is too broad, as it would include counsels, which are also rules and measures that induce persons toward actions that promote the good.[17] A counsel is a recommendation or piece of advice. The person giving the counsel provides what she takes to be a good reason for the advisee to adopt a particular course of action. Importantly, though, the kind of good reason involved in counsel imposes no moral necessitation: the advisee remains free to decide for herself whether or not to follow the recommendation. The same is true of petitions, which are requests from inferiors to superiors. Only laws, in the strict sense of the term, impose genuine obligations.[18]

3. *Promulgation by a Superior*. The claim that law is necessarily promulgated by a superior is closely related to the claim that obligation is given in the form of a law that commands. Indeed, the reason, according to Suarez, that obligation can never take the form of petition or counsel is that these lack the top-down dynamic that is necessary to effectively bridle the will. A petition 'is normally addressed by an inferior to a superior'.[19] To petition someone is, in a sense, to submit to that person, and Suarez seems to regard it as self-evident that one cannot issue effective, binding commands from a submissive position. A counsel, on the other hand, 'passes essentially between equals'.[20] Of course the person giving the counsel may be superior to the advisee in knowledge of the specific matter under discussion, but that is not the kind of superiority that can give rise to obligations. Only someone who is superior in power can issue laws, that is, genuinely efficacious ordinances with compulsory force.[21] Pufendorf agrees, arguing that 'an obligation is introduced into a man's mind by a superior'.[22] Even Kant, who rejects the idea that obligation has its source in the command of God or of another person, retains the idea that the moral law must come from a superior position. Kant distinguishes between a lower faculty of desire, which is determined pathologically, and a higher faculty of desire, which is determined

by the pure moral law. The 'solemn majesty' of the moral law is made manifest in the feeling of respect, which is the experience of the humiliation of our self-conceit.[23]

4. *Sanctions*. For many philosophers of the early modern period who have reflected on the nature of obligation, the superiority of the lawgiver has consisted entirely, or at least in large part, in his power to reward and punish. If there is anyone who recognises no superior who could impose necessity on him by means of sanctions, and who nonetheless in his actions promotes the good and avoids the bad, he cannot be understood to perform those actions from obligation. He does them, according to Pufendorf, rather 'out of his own good pleasure'.[24] Richard Cumberland, whose moral philosophy differs considerably from Pufendorf's, agrees on this point:

> There is nothing which can superinduce a necessity of doing or forbearing anything, upon a human mind deliberating upon a thing future, except thoughts or propositions promising good or evil, to ourselves or others, consequent upon what we are about to do.[25]

Importantly for Cumberland, these sanctions are not the *causes* of obligation, but rather the consequences that follow from our actions in accordance with 'the nature of things'.[26] Gluttony, for example, naturally leads to sickness, and breaking promises naturally leads others to distrust us.[27] We can learn these natural connections from sense experience, which is imprinted on our minds by God as if with a pencil.[28] It is through the empirically knowable nature of things that God manifests his will to us, so that what appear as merely natural consequences of various sorts of behaviour are revealed to be signs of God's law. 'In this discovery of the divine will consists the promulgation of the law of nature, and thence directly flows natural and moral obligation.'[29] John Locke has a different view of the relation between sanctions and obligation, arguing that

> it would be in vain for one intelligent Being, to set a Rule to the Actions of another, if he had it not in his Power, to reward the compliance with, and punish deviation from his Rule, by some Good and Evil, that is not the natural product and consequence of the Action itself.[30]

Although these philosophers disagree on the details, they share the idea that without sanctions, the wills of finite rational beings like us could not be constrained, and so there could be no obligation.

5. *Addressed to a Rational Being.* I noted above that the natural law-yers' distinction between petition, counsel and law has shaped the modern conception of obligation perhaps more than any other. I want to emphasise the 'perhaps', though, because there is a second distinction that has played a similarly influential role: the distinction between obligation and coercion. The point is straightforward: the threat of some evil consequent on my failure to perform a certain act may be necessary to obligate me to perform that act, but it is by no means sufficient. If, for example, someone points a gun at me and demands that I give him my money, I certainly have good reason to do so. But just as certainly, I would not be *obligated* to the mugger to hand over my money; I would merely be overpowered by him. Once again, Pufendorf expresses the point in an especially lucid way:[31]

Again, an obligation differs in a special way from coercion, in that, while both ultimately point out some object of terror, the latter only shakes the will with an external force, and impels it to choose some undesired object only by the sense of an impending evil; while an obligation in addition forces a man to acknowledge of himself that the evil, which has been pointed out to the person who deviates from an announced rule, falls upon him justly, since he might of himself have avoided it, had he followed that rule.[32]

In order to be obligated, in other words, I must be able to represent a rule of conduct to myself, recognise that it justly applies to me, and then 'judge [myself] worthy of some censure' if I fail to act in accor-dance with it.[33] Even though, according to Pufendorf, the rules of conduct have their origin in commands backed by sanctions, these rules can be obligatory only for rational beings who can recognise them as such and make them their own.[34]

6. *Priority of the Good.* One of the most pressing concerns for moral philosophy in the early modern period was to resolve the question whether an act was commanded by God because it was good, or whether the act became good simply in virtue of its having been commanded. The latter position has certainly had many defenders, including most notably Duns Scotus, William of Ockham, Martin Luther, John Calvin and René Descartes. But during the early mod-ern period, this position came increasingly under attack. One rea-son, emphasised by Leibniz, was that 'to say *stat pro ratione voluntas,*

my will takes the place of reason, is properly the motto of a tyrant'.[35] The tyrannical God suggested by the Cartesian position was seen as unlovable, and thus as entirely incompatible with the biblical God, whom believers were commanded to love more than anything else.[36] A second argument, advanced by a number of different moral philosophers of the early modern period, moves beyond specifically theological considerations. Arguing on the basis of the eternity of essences, these philosophers rule out the possibility that anyone could make an act good simply by commanding it. Ralph Cudworth makes what has been probably the most influential version of the argument. Writing explicitly in opposition to Hobbes's argument that there is no natural difference between good and bad, just and unjust, Cudworth argues, in an explicitly Platonic vein, that things are necessarily what they are:

As for example, things are white by whiteness, and black by blackness, triangular by triangularity, and round by rotundity, like by likeness and equal by equality, that is, by such certain natures of their own. Neither can Omnipotence itself (to speak with reverence) by mere will make a thing white or black without whiteness or blackness; that is, without such certain natures, whether we consider them as qualities in the objects without us according to the peripatetical philosophy, or as certain dispositions of parts in respect of magnitude, figure, site and motion, which beget those sensations or phantasms of black and white in us.[37]

The reason the natures of things cannot be determined merely by will, whether God's or anyone else's, is straightforward: if something with triangularity can be nonetheless not a triangle, or if something with justice can be nonetheless not just, then things can be what they are not, which implies 'a manifest contradiction'. And if contradictories could be true, then knowledge in general would be rendered impossible, for 'nothing would be certainly true or false'.[38] If Leibniz's and Cudworth's arguments are correct, then it must be the case that God commands what he commands because the commanded act truly is good, independently of the command.

7. *Objectivity.* The question whether or not a person is obligated to perform a particular act in a particular situation has typically been regarded as entirely objective. Whether a person is obligated, in other words, does not depend at all on her psychological make-up,

her moral intuitions, or even her theoretical commitments. All of these could conceivably point the moral agent toward the wrong conclusions. Samuel Clarke expressed this idea especially clearly when he wrote that 'some things are in their own nature *Good* and *Reasonable* and *Fit* to be done'.[39] The properties of goodness and fitness to be done, for example, are predicated of the act of promise keeping in much the same way the property of three-sidedness is predicated of triangles. In both cases someone who believed, for whatever reason, that the predicate term did not apply to the subject term would simply be mistaken. A similar idea lies at the basis of Kant's distinction between hypothetical and categorical imperatives: if practical necessitation depends on a subjective condition, such as the subject's having a particular desire, then it is not the necessitation proper to obligation. The idea of a merely subjective obligation is contradictory.

8. *Overriding.* All of the moral philosophers of the early modern period who reflected on obligation considered it as overriding every other kind of good. It is probably this insight more than any other that motivated figures like Suarez and Grotius to break with the older, Thomistic natural law tradition. As the first theorists of obligation explicitly noted, it can sometimes happen that acting in accordance with natural law works to our disadvantage. As Locke pointed out, for example, natural law obligates one 'to stand by one's promise, though it were to one's own hindrance'.[40] The good that the person could bring about by breaking the promise is overridden by the good of acting in accordance with the law. Immanuel Kant agreed, characterising the moral law as an imperative that commands categorically, reducing to nothing the competing claims of the inclinations. It is not the case, in other words, that the goodness of doing what one is obligated to do *outweighs* other kinds of goods; the point is rather that when we are obligated to perform a particular act, it is morally (though of course not physically) impossible to pursue a rival good instead.

The account of obligation that I advance in this book will not include all of these elements. And some of the elements that are included will be understood in senses that are different from those that would have been recognisable to early modern moral philosophers. This, of course, is not by itself a serious problem for my account, since none of the early modern theories of obligation included all of these elements or gave them all the same weight. The relevant question, which I will take up explicitly in the concluding chapter, is whether the account I propose differs so much from the outline sketched above that it no longer makes sense to think of it as an account of obligation at all.

1 Four Early Modern Accounts of Obligation

The eight elements outlined in the Introduction provide a sketch of the conception of obligation that was accepted, in broad terms at least, by the most important moral philosophers of the early modern period. But despite this broad agreement, philosophers disagreed sharply on the details. Disagreements about which elements were most essential to the phenomenon and which were less essential tended to revolve around a single question: in what, precisely, does the bindingness of obligation consist? Everybody agreed on the first point, that obligation is a kind of necessitation or bridling of the will. To say that a person is obligated to do *x* is just to say that the person is no longer at liberty to do as she pleases with regard to *x*. But what, precisely, is the nature of that necessitation? And just as importantly, what is the explanation or justification of the necessitation? Simplifying somewhat, we can say that one group of moral philosophers – the voluntarists – tended to emphasise elements two to four, focusing on the role of law, commanded by a superior and backed by sanctions, in accounting for the bindingness of obligation. A second group – the rationalists – tended to emphasise elements five to seven, focusing on the knowledge of objective goods that is available to us through our faculty of reason. For the rationalists, it is not the threat of sanctions, but rather our own understanding that obligates us. What I hope to show in what follows is that all of these philosophers found themselves in a situation much like Alice's in the Sheep's Shop: when they tried to get hold of obligation at the level of commands, the phenomenon slipped away to another shelf. And when they tried to fix it in place at the level of rational knowledge, it slipped away again.

Voluntarism

To show how this is the case, I will begin by describing the voluntarist account of obligation. I will focus specifically on two different accounts, starting with Martin Luther's, which places all of the emphasis on the role of command, and moving from there to Samuel Pufendorf's, which emphasises it somewhat less. What I aim to show is that all kinds of voluntarist accounts, from those that treat the command of a superior as wholly constitutive of obligation to those that treat it only as a necessary but not sufficient condition, end up letting the phenomenon as a whole slip through their fingers.

In *The Bondage of the Will*, Martin Luther argues in favour of a very strongly voluntarist position concerning the ground of obligation:

God is that Being, for whose will no cause or reason is to be assigned, as a rule or standard by which it acts; seeing that, nothing is superior or equal to it, but it is itself the rule of all things. For if it acted by any rule or standard, or from any cause or reason, it would be no longer the *will of* GOD. Wherefore, what God wills, is not therefore right, because He ought or ever was bound so to will; but on the contrary, what takes place is therefore right, because He so wills.[1]

This position, and the similar positions of Duns Scotus and William of Ockham, is motivated by the need to conceive God in a way that preserves his omnipotence. If the voluntarist thesis were false, so that God in fact commanded us to perform certain acts *because* those acts were right, then God's power would be limited by an order of moral truths independent of his will. The only appropriate way to understand the relation of obligations to God's will, then, is to understand the former as being brought into being solely by the latter. Of course the voluntarist is forced to pay a very steep price to maintain God's omnipotence in this way: if Luther's account is right, then God's commands must appear utterly arbitrary and perhaps even tyrannical. On a strictly theological level, the problem is that it is difficult to square these characterisations with the Greatest Commandment: 'Love the Lord your God with all your heart and with all your soul and with all your mind.'[2] But Luther is willing to bite the bullet on this point: it is our place, he thinks, to adore the mysteries of God's will and not to understand them.[3]

Indeed, Luther believes that we could not understand God's will even if we tried:

For if His righteousness were such, that it was considered to be righteousness according to human judgement, it would be no longer divine, nor would it in any thing differ from human righteousness. But as He is the one and true God, and moreover incomprehensible and inaccessible by human reason, it is right, nay, it is necessary, that His righteousness should be incomprehensible.[4]

According to Luther, then, God and human beings are so different from each other that they cannot constitute a single moral community: what seems best according to judgement from the human point of view need not have anything whatever in common with what God judges to be best. There is nothing for us to do, then, except to obey commands without even in principle being able to understand the reasons behind them.

This hyperbolically voluntarist account faces a very serious problem: in presenting God's reasons as completely closed off to human understanding, it effectively elides the distinction between obligation and coercion. As nearly every moral philosopher of the early modern period agreed, obligation is possible only as addressed to a rational being, who is able to judge for herself the rightness of the lawgiver's rules and thus to apply them to herself as the measure for her own conduct. If the lawgiver's reasons are completely inaccessible to the moral subject, then her own faculty of reason is left with hardly any role to play in her practical life. It is doubtful whether an account that reduces the role of practical reason to such an extreme degree can rightly be considered an account of obligation at all.

In *On the Law of Nature and Nations*, Samuel Pufendorf advances a considerably more sophisticated voluntarist account of obligation. Pufendorf's theory is like Luther's in the sense that both trace the origin of obligation back to God's commands. But the problems the two theories are meant to address are radically different. Luther, as we have seen, proposed his voluntarist account in response to a specifically theological need, namely to preserve the omnipotence of God. But as Christine M. Korsgaard has shown, Pufendorf's moral theory is distinctively modern, articulated in response to problems that developed on the basis of the newly emerging scientific worldview.[5] Specifically, Pufendorf accepts the truth of the mechanistic picture of the natural world. Thomas Hobbes gives vivid expression to this worldview at the very beginning of his *Leviathan*:

For seeing life is but a motion of limbs, the beginning whereof is in some principal part within, why may we not say that all *automata* (engines that move themselves by springs and wheels as doth a watch) have an artificial life? For what is the *heart*, but a *spring*; and the *nerves* but so many *strings*; and the *joints*, but so many *wheels*, giving motion to the whole body, such as was intended by the artificer?[6]

Where in such a mechanistic world is there room for something like an ought? What kind of sense can it make to say that I, *qua* machine made of springs, wheels and joints, am obligated to keep my promises or to refrain from lying? Somehow I really do experience myself as obligated to keep my promises. And I most certainly experience others as obligated to me to keep their promises. Pufendorf's voluntarist account is meant to explain how obligations like these can exist within the natural world.

Pufendorf's theory rests on a basic distinction, introduced at the very beginning of *On the Law of Nature and Nations*, between physical entities and moral entities. Physical entities are those whose movements are not guided by perception, or are guided only minimally by perception. Billiard balls, whose motions are determined by their own properties and by the ways they are affected by other bodies, are an example. Of course Pufendorf believes that human beings are physical entities, but he believes we are more than that as well. Human beings, unlike merely physical entities, are not determined by their natures to specific courses of behaviour; owing to their intelligence, they are able freely to choose their own actions. This freedom to choose is not unlimited, however: the behaviour of human beings is shaped by moral entities such as role requirements, marks of social rank and prestige, and prices, which do not produce physical changes directly, but which rather affect human behaviour by making 'clear to men along what line they should govern their liberty of action'.[7] These moral entities affect behaviour, in other words, only insofar as human beings represent the rules associated with them to themselves and, recognising their rightful authority, act in accordance with them. I recognise, for example, that I should fulfil the terms of the contracts I agree to, even though I am not necessitated in any specifically physical way to do so. When occasions arise for me to fulfil the terms of my contracts, I act according to the rule. How does this strange, non-physical 'should' enter into the world? Pufendorf's answer is that such moral entities must have been imposed, or 'superadded, at the will of intelligent entities, to things already existent and physically complete, and to their natural effects'.[8] In short, since moral entities are not natural properties of physical things, they can only have been added to the world in accordance with the wills of intelligent beings, and ultimately, in accordance with the will of God.

This claim about the origin of moral entities entails a strong voluntarist thesis. There can be no good of the specifically moral kind that is good in itself, without reference to the law. If something is morally good, then its goodness must consist ultimately in God's having commanded it. And this is exactly what Pufendorf claims:

> For if we consider reason, in so far as it is not imbued with an understanding and sense of law, or a moral norm, it might perhaps be able to permit man the faculty of doing something more expeditiously and adroitly than a beast, and to supply sagacity as an aid to his natural powers. But that reason should be able to discover any morality in the actions of a man without reference to a law, is as impossible as for a man born blind to judge between colours.[9]

Pufendorf relies in this passage on a distinction between two senses of good: the moral and the natural. This distinction is now very familiar, as it plays a central role in Kantian ethics, but it was still very new when Pufendorf articulated it, almost in passing, in chapter 7 of *On the Law of Nature and Nations*.[10] A natural good, according to Pufendorf, is 'a thing or an action [that] is understood to tend to a man's convenience or improvement'.[11] Examples of natural goods include things like nutritious food and actions like getting exercise. Natural goodness does not depend in the least on laws superadded by God to the physical properties of things. Indeed, nutritious food and exercise are good for human beings precisely because of our specific physical properties. Now if all goods were natural goods, the voluntarist thesis would appear considerably less plausible, since it is experience, and not command, that shows us what conduces to our convenience or improvement. But Pufendorf is committed to the claim that there is a second class of goods that are qualitatively distinct from natural goods, which are not determined by the physical properties of things, but simply by their relation to the law. To return to that favourite example of the early modern natural law theorists, it is good that I fulfil the terms of any contracts I agree to. The goodness of my doing so cannot be explained directly in terms of my natural properties in the way that the goodness of broccoli can; indeed, if I have agreed to a bad contract, it may well turn out to be naturally bad for me to fulfil it. I am obligated to fulfil the terms of the contract, then, not insofar as I am a natural being, but rather insofar as I am a moral being capable of representing laws to myself and of acting in accordance with them.

At this point, one crucial question remains unanswered: why are we obligated to do those morally good things that are commanded by the law? We are not, after all, obligated to pursue the natural goods that experience reveals to us. What is the relevant difference between these two cases? In answering this question, Pufendorf makes explicit reference to the third element of the general conception of obligation described in the Introduction: these laws are morally binding because they are promulgated by a superior. A superior, as Pufendorf understands it, is 'one who has both the strength to threaten some evil against those who resist him, and just reason why he can demand that the liberty of our will be limited at his pleasure'.[12] In this, Pufendorf explicitly rejects the Hobbesian conception, according to which 'God in his naturall Kingdome hath a Right to rule, and to punish those who break his Lawes, from his sole irresistable Power.'[13] God's might is sufficient only for coercion, not to create obligations; what is needed in addition is the legitimate authority to bind. The viability of Pufendorf's voluntarist theory of obligation is going to depend, then, on what precisely confers that legitimacy. Although his account on this point is considerably less detailed than we might like, it seems clear that Pufendorf means to ground the legitimacy of God's rule in an antecedent obligation of gratitude that we owe to him for having created us.[14] We are not, then, directly obligated by God's irresistible power, but are rather obligated to be obligated by it.

The addition of this antecedent duty of gratitude is necessary to preserve the distinction between obligation and coercion, which is so essential to the common understanding of obligation, but it preserves this distinction only at the price of undermining the voluntaristic nature of the theory. It was Ralph Cudworth who first advanced an argument for this position in *A Treatise Concerning Eternal and Immutable Morality*. Cudworth's argument has been taken up by numerous subsequent anti-voluntarist moral philosophers and has been widely held to have established conclusively the failure of all sorts of voluntaristic theories.[15] Any voluntarist theory, according to Cudworth, must be able to answer the question, why are we obligated to do what God commands? The answer to this question cannot be the voluntarist answer:

for it was never heard of that any one founded all his authority of commanding others, and others' obligation or duty to obey his commands, in a law of his own making, that men should be required, obliged, or bound to obey him.[16]

That is to say, it cannot be the case that we are obligated to follow God's commands on the ground that he has commanded us to obey his commands, for if we were not already obligated by God's particular commands, we would not be any more obligated by his meta-command. And so there must be some other ground for our obligation to obey. Pufendorf, of course, acknowledges this, positing an antecedent duty of gratitude as the source of our obligation to obey. But this move, by itself, does not resolve the difficulty, for we are still left with the question, why does our gratitude obligate us to obey God's commands? There are, broadly speaking, two possible answers to this question: a voluntarist answer and a non-voluntarist one. The voluntarist answer would be that we have obligations of gratitude to God because God has commanded that we act in such ways as express gratitude for benefits conferred upon us. But to argue in this way, of course, would be to argue in a circle.[17] The only remaining possibility is that our obligation does not derive ultimately from God's, or anyone else's, command. But to accept this conclusion is to renounce the voluntarist theory entirely.

What these considerations of Luther's and Pufendorf's theories show, I want to argue, is that any account that tries to get hold of obligation at the level of command or will ends up letting the phenomenon slip away. If, as in Luther's voluntaristic theory, God's will does all the work of creating obligations, then it turns out not to be obligations at all, but rather coercions, that his will produces. And if, as in Pufendorf's theory, the will of the superior must have some quality beyond irresistible power in order to produce obligations, then it turns out that the will of the superior is not really the source of obligations after all.

Rationalism

The accounts of obligation that emerged in direct response to the perceived failure of voluntarism tended to emphasise elements five to seven of the common conception of obligation, treating necessitation as grounded not in the will of a superior, effectively backed by sanctions, but rather in our own rational natures. These rationalist moral philosophers – the most important and influential of whom were Nicolas Malebranche, Ralph Cudworth, Gottfried Wilhelm Leibniz, Samuel Clarke and Christian Wolff – rejected the idea, common among voluntarist theorists, that moral community with God was impossible for beings like us. From this claim it was a short jump to the conclusion that sanctions were entirely unnecessary for moral necessitation. Knowledge of good and evil, for these thinkers, was not different in kind from knowledge of mathematics, logic or the natural sciences. Just as we have compelling reasons to assent to the claim that $2 + 3 = 5$ without needing to bring sanctions into it, so we have compelling reason to acknowledge the bindingness of the obligation to keep our promises and to refrain from wanton aggression.

It will be helpful to begin here by rehearsing some influential arguments in favour of the claim that we do in fact form a moral community with God. Among the most important of these was the one advanced by Nicolas Malebranche, whom David Hume regarded as the founder of rationalist moral philosophy.[18] Malebranche begins his *Treatise on Ethics* by drawing a distinction between sensibility and intelligibility. Sensibility, he argues, pertains to us merely as particular beings. When I stub my toe, for example, it is I, and no one else, who experience the pain. Of course others can experience pain as well, but it is always their own pain, not mine. My pain, then, is best understood as 'a modification of my own substance'.[19] Reason is not like this. The true idea of a triangle that I contemplate in my own mind is exactly the same as the true idea of a triangle that anyone else contemplates. 'Thus by means of Reason I have, or I am able to have, some society with God, and with all other intelligent beings, since all minds have the same good, or the same law as I have – Reason.'[20] The argument for the position that we share reason in common with God, and not merely with all the other human beings with whom we communicate, is only hinted at in the *Treatise on Ethics*, but is spelled out in more detail in *The Search after Truth*. First, I am certain that everyone perceives that $2 + 3 = 5$, and that it is not just a quirk of my own cognitive make-up. Reason, then, is universal. Second, I am certain that eternal truths are necessary. It is not just a coincidence, in other words, that all rational beings perceive that $2 + 3 = 5$; we all perceive this because it is necessarily true. Finally, it is clear that reason is infinite. I conceive clearly that there can be an infinite number of different triangles and that space extends to infinity, even though I cannot actually conceive each of the infinite possible triangles or every inch of the infinite space. Now the only reason that can be universal, necessary and infinite is God's. Insofar as I participate, however confusedly, in that reason, I am in community with God.[21] And insofar as my reason conceives ideas concerning what is better and worse, what is more and less worthy of being valued, I share a specifically moral community with God.

Leibniz reaches a similar conclusion by means of the argument, advanced in many different texts, that our praising God for his justice makes sense only on the assumption that we form a moral community with him. In Section 2 of his *Discourse on Metaphysics*, Leibniz raises the question, 'why praise [God] for what he has done if he would be equally praiseworthy in doing the exact contrary?'[22] If, for example, God rewarded and punished people in the afterlife in accordance with the virtue they practised during their lifetimes, we would describe his doing so as just. But on the voluntarist thesis, we would also have to describe God's rewarding and punishing people in inverse relation to their virtue, so that the good were damned to Hell and the evil were saved, as just. After all, it is God's will that creates by fiat the goodness and badness of things. Now if God had to be called just in every possible circumstance, no matter what he did, then the statement 'God is just' would be meaningless. The statement would only be contentful on condition that the term 'just' have a univocal sense in its application to God and to human beings. Given that we really are committed to the nonvacuity of the claim that God is just, it must be the case that the term is meant univocally.

But Leibniz's argument is not only about the vacuity of judging God to be just.[23] In his 'Opinion on the Principles of Pufendorf', he presents the argument slightly differently, bringing to the fore an idea that is essential to the rationalist ethical project. According to Leibniz,

> one must pay attention to this fact: that God is praised because he is just. There must be, then, a certain justice – or rather a supreme justice – in God, even though no one is superior to him, and he, by the spontaneity of his excellent nature, accomplishes all things well.[24]

Here the emphasis is placed on the fact that God has no superior. If God acts justly even though there is no superior whose commands guide his will, then, contrary to the voluntarist thesis, moral goodness can in fact be conceived independently of command. God acts justly on the basis of his understanding. Since we as rational beings participate, albeit to a limited degree, in the divine understanding, God's reasons for action can also be our own.

If Malebranche and Leibniz are correct about our ability to share in God's reason, then sanctions no longer have any role to play in obligating us. The work of moral necessitation is done entirely by right reason. Leibniz illustrates the point by means of a well-known thought experiment:

> Supposing, for example, that a Christian who is ill falls into the power of a Turkish doctor, by whom he is made to practice hygienic precepts that he already knew [to be efficacious] for some time, but which are now imposed on him coercively; when, afterwards, he is offered an occasion to escape, would he be obliged to [observe] temperance more than he had before his imprisonment? One or the other, then: either reasons oblige prior to force, or they do not obligate any longer when force fails.[25]

The Christian, in Leibniz's example, understands the benefits of the hygienic precepts, and this alone suffices to give him good reason to practise them. It should seem odd, Leibniz thinks, that he would only become obligated to practise them at the point when the Turkish doctor commanded him to do so and backed his commands with sanctions. The sanctions, we should conclude, play at best a supplementary role; the obligation itself has its source in the Christian's understanding.

The necessitation proper to obligation has its source in a particular feature of our rational nature, namely that we cannot help but assent to what we perceive clearly and distinctly. Descartes provides what is perhaps the most familiar statement of this idea in his *Principles of Philosophy*, arguing that 'we are by nature so disposed to give our assent to what we clearly perceive that we cannot possibly doubt its truth'.[26] This is true even for those who are 'argumentative and stubborn', and who thus have a strong incentive not to assent.[27] Malebranche puts the point in a way that brings it somewhat closer to specifically moral concerns: clear and distinct perceptions 'oblige the will to give its consent'.[28] We cannot, in other words, refrain from giving our consent 'without feeling an inward pain and the secret reproaches of reason'.[29] Samuel Clarke expresses the same point more forcefully: certain moral truths 'are so notoriously plain and self-evident that nothing but the extremest stupidity of Mind, corruption of Manners, or perverseness of Spirit could possibly make any Man entertain the least doubt concerning them'.[30] And Christian Wolff gives the most explicitly moral formulation of the point:

The knowledge of good is a motive [*Bewegungsgrund*] of the will. Whoever distinctly conceives those free acts of man that are good in and of themselves will recognize that they are good. And therefore the good that we perceive in them is a motive for us to will them. Now, because it is not possible for something to be a motive both to will and not to will, it cannot happen that one does not will an inherently good act if one distinctly conceives it.[31]

To understand, in sum, is to find oneself rationally constrained to assent. And to assent is to find oneself rationally constrained to will accordingly.

The last step in this reconstruction of the general rationalist argument is this: if there is genuinely moral necessitation, it must take the form of rational necessitation. Wolff states the point explicitly, arguing that

virtue can exist with natural obligation alone; everything beyond that works simply as an outer compulsion . . . Accordingly, if one wants to guide man, one can do it in two ways: one guides him either through compulsion, like a beast, or through the aid of reason, like a reasonable creature. With the former I have, in ethics, nothing to do.[32]

If a person is directed by means of force to do what is good and to avoid what is bad, then his conduct is not different in kind from that of a domesticated animal. If a cow does what it is constrained by force to do, it should seem odd to ascribe any specifically moral worth to the cow's act. It should, according to Wolff, seem just as odd to us to attribute moral worth to the good acts of a human being when those acts have been produced by coercion. An act has moral worth, then, only when it is done because the agent recognises, by means of his own reason, that the act is right.

With this argument, the rationalists thought they had followed obligation up to the very top shelf, where it could not possibly escape from them. If the necessitation proper to obligation was not to be found in the command of another, then it must be found in our own reason. But Jean Barbeyrac, the translator of many of the natural law classics into French, and himself an important philosopher in the natural law tradition, advanced two different arguments designed to show that reason could not be the source of moral necessitation. The first argument that I would like to address calls upon the well-known principle that one cannot impose necessity on oneself: 'if he on whom necessity is imposed is the same as he who imposes it, then he will be able to release himself from the necessity whenever he sees fit; in other words, there will be no true obligation'.[33] In short, if I have the power to bind my own will, then that same power enables me to unbind it. Barbeyrac's argument here depends on two important interpretations of the rationalist argument: first, it assumes that 'our reason . . . is, at bottom, nothing other than ourselves' and second, it assumes that we – that is, our reason – *impose* obligations on ourselves.[34] But these assumptions, and the argument as a whole, do not adequately capture the 'can't-help-but' character of necessitation as it is described by the rationalist moral philosophers. It is not the case that reason imposes on itself the necessity of assenting to whatever it perceives clearly and distinctly; rather, we, as rational beings, find ourselves compelled, irrespective of our preferences, to assent to such truths. If this is the case, then we are not in fact free to unbind ourselves in the way that Barbeyrac suggests.

Barbeyrac's second argument, though, does point out a genuine difficulty for rationalist accounts of obligation. Let us grant what Barbeyrac seems to have denied, namely that reason finds itself necessitated – and does not impose on itself the necessity – to assent to whatever it recognises clearly and distinctly to be true. In the specific case of moral experience, what is clearly and distinctly perceived is something's truly being good, or its truly having a greater value than some other thing. But this clear and distinct perception, along with the assent that we experience ourselves as necessitated to give, is not enough to get us to obligation: 'That there is such and such a relation of equality and proportion, of propriety or impropriety, in the nature of things, commits us only to *recognizing* that relation.'[35] Taking an example from Malebranche, let us suppose that we recognise it as plainly true that a coachman has a greater degree of perfection than a horse. Based on this recognition, we ought, according to Malebranche, to esteem the coachman more than the horse. But whence derives this 'ought'? How do we cross the gap that separates recognition of a truth from the obligation to act in some particular way on the basis of that recognition? Wolff seems to provide an answer to this question when he notes that the perception of a good gives us a motive to will the good. But of course there remains a gap between the idea of having a motive to do something and being necessitated to do it. Insofar as rationalist moral philosophers borrow their model of moral necessitation from the kind of assent we cannot help giving to speculative truths, they lack the conceptual tools that would be necessary to close that gap.

Following Pufendorf, Barbeyrac insists that only command can close the gap. But this move once again invites a kind of Cudworthian objection, which, combined with Barbeyrac's anti-rationalist arguments, looks to be fatal to any rationalist or voluntarist account of obligation whatever. If command genuinely obligates, and does not merely coerce, then it must do so in virtue of some prior obligation. That prior obligation must have its source either outside us, in the command of another, or within us, in our own understanding. As we have seen, the first option is incoherent: we cannot be obligated to act in accordance with commands by another command. But if the purported obligation to follow commands is discerned by our own faculty of reason, for example by our perceiving clearly and distinctly that God has legitimate authority to issue them, then, for reasons we have just seen, we once again fall short of moral necessitation. And with this it seems as if obligation has eluded the grasp of moral philosophers once again, passing through the ceiling as quietly as possible, as if it were quite used to it.

Egoism

But voluntarism and rationalism do not exhaust the possibilities for thinking about moral obligation. Two other theories – egoism and sentimentalism – emerged in the early modern period as important attempts to get a grip on the phenomenon. The argumentative strategies of both these theories can be understood with reference to a distinction that Francis Hutcheson introduced in his *Illustrations upon the Moral Sense* between what he called exciting reasons and justifying reasons.[36] When we ask for the reason of some action, we sometimes want to know which fact about the situation excited the agent to perform it. If someone were to ask me the reason why I made a pot of coffee this morning, for example, I would point out that coffee has caffeine in it. It is that fact about coffee that provided me with the motivation to prepare it. But sometimes when we ask for the reason of an action, we want to know which feature of that action makes it worthy of being approved. This asks after what Hutcheson calls the justifying reason. If someone asks me why I donate some percentage of my income to Oxfam, I would point out that my doing so improves the lives of people who are in difficult circumstances. That is the feature of the act that makes it seem good, or worthy of moral approval, to me.

Now it often happens that these two reasons do not line up. Of course if I do something I know to be morally bad, say for the sake of self-interest, then the exciting reason cannot be the same as the justifying reason, since there is no justifying reason at all. But also, if I do something I ought to do in order to avoid punishment or to gain some kind of reward, then my exciting reason is different from my justifying reason. Voluntarist moral theories, which locate the bindingness of obligation in the exciting reasons (commands promulgated by superiors and, most importantly, backed by sanctions) and not in the justifying reasons, present this as the normal case of moral action. This, translated into Hutcheson's terms, was the basis of Cudworth's criticism: if a person is obligated to keep her promises, the obligatoriness cannot come solely from the superior's command that she do so. There must be some justifying reason in addition to the exciting reason to support the act of obeying the command. Rationalist theories, on the other hand, locate obligatoriness on the side of justifying reasons, and insist that these reasons must have their source in human understanding. But as Barbeyrac argued, and indeed as Hutcheson and David Hume argued even more forcefully, mere understanding cannot function as an exciting reason: merely knowing that promises in general ought to be kept does not motivate anyone actually to keep them.[37]

If the failures of voluntarism and rationalism can be understood in terms of their entailing a disconnect between exciting and justifying reasons, then perhaps we can get a secure hold on obligation by means of an account that treats the two kinds of reasons as identical. This, broadly speaking, was the strategy of egoist and sentimentalist moral theories. These two theories share many features in common. In opposition to the voluntarist accounts favoured by many of the natural law theorists, both egoism and sentimentalism explicitly deny that laws promulgated by superiors play any role in obligating moral agents. Of course these theories do not deny that coercive laws play an important role in encouraging people to do what they ought; they merely deny that the laws themselves are sources of obligation. As a result of this denial, both theories advance a version of what I earlier called the 'can't-help-but' account of necessitation. For the rationalists, this can't-help-but account has its basis in our intellectual nature: once we perceive an idea clearly and distinctly, we are unable to withhold our assent. The egoists and sentimentalists, on the other hand, ground this kind of necessitation in an empiricist account of human nature, which takes sensibility as basic. Given the way we are naturally constituted, we cannot help but take certain facts as exciting reasons for action. (The egoists and sentimentalists disagree on what these facts are.) And according to both theories, the exciting reasons for action are also the justifying reasons; if this were not so, then the purported obligations would be better described as compulsions, and we would once again lose the phenomenon we are trying to capture.

The egoist conception of obligation is most closely associated with the work of Thomas Hobbes. In his *Leviathan*, Hobbes explains that he grounds 'both the duty and liberty of subjects, upon the known natural inclinations of mankind'.[38] These known natural inclinations are broadly egoist: any voluntary act has as its object some good for the agent.[39] Given this egoistic psychological constitution, we cannot help but pursue our own interests, and herein lies the necessitation that is proper to obligation. So, for example, the 'first and fundamental law of nature', according to Hobbes, is 'to seek peace and follow it'.[40] This law obligates us *foro interno*, or in conscience, because one of the goods we cannot help but seek is our own preservation. In a state of war, where all people are roughly equal in their ability to inflict harm and in their susceptibility to receive harm from others, our lives are in constant danger. Since we cannot effectively pursue goods for ourselves when our most fundamental good is insecure, we must strive to bring about conditions of security. The obligatory force of the natural law, then, has as its basis a hypothetical imperative: if you want to preserve yourself, then you must seek peace.[41] In this account, there is no gap between the exciting reason and the justifying reason: we are motivated to pursue peace because doing so is conducive to preserving ourselves, and it is good that we pursue peace for the same reason.

There is considerable debate about whether this psychological egoist reconstruction adequately captures Hobbes's view of obligation. But there can be no doubt that Baron d'Holbach held such a position. In his *Morale Universelle*, Holbach expresses the psychological egoistic thesis clearly and straightforwardly: 'All of the passions, interests, wills, and actions of man have as their constant object nothing but the satisfaction of the love he has for himself.'[42] Holbach's conception of obligation follows directly from this description: 'Moral obligation is the necessity of doing or avoiding certain actions for the sake of the well-being that we seek in social life.'[43] This does not mean that we are obligated to act selfishly, in the everyday sense of the term. As it turns out, in fact, the kinds of acts that are obligatory or prohibited on Holbach's account line up very closely with the acts that are obligatory or prohibited on most rival accounts. For example, Holbach believes, like nearly every early modern moral philosopher, that we are obligated to act beneficently. For Holbach, though, the reason we ought to act beneficently is that doing so makes it more likely that others will benefit us in turn.[44] Failure to act beneficently, on this account, is not so much a character flaw as a failure of instrumental rationality; the wrong is ultimately a wrong to oneself.

The egoists' claim that exciting reasons (self-interest) and justifying reasons are ultimately the same is plausible only if the results produced by the theory correspond at least roughly to our intuitions about morality. If it turns out, for example, that we ought frequently to lie, break promises or engage in unprovoked acts of violence, then we have strong reason to reject egoism as a successful account of moral obligation. Hobbes raises this kind of concern about his own theory in a well-known passage from *Leviathan*:

The fool hath said in his heart: 'there is no such thing as justice'; and sometimes also with his tongue, seriously alleging that: 'every man's conservation and contentment being committed to his own care, there could be no reason why every man might not do what he thought conduced thereunto, and therefore also to make or not make, keep or not keep, covenants when it conduced to one's benefit.'[45]

If I enter into a contract, for example, and later come to realise that I will most likely lose money on it, it seems, on Hobbes's account, that my obligation to fulfil the terms of the contract should disappear. This is the position that Hobbes attributes to the fool, and which, in order to preserve the plausibility of his own theory, he attempts to refute. Despite appearances, according to Hobbes, we do in fact have compelling, though indirect, self-interested reasons to uphold the terms of contracts we have entered into by mistake. Without mutual trust of the sort that is exemplified most clearly in the norm of upholding the terms of contracts, there can be no commonwealth. The state of affairs in which there is no commonwealth is 'a condition of war of every man against every man', which is incompatible with everyone's interests.[46] Insofar, then, as the fool has an interest in maintaining himself under the protection of the commonwealth, he has a compelling interest in upholding the terms of his contracts. Therefore, he is obligated to do so.

Is it really the case, though, that isolated acts of contract breaking will imperil either the existence of the commonwealth or the fool's continued membership in it? Couldn't a clever fool violate the terms of a contract without anyone's ever knowing about it? If the answer to this question is yes – and it certainly seems that it is – then shouldn't we say that the fool is at least sometimes obligated to violate the terms of contracts? Hobbes insists that he would always be wrong to do so, even in cases where he was quite sure he could avoid detection. Hobbes's argument is not as clear on this point as we might like, but he seems to base his conclusion on considerations of the worst-case scenarios. It would be extraordinarily difficult for even the most clever and far-sighted person to know for certain that his wrongs would go undetected. And even if there is only a 1 in 10,000 chance that he would be caught, the fool must take into account the disastrous consequences that would follow: he would have to be expelled from the commonwealth. There can be no result that would be worse than that. On the other hand, if he upholds the terms of his bad contract, he will suffer at very worst a much lesser harm.[47] And so, although it is not literally impossible that the fool might promote his self-interest more effectively by breaking contracts on some occasions, he could in fact never know with sufficient certainty which occasions those were. Therefore, he is obligated to uphold the terms of his contracts on every occasion.

This account is implausible, to say the least. Given Hobbes's project of reducing obligation to motivation, we would need to believe that real-world actors are sufficiently motivated by the extremely remote possibilities of the worst-case scenarios he imagines. There is little reason to believe they are. But even if moral actors did reason this way with regard to contracts, it is very difficult to see how this kind of reasoning would support other traditional obligations, such as the obligation to beneficence. The point is summarised neatly in a marginal heading in Hutcheson's *Illustrations upon the Moral Sense* where the egoist theory is being discussed: the theory 'does not answer the Appearances'.[48] A father, for example, does not seem to experience his obligation to take care of his children as arising from a calculation of the benefits that will accrue to him for doing so. Of course it is not impossible that he connects his obligation to such a calculation unconsciously. But, Hutcheson argues, it is odd to resort to such an extravagant hypothesis when more intuitive explanations lie close to hand:

Whatever confusion the Schoolmen introduced into Philosophy, some of their keenest Adversaries threaten it with a worse kind of Confusion, by attempting to take away some of the most immediate simple Perceptions, and to explain all Approbation, Condemnation, Pleasure and Pain, by some intricate Relations to the Perceptions of the External Senses. In like manner they have treated our Desires or Affections, making the most generous, kind and disinterested of them, to proceed from Self-Love, by some subtle Trains of Reasoning, to which honest Hearts are often wholly Strangers.[49]

Our everyday experience in the world strongly suggests that we can be effectively motivated by perfectly familiar, other-directed feelings. And moreover, these are just the sorts of feelings that we seem to experience as making moral demands on us, imposing a kind of necessitation authoritatively and immediately, without the need for far-reaching and dubious calculations of self-interest.

Sentimentalism

Sentimentalist moral philosophers – most prominently, Francis Hutcheson and David Hume – argue that these sympathetic feelings are the true grounds of obligation. Reconstructing a general sentimentalist argument from the works of these two philosophers, we can see how they attempt to fix obligation in its place by means of a series of disjunctive syllogisms. First, the source of obligation must be either external or internal. In *An Inquiry into the Original of our Ideas of Beauty and Virtue*, Hutcheson presents a version of an argument we have already discussed to show that the source cannot be external, that is, in the will of a superior who issues commands backed by sanctions: if the goodness of actions is constituted by God's commanding them, then claims that God's commands are good would reduce to the tautological claim that God's commands are God's commands. Assuming we intend to say something meaningful when we praise God, it must be the case that goodness has a meaning independent of God's commands.[50]

This means that the source of obligation must be internal. More specifically, the goodness whose meaning pre-exists God's commands must have its source either in reason or in impressions. Hutcheson and Hume present many different arguments to show that reason cannot be the source of obligation, but I will focus only on two of the most important. First, the sense we have of ourselves as obligated seems to be immediate, and thus more like a sensation than a rational conclusion. If I see a child about to wander out into a busy street, for example, I perceive the goodness of stopping her as directly as I perceive the redness of her coat. I do not seem to engage in any kind of rational deliberation that would have as its conclusion the goodness of stopping the child.[51] Second, obligation is a kind of necessitation. Reason, though, is merely the faculty by means of which we discover truths and falsehoods. And as Barbeyrac had argued against Leibniz's rationalist account, there is a wide gap between recognising something to be true and being necessitated to act in accordance with that recognition. This is not to say, of course, that our faculty of reason plays no role whatever in our moral deliberation. Suppose, for example, that I believe I ought to enrol my child in an expensive private school. This belief is grounded on the prior beliefs that I ought to do what I can to maximise my child's opportunities to lead a happy and fulfilling life and that enrolling him in the private school will contribute to that end. But then suppose I learn that the private school in question actually performs worse than the local public school. At that point, I would conclude that I had been mistaken in thinking I was obligated to send my child to the private school. This may look like a case of reason (the faculty of discovering truths and falsehoods) determining my obligation, but Hume and Hutcheson deny that it is: the faculty of reason can provide normative guidance only if I am already committed to achieving some good, in this case, the well-being of my child. And that commitment does not have its source in reason, but rather in my natural affection for my child. It is that affection that is the source of necessitation; reason functions only as an accessory.[52] As Hume famously put it in his *Treatise of Human Nature*, 'reason is, and ought only to be the slave of the passions, and can never pretend to any other office than to serve and obey them'.[53]

If this line of argumentation is correct, then it must be the case that morality 'is more properly felt than judg'd of'.[54] The only question that remains is, what is the relevant kind of feeling? Both Hutcheson and Hume present two broad alternatives: the relevant feeling is either self-love or benevolence. We have already examined one of the sentimentalist arguments against the view that self-love lies at the basis of obligation, namely that the egoist account of moral deliberation 'does not answer the Appearances'. But both Hutcheson and Hume provide many other arguments against the egoist account as well. The first of these that I would like to address captures an intuition that is common to most of the major philosophers in the voluntarist, rationalist and Kantian traditions: far from grounding obligation, self-love provides us with the most powerful impulse to disregard our duties. For natural law theorists like Grotius and Pufendorf, for example, it is precisely our self-seeking desires, which always threaten to disturb our natural sociableness, that make law necessary in the first place. Hume puts the point even more forcefully than Grotius:

But 'tis certain, that self-love, when it acts at its liberty, instead of engaging us to honest actions, is the source of all injustice and violence; nor can a man ever correct those vices, without correcting and restraining the *natural* movements of that appetite.[55]

Of course this is exactly the kind of claim that Hobbes and, more explicitly, Holbach deny. They insist that self-love, rationally pursued, yields obligations that correspond very closely to the ones that are familiar from the natural law tradition. But for the sentimentalists, this claim is as implausible as the egoists' picture of moral psychology.

The second argument that I would like to examine is advanced by Hume in *An Enquiry Concerning the Principles of Morals*. Hume acknowledges that, since our own interests are so closely bound up with the good of the community, it is at least plausible to assume that our apparent concern for the community is best understood as a modification of our self-love. But although this account has the virtue of theoretical simplicity, it accounts very badly for our experience. Hume refers here to a well-known line from Horace's *Art of Poetry*: 'Just as the human face will smiles return to those who smile, it mourns with those who mourn.'[56] We do, in other words, have sympathetic connections with others, and these cannot plausibly be understood as relations ultimately grounded in self-interest. When we are at the theatre, for example, we find that the mood conveyed by the actors is contagious; we pick up on the feelings of joy or sorrow even though our interests are not affected by the fictional events taking place on stage. Indeed, even if we came in at the middle of the play and were unfamiliar with the story, we would be affected by the mood in the theatre.[57] If this description of our affective relations to others is correct, then it seems we have no compelling reason to accept the egoists' counterintuitive account of moral motivation.

A third argument, advanced by both Hutcheson and Hume, makes a similar point. When we contemplate actions by historical figures who have contributed to the well-being of their contemporaries, we find that we cannot help feeling a sentiment of approval, even though the actions do not contribute in any way to our own self-interest. An even stronger argument is based on the fact that we cannot help giving our moral approval to actions that are widely beneficial, even when those actions oppose our own self-interest. Hutcheson proposes as an example

some resolute Burgomasters, full of Love to their Country, and Compassion toward their Fellow-Citizens, oppress'd in Body and Soul by a Tyrant, and Inquisition, [who] with indefatigable Diligence, public Spirit, and Courage support a tedious perilous War against the Tyrant, and form an industrious Republick, which rivals us in Trade, and almost in Power.[58]

To approve of the Burgomasters' actions, we must identify sympathetically with their countrymen and judge the case from their perspective, not our own. This, according to Hutcheson, is exactly what we naturally do. Finally, we might ask whether we experience a similar sort of moral approval for actions clearly motivated by self-interest. Hutcheson thinks we do not. If a person acts in accordance with his own self-interest, and in the process does no wrong to anyone else, we regard his actions as morally indifferent: not worthy of blame, but not worthy of any kind of specifically moral approbation either.[59] All of this suggests that our moral judgements are determined by the feeling of benevolence.

As we have seen, obligation eluded the grasp of voluntarist and rationalist theories, owing in large part to a gap entailed by both theories between the exciting and the justifying elements of the phenomenon. Hutcheson attempted to close the gap between these elements, treating the good as an object of the moral sense and treating that sense's perceptions as providing sufficient exciting reasons for action. But the sentimentalist solution to the problems that plagued voluntarist and rationalist theories introduces a new problem: it fails to capture the specifically normative sense of justification. John Balguy, a contemporary of Hutcheson's, advanced an argument to this effect in his *Foundation of Moral Goodness*. Balguy's argument against Hutcheson's sentimentalism resembles Hutcheson's own argument against voluntarism. Hutcheson believes that our moral sense was given to us by God. But given this account, 'it is natural to ask, what it was that determined the Deity to plant in us these Affections rather than any other'.[60] The most plausible answer to this question would be that God gave us a moral sense that approved of benevolence precisely because benevolence really is a good thing. But of course Hutcheson could not accept that answer without giving up a point that is central to the sentimentalist theory, namely that the goodness of an act consists in its being approved by the moral sense, much as the redness of an apple consists in its being perceived as red by people endowed with normal capacities for vision. And so Hutcheson responds by asserting that God himself has a moral sense that approves of benevolence, and that that moral sense gave him sufficient exciting reasons to create us with such a moral sense, since doing so could be calculated to bring about the most good for his creatures.[61] But this only pushes the same question back a step: why does God himself have a disposition favouring benevolence? Again, the most plausible answer is that God has such a disposition because benevolence really is good. The other option is to assert that God just happens to have such a disposition; if he had had some other kind of moral sense – say one that approved of unprovoked cruelty – then he would have created us with the same sense, so that unprovoked cruelty would be good. But the idea that God just happens to have a certain kind of moral sense conflicts with our idea of God as necessarily good and introduces an unacceptable arbitrariness into the foundation of morality.[62] It must be the case, then, that God approves of benevolence because benevolence really is good, independently of what his or our moral sense suggests. In other words, it is not the case that benevolence is good because our moral sense approves of it; rather, our moral sense approves of benevolence because benevolence really is good.

Even if Hutcheson had not sought a divine ground for our moral sense, the sentimentalist theory would still face problems similar to the kind that Balguy emphasised. Let us suppose that we do have a moral sense that presents acts of benevolence as good. It still remains an open question whether benevolence really is good, and if so, what about it is good. As rational beings, we do not take the evidence of our senses at face value, and there does not seem to be any reason why we would treat the purported moral sense any differently. As Balguy notes in *The Foundation of Moral Goodness*, 'to suppose Reasonable Beings unconcerned with the Reasons of Things, is to suppose them reasonable and unreasonable at the same time'.[63] And as Christine M. Korsgaard has persuasively argued, the problem of normativity arises precisely in the reflective act by which we step back from the givens of our moral experience and ask ourselves whether apparently obligating reasons are genuinely obligating reasons: 'A lower animal's attention is fixed on the world. Its perceptions are its beliefs and its desires are its will . . . The reflective mind cannot settle for perception and desire, not just as such. It needs a *reason*.'[64] The mere fact that our moral sense approves of benevolent acts, then, cannot obligate us to act on that sense. As rational beings, we experience the moral sense as standing in need of further justification, and we recognise ourselves as genuinely obligated only when the process of justification has reached a successful conclusion. To treat the deliverances of the moral sense as both justifying and exciting reasons, then, is to prematurely cut off the process of reflection that gives rise to the normative question in the first place. Because of this, the phenomenon of obligation slips away from the level of moral sense where the sentimentalists try to grab it.

2 The Copernican Revolution in Ethics

Reflection as the Source of the Problem of Normativity

In *The Sources of Normativity*, Christine M. Korsgaard argues that the problem of normativity arises for us because of the reflective structure of our consciousness. To reflect, as Korsgaard understands it, is to 'back up' from the given contents of our consciousness, 'to distance ourselves from them, and to call them into question'.[1] Because of our capacity for reflection, we do not take the contents of our consciousness at face value. To take an example from theoretical reason, I perceive the sun as rising from the eastern horizon, while I perceive myself as occupying a static position. But perception is not the same thing as belief. I can back up from the perceived content of consciousness and call it into question: is what I am seeing really what it gives itself to be? Is the sun really rising, while my own position remains static? In sum, ought I to believe that the sun is really rising from the eastern horizon? Given the reflective structure of human consciousness, I cannot avoid asking questions of this kind. And once these questions arise, I cannot effectively will them away, commanding myself to take the perception as belief. The perception itself comes to be given as questionable. It only ceases to appear that way once I have discovered a compelling reason to take it either for what it gives itself to be or for something else. Once I have discovered such a compelling reason, that particular normative problem disappears: I know that I ought not to believe that the sun really rises from the eastern horizon.

The specifically moral import of Korsgaard's idea is that as long as I am able to step back from some given content of consciousness, which purports to present me with a sufficient reason for acting in accordance with it, and raise the question whether I in fact ought to act in accordance with it, my will is not necessitated, and so I am not genuinely obligated. A banal, everyday example will bring out Korsgaard's point most clearly. Suppose I have a desire to eat a bar of chocolate. That desire is certainly present in my consciousness as a reason to eat the bar of chocolate. Nonetheless, it would be a very odd use of language to say that my desire for the bar of chocolate obligates me to eat it. As Korsgaard notes, for rational beings like us, desire is not the same as will; I can step back from the felt desire and ask myself whether it really does give me a compelling reason to eat the bar of chocolate. What this means is that the desire itself cannot necessitate my will, and thus cannot ground any obligation. This is especially obvious if I step back from the desire and conclude that I ought not to eat it. But even if I do decide that I ought to eat the bar of chocolate, it is the successful conclusion of a process of reflection, and not the initial desire, that provides me with the ultimately compelling reason. As Korsgaard memorably puts the point, 'if the problem springs from reflection then the solution must do so as well'.[2]

With this conception of moral reflection in mind, we can look back to the major theories of obligation that emerged in the early modern period and see clearly why the phenomenon eluded their grasp. Beginning with voluntarism, we can see that a command, issued by a superior and backed with sanctions, certainly presents itself as a reason to act in accordance with it. But of course a rational person can step back and ask herself whether she is genuinely obligated to do what she been commanded to do. This is especially obvious in cases in which the command seems *prima facie* unjust. We can see clearly in such cases that the command does not necessitate directly. Rather, if it turns out that the person really is obligated to do what she was commanded to do, then the source of that obligation will have been the process of reflection by which the command was put to the test, and not the command itself. The rationalist seems closer to Korsgaard's view, taking the nature of things, as disclosed to us in clear and distinct conceptions, as the ground of obligation. But once again, we can see that clear and distinct conceptions do not directly necessitate our wills; we are able to step back from them and ask whether we are genuinely obligated to act in accordance with them. To take an example from Malebranche, suppose we do in fact conceive clearly and distinctly that a fly has a greater degree of perfection than a stone; we can reflect on that conception and ask ourselves whether we have compelling reasons to act in such a way as to show greater esteem for the fly than for the stone. The mere conception does not obligate by itself. (This was also Barbeyrac's criticism of the rationalist position.) A similar argument applies to moral sense theory: the sense of approval that I feel when I contemplate acts of benevolence does not by itself yield any obligation to act benevolently; I can step back from the moral sense and ask myself whether what it shows to be morally good really is. If I ultimately judge that the moral sense was correct, then once again it will have been the process of reflection that functioned as the ground of obligation, and not the moral sense. And of course the same sort of argument applies to egoistic accounts of obligation.

Kant and the Copernican Revolution in Ethics

In all of these theories, we find a gap, opened up by the act of reflection, between the appearance of a purported reason for action and the necessitation to perform that action. It is this gap that accounts for their failure to fix the phenomenon of obligation in its place. We look for obligation at the level where it seems to be given – at the level of a superior's command, or of the rationally conceivable nature of things, or of self-interest, or of moral sense – but the act of reflection ceaselessly takes it up and displaces it. To present the problem in this way is to point in the direction of a possible solution: if it could be shown how the appearance of something as good was given immediately with the experience of its moral necessity, then the process of reflection that displaces obligation would come to a halt. That is to say, the act of backing up by which we put into question the obligatoriness of some purported good would no longer make sense, since the obligatoriness would already form an integral part of the sense of the perceived good.

This, I want to argue, is exactly the strategy that Immanuel Kant pursues in his Copernican Revolution in ethics. In the Preface to the B edition of his *Critique of Pure Reason*, Kant famously compared his proposed methodology for solving long-standing problems in metaphysics to the Copernican turn in astronomy:

Up to now it has been assumed that all our cognition must conform to the objects; but all attempts to find out something about them *a priori* through concepts that would extend our cognition have, on this presupposition, come to nothing. Hence let us once try whether we do not get farther with the problems of metaphysics by assuming that the objects must conform to our cognition, which would agree better with the requested possibility of an *a priori* cognition of them, which is to establish something about objects before they are given to us.[3]

According to Kant, all systems of metaphysics prior to his own have assumed the truth of transcendental realism, that is, the idea that appearances, or the objects of our cognition, are 'things in themselves, which would exist independently of us and our sensibility and thus would also be outside us according to pure concepts of the understanding'.[4] Knowledge, on this transcendental realist account, would be the adequation of our cognition to the natures of the objects known. This common-sense conception of cognition renders genuine metaphysical knowledge impossible, since there is no compelling reason to believe a priori that our concepts correspond to the natures of the objects. If metaphysical knowledge is to be possible, then, it must rather be the case that the objects correspond to our cognition. This position, which Kant calls transcendental idealism, holds that objects can only appear to us as such insofar as they conform to the conditions of our essentially discursive understanding. On this account, our understanding gives the law that makes nature possible in the first place as something that can be known.[5] In the *Groundwork of the Metaphysics of Morals*, and even more explicitly in the *Critique of Practical Reason*, Kant proposes a similar Copernican Revolution in our understanding of obligation. All ethical systems prior to his own, Kant argues, began with an attempt to discover the nature of the good. The moral law, then, was conceived as secondary, determined on the basis of the independently existing good. But this way of proceeding, roughly analogous to the transcendental realist procedure in metaphysics, yields exactly the sorts of problems that Korsgaard emphasises: it leaves a gap between the recognition of something as good and the necessitation to do it. Specifically, Kant believes that all ethical theories that take an independently existing good as the ground for the determination of the will must treat self-love as the principle of morality.[6] But the principle of self-love, according to Kant, can never yield any obligation, since it would counsel us to do

exactly what we would have done anyway, had the notion of a specifically moral good never entered our consciousness. What is missing, in other words, is the element of necessitation. If obligation is to
be possible, then, it must be the case that our practical reason is legislative. In this case, it would be the moral law 'that first determines
and makes possible the concept of the good, insofar as it deserves this
name absolutely'.[7] If the law itself gives the good to appear as such,
then goodness is given immediately with its *vim obligatoriam*, and the
question of normativity finds its definitive solution.

If this Copernican strategy in ethics can be made to work – and we
should certainly take the 'if' seriously – it would enable Kant's theory
to account very well for all but two of the elements of the general conception of obligation described in the Introduction. First, expanding
on the point suggested above, it would provide a compelling account
of the element of necessitation. If the goodness of an action is not
given immediately with its obligatoriness – as all non-Kantian theories suppose – then we must search beyond the perceived goodness
of the act for what Hutcheson called an exciting reason to perform
it. And as we have seen, Kant believes that the only possible exciting
reason other than the motive of duty is self-love. This claim, of course,
has been very controversial, as it has seemed to suggest that all actions
not motivated by the specifically Kantian formulation of the moral
law are undertaken for selfish reasons. But if we take Kant to mean
simply that all such exciting reasons must be self-regarding, in the
sense that they necessarily make reference to the subjective condition
of the person who is reflecting on what to do, then his claim will seem
less controversial. In deciding whether I have a compelling reason to
follow a command, for example, I must take into account whether I
am willing or able to suffer the penalties that back up the command.
This is a fact about my own subjective condition. Thus, whether I
decide to obey the command or to disobey it, I do so for reasons that
are ultimately self-regarding. These self-regarding reasons fall short of
what we could reasonably call necessitations. If I know, for example,
that I will be fined $10,000 for violating some command, and I decide
that I am unwilling to part with that much money, then I certainly
have what Kant calls a prudential reason to obey the command. But
I would not be necessitated in any robust sense of the term; someone
else, subject to exactly the same command, who was much richer
than me, or simply had less aversion to losing $10,000, might very

well have good reasons to disobey the command. Neither of us is necessitated insofar as we choose with reference to our own subjective conditions. If, on the other hand, the obligatoriness of the act is given immediately with its perceived goodness, then I do not need to search for any self-regarding exciting reason. The moral necessity in that case would be objective, and thus ineluctable.

Next, the Kantian theory accounts nicely for the intuition, emphasised especially by many of the natural law theorists, that obligation is given in the form of a law promulgated by a superior. As we have already seen, Kant believes that our faculty of reason is legislative in the area of morality. The moral law originally gives the good that it commands us to do, in something at least roughly like the way the criminal law establishes the legal existence and definition of extortion, which it forbids us to commit. Even though the moral law has its source in our own reason, we experience it as being promulgated from a superior position. This is possible, Kant thinks, because human beings possess both a higher and lower faculty of desire. Our higher faculty of desire is entirely rational, determined by the moral law itself. If we were fully rational beings, then our wills would be holy, like God's; we would act in accordance with the moral law simply as a matter of course. But we are not fully rational beings; we are also sensible beings with sensible needs, and so we cannot help taking considerations of our own well-being as important reasons for action. This sensibly determined faculty of desire is what Kant calls the lower faculty. Because finite rational beings like us have both a higher and a lower faculty of desire, and because we experience the higher faculty as both restricting our pursuit of our pathologically determined interests and striking down our natural esteem for ourselves, we cannot help viewing the law as having a 'solemn majesty'.[8]

One element from the general conception of obligation that the Kantian theory does not capture is the idea that the law must be backed by sanctions. Natural law theorists distinguished between the indicative and the preceptive functions of law. As indicative, the law merely points out what is intrinsically good and what is intrinsically bad. Some natural law theorists, including most prominently Gregory of Rimini, held that natural law was only indicative law. But others – most notably Suarez – held that the natural law was law in the fully proper sense, that is, both indicative and preceptive. As preceptive, the law goes beyond merely indicating what is good and bad, commanding us to do the former and forbidding us from doing the latter. Since the natural law theorists understood moral law on the model of political law, they could conceive of the preceptive function of law only as grounded in sanctions. Kant, like Suarez, believes that the moral law is both indicative and preceptive. But Kant does not borrow his model of lawgiving so directly from the political sphere, where one agent imposes the law on another. For Kant, the source of the moral law is our own reason. Since the Kantian moral law at once indicates what is morally good and necessitates us to do it, there is no need for any sanctions to support it. Indeed, the addition of sanctions would ruin the necessitation of the law, presenting the subject with self-regarding reasons to obey.

The other element of the general conception of obligation that Kant's theory does not capture is the priority of the good. This element, emphasised especially by the rationalist moral philosophers, was viewed as necessary to avoid arbitrariness. If God did not issue commands with a view to what was good independently of his will, but rather made things good merely by means of his commands, then it would be entirely possible that acts of unprovoked aggression could be good, even though they lacked the objective property of goodness.[9] But the variation of the Euthyphro problem that concerned the rationalist moral philosophers does not arise within Kant's system. For transcendental idealism, the legislation of the faculties of understanding and reason can in no way be understood as arbitrary, or in Kant's German, *willkürlich*, since that legislation is the very condition of possibility for the objective, rationally ordered worlds of nature and morality. Of course this view is counterintuitive from the perspective of the transcendental realism that forms such an important part of both our theoretical and practical common sense. But, if Kant's argument is correct, it turns out that arbitrariness would actually be the consequence of the transcendental realist position, and not of the transcendental idealist position. That is to say, if the good is determined independently of the legislation of pure practical reason, then the obligatoriness of acting on that good cannot be objective. The question whether or not to act on the good would be subjective, based on the different circumstances of different agents. If obligation is to be genuinely objective, binding on all rational beings simply in virtue of their rationality, then it must be the case that the moral order has its origin in the legislation of reason.

The Argument of the Collins Lectures

Of course Kant's Copernican theory can provide a compelling account of obligation only if it can be shown precisely how the appearance of the moral good can be given immediately with its obligatoriness. In the remainder of this chapter, I want to show that the different stages in the development of Kant's ethical theory can be understood as progressively more adequate attempts to conceive that immediacy. I will examine three different Kantian accounts, beginning with an argument he advanced in his lectures on ethics, delivered in the winter semester of 1784–5, just prior to the publication of his *Groundwork of the Metaphysics of Morals*. I will then consider the better-known argument of the *Groundwork* itself, emphasising the ways in which it fails to demonstrate the objective validity, or bindingness, of the moral law. Finally, I will consider the argument that Kant advanced in the *Critique of Practical Reason*, focusing specifically on his doctrine of the fact of reason. I will argue that it is this latter doctrine, imperfectly formulated as it is, that provides the key to an adequate understanding of the phenomenon of obligation.

In the lectures on ethics that he delivered in the winter semester of 1784–5, commonly referred to as the Collins lectures, Kant introduces a distinction between what he calls the principle of appraisal of obligation and the principle of its performance or execution.[10] The principle of appraisal of obligation is the principle by which moral subjects judge whether actions are morally good or bad. The principle of its performance, on the other hand, is the subject's motivation to do what she has judged to be morally good. Kant believes that other philosophical systems have confused these two principles, as a result of which 'everything in morality has been erroneous'.[11] Specifically, Kant believes that other moral theories have mistakenly treated the principle of performance as if it functioned as a principle of appraisal, providing the norm by which moral goodness and badness could be judged. The problem with doing so is that motives are only subjectively valid, whereas obligation must be objectively valid. Before addressing the question of motivation, then, it is necessary to discover the principle of appraisal. Where should we seek such a principle? Kant arrives at an answer to this question by means of a process of elimination. Given the account of cognition that he had advanced in the *Critique of Pure Reason*, the only two candidates for the source of the principle of appraisal are feeling and understanding. Now principles based on feeling, or pathological principles, can be of two kinds: either they are based on physical feelings, and aim at the satisfaction of all of our inclinations, or they are intellectual feelings, and aim specifically at satisfying the inclination to morality. Pathological principles based on physical feeling are plainly inadequate, as they refer only to the contingent subjective conditions of moral agents. And the idea of a pathological principle based on intellectual feeling, Kant thinks, 'is in itself an absurdity', since we cannot have any kind of feeling directed toward objects of the understanding.[12] The principle of appraisal of obligation, then, must have its source in the understanding.

In order to articulate a determinate conception of the principle of appraisal, then, it will be necessary to examine the faculty of understanding. It will be recalled that, according to the system of transcendental idealism advanced in the first *Critique*, the faculty of understanding is legislative for the domain of nature. This entails that the understanding is a faculty of rules:

Sensibility gives us forms (of intuition), but the understanding gives us rules. It is always busy poring through the appearances with the aim of finding some sort of rule in them. Rules, so far as they are objective (and thus necessarily pertain to the cognition of objects) are called laws.[13]

But the understanding does not merely discover laws that are already there in nature, independent of our reason. Rather, the understanding is the faculty that first provides the domain of nature with its lawfulness, making it possible as an object of knowledge in the first place. This is what it means to call the faculty of understanding legislative: it is a spontaneous, lawgiving faculty, and not merely a receptive one. With this basic characterisation of the faculty of understanding, we can see what the principle of appraisal of obligation must be:

All morality is the relationship of the action to the universal rule. In all our actions, that which we call moral is according to rule – this is the essential part of morality, that our actions have their motivating ground in the universal rule.[14]

This, of course, is very similar to what Kant will later describe as the Categorical Imperative. We can determine whether an act is morally permissible or not by asking, 'what becomes of the action if it is taken universally? If, when it is made into a universal rule, the intention is in agreement with itself, the action is morally possible; but if not, then it is morally impossible.'[15] In the latter case, we are obligated not to perform it.

Given that the faculty of understanding determines the moral goodness or badness of actions, how are we to understand the principle of performance? How can we understand the element of necessitation that is inseparable from the phenomenon of obligation? In the *Lectures*, Kant insists that we cannot give an entirely satisfactory answer to these questions:

Nobody can or ever will comprehend how the understanding should have a motivating power; it can admittedly judge, but to give this judgement power so that it becomes a motive able to impel the will to performance of an action – to understand this is the philosopher's stone.[16]

But we can, Kant seems to suggest, at least point in the direction of an answer. Because the understanding necessarily judges in accordance with rules, it resists whatever cannot be thought in the form of a rule. The understanding views actions contrary to the rule as abhorrent, and is therefore averse to them.[17] As Kant expresses the point in a note from his handwritten literary remains, 'that through which the supreme power contradicts itself is a natural and necessary object of aversion'.[18] How that aversion comes actually to be felt in a way that can move our wills, we cannot say, but at minimum we know that the ground of the aversion lies in the resistance of the understanding.

Because it is the same faculty that judges the morality of actions and imposes the resistance that, by whatever means, moves the will, it appears as if Kant has provided an account that shows how the goodness of an action can be given immediately with its binding character. But this appearance is deceptive. In one important point, Kant's argument resembles rationalist arguments of the kind advanced by Malebranche. For Malebranche, it is our faculty of reason that serves as the principle of appraisal of obligation. Because we participate in God's own reason, we are able to conceive practical truths established by God. But what motivates us to assent to these truths, which we perceive clearly and distinctly? For Malebranche, it is the fact that if we do not, then we will feel 'an inward pain and the secret reproaches of reason'.[19] This experience of pain certainly makes it likely that we will in fact assent, but it does not go so far as to necessitate assent. The same kind of problem arises in Kant's account from the Collins lectures. Lack of lawfulness may indeed be a natural and necessary object of aversion for the understanding, but that feeling of displeasure is insufficient to produce necessitation. At best, it could give rise to a hypothetical imperative to act lawfully: if we want to avoid the feeling of displeasure caused by contradiction, then we should only act on maxims that can function as universal laws. Given the experience of displeasure, the agent has room to back up and ask himself whether that feeling gives him a sufficient reason to avoid the unlawful act. The feeling, connected to the perception of the wrongness of an act, does not immediately necessitate the will not to perform the act. If, for example, the agent found the displeasure not to be especially strong, or if he concluded that the pleasure likely to be produced by the unlawful act outweighed the displeasure, then he would lack a compelling reason to avoid the act. On Kant's account from the Collins lectures, then, the determining ground of the agent's will would be subjective, no matter whether he eventually chose to act lawfully or unlawfully. As a result, it fails as an account of obligation.

The Argument of the *Groundwork*

In the *Groundwork of the Metaphysics of Morals*, Kant introduces a new argument intended to show that the moral law not only indicates what is morally good and bad, but also obligates by means of commands that necessitate the will. The *Groundwork* is divided into three sections, the first two of which are meant to determine the supreme principle of morality. In Section One, Kant argues analytically, beginning with common rational knowledge of morality, or our unreflective, pre-philosophical moral common sense, and deriving from this the philosophical, that is, clear and abstract, principle of morality. In Section Two, Kant argues that popular moral philosophy is mistaken in grounding its principles on a hodgepodge of empirical observations and poorly worked out rational principles. Instead of this, he argues that all morality must be grounded a priori in reason. From there, Kant proceeds to give a much more thorough account of the purely rational principles of morality than he had given in Section One, culminating with his account of autonomy as the supreme principle of morality. It is important to note here that both of these sections take for granted the idea, well established in our moral common sense, that morality imposes genuine obligations on us. But of course it is entirely possible that our moral common sense is wrong on this point. It may be the case that morality is an 'empty delusion' and 'a chimerical idea without any truth'.[20] In other words, Sections One and Two describe what the supreme principle of morality would be, assuming it were objectively valid. Section Three, then, attempts to give a deduction of the moral law, demonstrating that we are genuinely obligated by it.

Kant begins Section One of the *Groundwork* with the claim that 'it is impossible to think of anything at all in the world, or indeed even beyond it, that could be considered good without limitation except a good will'.[21] Kant attributes this view to our moral common sense. We can all recognise, without any specifically philosophical reflection, that other qualities we typically regard as good, such as intelligence, courage and wealth, can be bad under certain circumstances. Intelligence, for example, can be put to use for evil ends. The value that we place on these goods, then, is conditional: they are good as long as they are put to use in a good way. Their goodness, in other words, depends on the goodness of the will. We can also recognise, again without any philosophical reflection, that the good will 'is not good because of what it effects or accomplishes, because of its fitness to attain some proposed end, but only because of its volition, that is, it is good in itself'.[22] For example, if a neighbour rushes into a burning house to save a child who, unbeknownst to the neighbour, had already died, we do not regard his act as morally worthless. The goodness of the act does not consist in the saving of the child's life, but in the volition itself. From this conception of the good will, which 'already dwells in natural sound understanding', Kant attempts to extract some properly philosophical principles concerning duty.[23] First, he concludes that an action has moral worth only if it is done from duty. That is to say, we do not give people a specifically moral kind of credit for performing acts motivated by inclination, since those are exactly the sorts of acts they would have performed if they had lacked the concept of duty altogether. Next,

Kant concludes that the moral worth of an action is not to be found in the effect of that action, but rather in the principle of the volition. Finally, he concludes that 'duty is the necessity of an action from respect for law'.[24] This last principle follows straightforwardly from the other two. Given these principles, the obvious question we want to answer is, 'what kind of law can that be, the representation of which must determine the will, even without regard for the effect expected from it, in order for the will to be called good absolutely and without limitation?'[25] Because such a will cannot be determined by the goodness of the end at which it aims (since the goodness of that end could only be conditional), the law cannot be a particular law. The only remaining possibility, then, is that the mere form of lawfulness must determine the will. And from this, Kant derives the first formulation of the Categorical Imperative: 'I ought never to act except in such a way that I could also will that my maxim should become a universal law.'[26]

In Section Two of the *Groundwork*, Kant begins with a criticism of popular moral philosophy, which attempts to derive the principles of morality, in part at least, from experience. This way of proceeding, Kant thinks, is detrimental to morality, since experience can never provide us with examples of actions done from the motive of duty. If we examine human conduct empirically, it appears as if action is always undertaken on the basis of sensible motives, which all reduce to the motive of self-love. In order to arrive at a rigorously philosophical account of morality, then, we must begin with a metaphysics of morals, that is, with an a priori determination of the faculty of practical reason. This is what Kant provides in Section Two. Specifically, he presents an account of rational agency in general, from which he derives a whole set of principles and concepts, including the five different formulations of the Categorical Imperative, the distinction between hypothetical and categorical imperatives, the distinction between dignity and price, and the distinction between autonomy and heteronomy. In the following paragraphs, I will focus only the part of Kant's argument that pertains to autonomy, as this is the concept that is especially relevant for his attempted deduction of the objective validity of the moral law in Section Three.

The properly philosophical account of rational agency that Kant develops in Section Two begins with a premise that will be decisive for everything that follows: 'Everything in nature works in accordance

with laws. Only a rational being has the capacity to act in accordance
with the representation of laws, that is, in accordance with principles,
or has a will.'[27] This minimal condition of rational agency is not discovered empirically, by observation of what rational agents actually
do. Rather, the principle simply elucidates the concept of rational
agency, irrespective of whether such agency can be found in experience. We do not think of water as a rational agent when it changes its
state at 32° Fahrenheit, since it does so in accordance with laws that
are effective without the water's representing them to itself. Rational
agents, on the other hand, act not on the basis of rules that determine
their behaviour from the outside, as it were, but rather on the basis
of rules that they represent to themselves. To act rationally, in other
words, is to act on the basis of maxims. When I go to the grocery store
to buy a carton of milk, I always stop at the cashier and pay before I
leave the store. I do not do this in the same way that water changes
its state at 32° Fahrenheit. Rather, I do so because the act of acquiring a carton of milk falls under a rule, or maxim, that I represent to
myself in the relevant circumstances. What we mean when we say
that I have a will is just that I have this ability to act on the basis of
maxims. And as Kant had intimated in Section One, and as he states
more explicitly in Section Two, my will is morally good, or good without qualification, when I act in accordance with maxims that I can at
the same time will to be universal laws. But because I am a rational
being who is at the same time a sensible being with sensible needs, I
cannot help but take particular, subjective considerations into account
when I act. I do not, therefore, act in accordance with universalisable
maxims simply as a matter of course. And that is why the moral law
is present to my consciousness in the specific form of a command or
imperative.

Still proceeding analytically, merely elucidating the concept of
rational agency, we can ask, what are the properties of a will that
would be able to determine itself by the mere representation of the
form of lawfulness? Kant's answer is that such a will would necessarily be autonomous. By autonomy, Kant means 'the property of
the will by which it is a law to itself (independently of any property
of the objects of volition)'.[28] The parenthetical clause in this definition is especially important. By describing the will as a law to itself,
Kant does not mean simply to deny that human action is entirely
determined by external stimuli. Such an interpretation of autonomy

would render the distinction with heteronomy, which Kant clearly intends to play an important role in his moral theory, practically meaningless. Autonomy, then, must amount to more than merely acting from maxims. The independence Kant has in mind is rather what Henry E. Allison describes as

a motivational independence, that is, a capacity for self-determination independently of, and even contrary to, [our sensible] needs. Positively expressed, a will with the property of autonomy is one for which there are (or can be) reasons to act that are logically independent of the agent's needs as a sensuous being.[29]

If I am autonomous, then, I am capable of disregarding my difficult financial circumstances as I deliberate about whether I should make a lying promise, and of disregarding my antipathy toward other human beings as I deliberate about whether I should make it my policy to contribute to their happiness. I am able effectively to determine my will merely by a consideration of whether the maxim in each case could serve as a universal law. Once again, we can never be certain, judging empirically, whether anybody's will has ever determined itself in this way. This is true even in our experience of ourselves. Kant's argument in this section is merely analytic: if there is such a thing as a rational will, then it would have to be an autonomous will. And if duty is not 'everywhere an empty delusion and a chimerical concept', then it must be the case that the will's own law – the Categorical Imperative – is objectively valid for finite rational beings like us.[30]

Section Three of the *Groundwork* is devoted to demonstrating that we really are bound by the moral law. Much of the difficulty involved in this demonstration can be traced back to the fact that the Categorical Imperative, in all of its formulations, is 'an a priori synthetic practical proposition'.[31] The validity of hypothetical imperatives is much easier to demonstrate because they are analytic practical propositions. Kant thinks of them as analytic because the necessitation to will what the imperative commands is 'contained in' the willing of the end, which is already given. So, for example, if I want to preserve my perfumes in their proper condition, I must store them in a cool, dark place. Supposing that I really do will that as an end, I cannot, as a rational being, fail to will the means. That this is so can be seen from the fact that if anyone saw me putting my fragrances into a cool, dark place, she would not understand me to be doing two different things: the act of putting the fragrances into the cool, dark place would not be seen as adding anything new to the act of preserving them in their proper condition.[32] Of course the hypothetical imperative does presuppose a synthetic *theoretical* judgement, namely that storing fragrances in a cool, dark place contributes to maintaining them in their proper condition. But taking that background synthetic knowledge as given, the practical principle itself is analytic: since it is true that preserving perfumes in their proper condition does require storing them in a cool, dark place, the necessitation of doing so is contained in the will to preserve them. The Categorical Imperative cannot be analytic in this way precisely because it does not take the willing of any end as already given. This is what it means to say that the Categorical Imperative commands unconditionally. Thus, the necessitation to act in accordance with the principle of autonomy is something new, and not just the result of unpacking the meaning of an already given volition. Because this synthetic judgement is also a priori (since, as Kant had shown in Section Two, we cannot discover it in experience), we are left with the difficult problem, parallel to that of the categories in the first *Critique*, of showing that it is objectively valid, that is, that we are genuinely obligated by it, and that it is not merely an idea in our minds. This demonstration, just as in the first *Critique*, takes the form of a deduction.

In carrying out the deduction of the objective validity of the Categorical Imperative, Kant must be careful not to presuppose in any way the genuineness of our experience of ourselves as unconditionally obligated, since that genuineness is exactly what is in question. This means that Kant must somehow demonstrate the legitimacy of the moral law entirely on the basis of non-moral premises. In the first subsection of Section Three, Kant begins his argument by developing a conception of freedom that follows analytically from the mere concept of a free will. According to Kant, will is 'a kind of causality of living beings insofar as they are rational'.[33] And to call a will free is just to say that it is not determined in its causality from without. This negative conception of freedom – its *not* being determined from without – yields a positive conception of freedom once we take into account the necessary connection between causality and laws. Since 'lawless causality' is a contradiction in terms, we must assume that the will exercises its causality in accordance with laws. Those laws in accordance with which the free will exercises its causality cannot come from outside the will, as this would render it unfree. This insight leads directly to the main conclusion of the first subsection of *Groundwork* III: if the will is free, then the law in accordance with which it exercises its causality must be its own, which is just to say that the free will necessarily acts autonomously. Since autonomy of the will is the supreme principle of morality (as Kant had demonstrated analytically at the end of Section Two), it follows that 'a free will and a will under moral laws are one and the same'.[34]

So far in the argument, Kant has not taken for granted in any way the genuine bindingness of the moral law. All he has shown is that *if* the will is free, then its law is necessarily the moral law. But in beginning the argument this way, Kant seems to have painted himself into a corner. For the deduction to succeed, he must show that we are in fact free in the relevant sense. One of the most important conclusions of the *Critique of Pure Reason*, though, was that we could not demonstrate the reality, or even the possibility, of freedom theoretically. If that conclusion is correct, then it seems as if the only way left open is to demonstrate the reality of freedom from the practical point of view. And that is exactly the kind of argument Kant pursues in the second subsection of *Groundwork* III:

every being that cannot act otherwise than *under the idea of freedom* is just because of that really free in a practical respect, that is, all laws that are inseparably bound up with freedom hold for him just as if his will had been validly pronounced free also in itself and in theoretical philosophy.[35]

Reason, in its practical use, cannot help regarding itself as acting on its own principles, independently of alien influences, and so it cannot help regarding itself as acting under the moral law. But is this true? It certainly seems as if we could understand the activity of practical reason entirely prudentially, as choosing the best means to ends that are given independently of reason. Indeed, many of the most important moral philosophers in the history of western philosophy have viewed practical reason in just that way. If we cannot act otherwise than under the idea of freedom, this seems to be because the alternative – thinking of our wills as influenced by alien causes – would undermine the categorical nature of our moral judgements. We must think of ourselves as free in the strong Kantian sense of the term, then, because we experience ourselves as unconditionally obligated. But the objective validity of this experience is exactly what is in question. To assume the genuine bindingness of obligation at this stage is to argue in a circle: we posit freedom as an explanation for the possibility of obligation, and then we posit obligation to demonstrate that we really are free, which in turn confirms that we really are obligated.

As Kant makes clear in the third subsection, he is aware that he has begged the question in the argument developed over the first two subsections.[36] His reason for introducing the fallacious argument in the first place, it seems, was to highlight the necessity of demonstrating the reality of freedom from non-moral premises. But given the results of the first *Critique*, it is not immediately obvious what sort of non-moral premise could yield the desired result, since he cannot present the reality of freedom as something known through the theoretical use of reason. In the argument developed in the third subsection of *Groundwork* III, Kant attempts to thread the needle by appealing to the difference between the two *standpoints* that we cannot help adopting. Kant gets this new argument off the ground by attributing to common sense one of the most basic insights of transcendental idealism, namely the distinction between appearances and things in themselves. We arrive at this distinction from our experience as knowers of the world: we become aware of the objects that we cognise only when they affect us, and this leads us to the conclusion that the objects as they affect us are not the same as the objects as they are in themselves, independently of their effects on us. From this conclusion follows a second distinction, this time between a world of sense and a world of understanding, the latter of which is the ground of the former. Crucially for Kant's argument, the distinction between the two worlds applies to us as well as to the other objects we encounter in experience. We know about ourselves empirically, as objects within the world of sense, but we must also belong to the world of understanding as things in ourselves. We become aware of our belonging to a world beyond the world of sense when we reflect on our faculty of reason, which is purely spontaneous and which provides us with ideas that go beyond anything given in experience. Thus, we cannot help taking two different standpoints on ourselves: as members of the world of sense, we view ourselves as subject to the same sorts of natural

laws that govern all the other objects of experience, that is, as heter-
onomous, but as members of the world of understanding, we view
ourselves as transcending the world of sense, and thus as free. Since
we cannot help taking up the former standpoint, we cannot help
thinking of ourselves as acting under the principle of autonomy.

The deduction of the objective validity of the moral law is completed in the fourth subsection, where Kant attempts to account for
the imperatival character of the moral law and for the legitimacy of
the demand it makes on us. The key to the argument is that as finite
rational beings, we necessarily occupy both standpoints at once. If
we took only the standpoint of the world of understanding, then we
would view our actions as proceeding from the principle of autonomy simply as a matter of course. But we also take the standpoint of
the world of sense, from which we view our own actions as determined heteronomously, by our inclinations. We thus experience a
gap between what we perceive ourselves to be doing and what we
would do if we belonged solely to the world of understanding. It is
in this gap that the phenomenon of the 'ought' arises. Because we
conceive the world of understanding as the ground of the world of
sense, and because we do not experience the world of sense as in
any way the ground of the world of understanding, we cannot help
recognising the moral law as authoritative for us. And because we
do not experience ourselves as acting in accordance with that law
as a matter of course, we cannot help experiencing the law as commanding us.

The correctness of this deduction, Kant believes, can be confirmed
(but, importantly, not established) by consulting experience. Even
'the most hardened scoundrel', when confronted with examples of
morally good action, wishes he could disburden himself of his inclinations and act steadfastly in accordance with the moral law. The scoundrel experiences his will as being determined heteronomously in the
world of sense, but at the same time he acknowledges the authority
of the moral law, which he would like to live up to. The scoundrel's
experience of the authoritativeness of the ought makes sense only on
the supposition that he adopts the standpoints of the world of sense
and the world of understanding simultaneously.

Kant scholars, for the most part, have been unconvinced by the
Groundwork III deduction, and rightly so. I want to focus here on
two problems with the argument that are especially relevant to

my project in this book. Both of these problems arise from Kant's attempt to locate the bindingness of obligation in the gap that separates the practical subject understood as a member of the world of understanding from that same subject understood as belonging to the world of sense. The first problem was pointed out already in 1792 by Karl Leonhard Reinhold in his *Briefe über die Kantische Philosophie*. Reinhold argued that if the moral law is the causal law of the free will, that is, the will conceived as belonging to the world of the understanding, then we have no way to explain how we in the sensible world could ever freely act in a manner contrary to the law: 'as soon as it is assumed that the freedom of the pure will consists merely in the self-activity of reason, one must also concede that the impure will, which is not effected through practical reason, is in no way free'.[37] If the impure will is not free, then we cannot think of it as the addressee of an imperative that is morally binding. Recalling the fifth element of the general conception of obligation described in the Introduction, obligation is only possible for a being that can represent the law to itself and take it as a reason for action, even when the inclinations pull in another direction. The supposed addressee of the imperative, considered as a sensible being and thus as governed entirely by the laws of nature, cannot do this.[38] But second, even if the impure will were somehow capable of recognising the law as such and taking it up as the norm for its actions, it is not at all clear why it would experience itself as necessitated to do so. Kant's own account seems to rely on two points: first, that the world of the understanding has a kind of priority insofar as it is the ground of the world of sense and second, that the finite rational being would act in accordance with the moral law simply as a matter of course if it were a purely rational being. But these points do not entail the conclusion that Kant needs. Specifically, it would not be irrational for the sensible will, assuming it were somehow able to reflect on its position vis-à-vis the law, to concede that it would act in accordance with that law if it were a pure will, but to deny the practical relevance of that point on the grounds that it is not in fact a pure will. The sensible will might view action in accordance with the law as an ideal to aspire to, but it would not be properly necessitated. For these reasons, and for many others besides, the bindingness of obligation cannot be located in the gap between the pure will, conceived as addressor of the moral law, and the sensible will, conceived as the addressee of the law.

The Fact of Reason

Having recognised the failure of the argument of *Groundwork* III, Kant pursues an entirely different argumentative strategy in the *Critique of Practical Reason*, denying both the necessity and the possibility for any kind of deduction of the moral law. The objective validity of the law, Kant insists, 'has no need of justifying grounds', but is given rather as 'the sole fact of pure reason'.[39] This fact is absolutely basic: 'one cannot reason it out from antecedent data of reason, for example from consciousness of freedom'.[40] The fact of reason is thus 'apodictically certain';[41] it 'forces itself upon us of itself as a synthetic a priori proposition that is not based on any intuition, either pure or empirical'.[42] The argument Kant gives to demonstrate that this is so is in one sense the reverse of the argument he gives in the *Groundwork*. After having completed his deduction there, Kant brought in the example of the hardened scoundrel as a bit of extra support for a point he took to have already been satisfactorily established. In the second *Critique*, though, the kind of moral experience exemplified by the scoundrel is made to carry the whole weight of the argument. Kant asks us to imagine a prince demanding that his subject 'give false testimony against an honorable man whom the prince would like to destroy under a plausible pretext'.[43] We are to suppose further that the prince threatens the subject with immediate execution if he refuses to give the false testimony. Is the subject in this example able to do what the moral law commands – to tell the truth – and thus to override his natural and powerful inclination to preserve his life? Kant believes the answer is obviously yes. That is not to say, of course, that the subject would succeed in following the moral law. The important point, though, is that he would certainly regard himself as being capable of it. And this, Kant thinks, is simply because he knows he ought to do it. *That* he ought to do it is never an open question; his consciousness of his unconditional obligation to tell the truth is just a fact, which is given immediately and which cannot be concluded from any other data of reason.

As Henry E. Allison has noted, this notion of the fact of reason 'has been greeted with even less enthusiasm than the ill-fated attempt at a deduction of the moral law in *Groundwork* III'.[44] Hegel, for example, described the supposed fact as 'the last undigested lump in our stomach, a revelation given to reason'.[45] Schopenhauer characterised it as 'a Delphic temple in the human soul'.[46] And Rüdiger Bittner has characterised it as 'an ad hoc solution, one that secures a seemingly indispensable premise by means of a doctrine introduced only to this end'. Instead of presenting an argument to defend the objective validity of the moral law, Kant 'simply cuts off criticism'.[47]

Despite the central importance of the fact of reason in the argument of the second *Critique*, Kant never presents an unambiguous account of what the fact is supposed to consist in or of the relation in which it is supposed to stand to reason. In the passage where it is first introduced, the fact of reason is characterised as the consciousness of the fundamental law of pure practical reason.[48] But as Lewis White Beck has pointed out, this can be understood in two importantly different ways. On the one hand, it could be interpreted to mean that the moral law is itself the fact, which is 'known by pure reason as its object, modo directo'.[49] On this account, the doctrine of the fact of reason would amount to a kind of intuitionism. On the other hand, one could interpret Kant to mean that our consciousness is itself the fact of reason. On this account, it is simply a fact, irreducible and apodictically certain, that we are conscious of the moral law as authoritative.[50] The distinction between these two interpretations can be characterised as a distinction between a consciousness-of and a consciousness-that, respectively.[51]

For the interpretation of the fact of reason as something of which we are conscious, the facticity of the fact consists in its being given immediately, like an intuition. One sees that the moral law is authoritative just as one sees that the coffee is brown. One's consciousness of the coffee as brown is basic and irreducible; it is not the conclusion of any chain of reasoning. Likewise, the moral law as authoritative would be given directly, and not as a result of any kind of deduction. If this were the correct interpretation of the fact of reason, then Paul Guyer would certainly be correct in his characterisation of the argument as so much 'foot-stamping'.[52] Such an intuition would be at best what Beck calls a putative intuition, that is, one 'which seems to be a real intuition, but which in fact may or may not be'.[53] Intuitions in general are not self-guaranteeing; it is always possible that we might be mistaken about them. If this is true for everyday intuitions like those of colour, then it is certainly true for the more dubious intuition of the moral law. Thus if there really is such a phenomenon as the fact of reason, with its characteristic apodicticity and a priority, then this fact cannot take the form of a consciousness-of.

The second interpretation, according to which the fact of reason is the consciousness that the moral law is authoritative, appears to be similarly problematic. What the concept of the fact of reason needs to establish is that the moral law is objectively valid for finite rational beings like us. To show that we are conscious that the moral law is authoritative, however, is only to show that it is subjectively valid. There is, in other words, a vast difference between the claim that we are conscious that the moral law is authoritative and the claim that the moral law really is authoritative.[54] This problem with the consciousness-that interpretation can be avoided, however, by an account that would construe the fact of reason as a constructed fact. Such an account is advanced by Paweł Łuków in his article 'The Fact of Reason: Kant's Passage to Ordinary Moral Knowledge'. For Łuków, the fact of reason is a consciousness-that, but one that is given only problematically, not as an 'indubitable, self-evident datum of reason'.[55] It is a fact, in other words, that we experience ourselves as constrained by the moral law. But as rational beings we do not just take this experience at face value. Rather, the fact of this experience 'must be provisionally adopted and examined' in order to determine whether it is consistent with our broader account of practical reason.[56] By presenting the fact of reason in this way as merely problematic, the constructivist account avoids the previously mentioned objection to the consciousness-that interpretation. But, I want to argue, in doing so it makes itself vulnerable to a new objection, namely that the fact of reason seems to be precisely the kind of thing that cannot be adopted merely provisionally. This is suggested by Kant's insistence that the moral law, as an apodictically certain fact, is 'firmly established of itself' and that its objective reality 'cannot be proved by any deduction, by any efforts of theoretical reason, speculative or empirically supported'.[57]

Of the two plausible interpretations of the fact of reason, then, neither yields a satisfactory account of the bindingness of obligation. Nonetheless, I want to argue that there is something importantly right in Kant's argumentative strategy here and that the key to producing a more adequate account of the bindingness of obligation consists in pursuing a somewhat modified version of that strategy. If the fact of reason is to play the role that Kant clearly meant it to play, namely that of rendering unnecessary any deduction of the objective validity of the moral law, then it must be understood in such a way as to present the practical subject as most basically responsive. The problem that Kant means to solve is the one that Korsgaard articulated in *The Sources of Normativity*: as beings who are capable of reflection, we can always back up from apparent reasons for action and ask ourselves whether they are ultimate and authoritative reasons. As long as we are able to step back in this way, our putative obligations remain merely provisionally valid. The bindingness of obligation, then, must have its source in some experience from which we cannot step back and reflect. The only such experience, I want to argue, would be that of finding ourselves responsive to something like the moral law always already. The moral agent would need to be understood as something other than a self-identical, fully formed subject who would experience putative obligations and then autonomously determine their validity or invalidity. Rather, the very act of stepping back from the purported reason for action and testing its objective validity would be understood as responsive to a law whose validity the subject could not help accepting. One could not be a practical subject at all, then, without having responded always already.[58] In the following chapters, I will argue that we can produce such an account by reinterpreting Kant's fact of reason as a fact of sense.

3 Perceptual and Expressive Sense

In the Preface to his *Phenomenology of Perception*, Maurice Merleau-Ponty writes that 'because we are in the world, we are condemned to sense'.[1] We cannot effectively bracket sense, treating it as a potentially naïve prejudice of the natural attitude about which we must suspend our judgement. That we are immersed in sense always already cannot be doubted even in principle, for the very attempt to bracket our natural commitment to it is itself already responsive to a meaningful context. Sense, then, is irreducible. It does not originate in subjective, intentional acts; to be a subject at all, rather, is to find oneself subjected to it. To be in the world just is to be exposed to a 'perpetual pregnancy' and 'perpetual parturition' of sense without being able to master it.[2] To say that we are condemned to sense, though, is not to suggest that we receive the sense of the world wholly passively, in something like the way that wax receives a seal. We receive sense only insofar as we actively intend it. But this activity of intending is necessarily an active passivity: we can intend the sense of the world only by gearing into it, and thus by rendering ourselves receptive to it. In order to understand a novel, for example, I must do more than merely open my eyes and turn them toward the book; I must actively read, animating the black marks on the page with a meaning-bestowing intention. But of course not just any meaning-bestowing intention will do. I must intend the sense in a way that is responsive to the meaning that the words themselves adumbrate. To be condemned to sense, then, is to find ourselves given over always already to a dynamic of sense in which we find ourselves indissociably active and passive, subject and subjected.

This condemnation to sense is a fact: it is 'firmly established of itself' and cannot be reasoned out 'from any antecedent data of reason'.[3] To be a practical agent in the world is to find oneself subjected to this fact always already. We cannot back up from it and put its objective validity decisively to the test, since the very act of backing up would be responsive to the adumbrated sense of the world, and would thus confirm our condemnation. Our being obligated, according to the Merleau-Pontian account that I will develop in this chapter, thus consists in the impossibility of our not responding to the sense to which we find ourselves condemned. In what follows, I will begin by arguing that we can draw an account of obligation from *Phenomenology of Perception*. This account locates the necessitation proper to obligation in a normativity that is inherent in perceptual experience itself. Next, I will show how the perception-based account fails to capture both the second-personal and the moral character of the phenomenon of obligation. The remainder of the chapter will be devoted to articulating what I take to be a better Merleau-Pontian account of obligation, focusing on the philosophy of expression he developed in his works of the late 1940s and early 1950s, and most importantly in *The Prose of the World*. More specifically I will argue, borrowing from the work of Bernhard Waldenfels, that the bindingness of obligation consists in the impossibility of not responding to the claims made against us by others, who are present to us, whether we like it or not, as 'self-originating sources of valid claims'.[4]

Normativity in Perceptual Experience

In order to show how the bindingness of obligation is grounded in the fact of sense, it will be necessary to begin by clarifying the sense of the sense to which we find ourselves condemned. This, of course, is no easy task. As Hegel explained in the passage from the *Aesthetics* that we discussed in the Introduction:

'Sense' is this wonderful word that is used in two opposite meanings. On the one hand it means the organ of immediate apprehension, but on the other hand we mean by it the sense, the meaning, the thought, the universal underlying the thing.[5]

Which of these – sensible sense or intelligible sense – is the one that we find ourselves immersed in and responsive to always already, such that it can function as the ultimate source of normativity? In the introductory chapters of *Phenomenology of Perception*, collectively titled 'Classical Prejudices and the Return to Phenomena', Merleau-Ponty demonstrates that neither of these senses of sense is basic, and that both of them are best understood as abstractions from a more originary dimension of our being-in-the-world. The first chapter, '"Sensation"', examines the idea of a purely sensible sense, completely uncontaminated by intelligible sense. If such a purely sensible sense were ever given in our experience, it would be given as 'an undifferentiated, instantaneous, and punctual "jolt"'.[6] But even those who argue for the existence of these insignificant, unmediated qualia concede that they correspond to nothing in our actual experience. As Gestalt theory has demonstrated, the most basic sensible given is that of a figure against a background. If I see something as apparently simple as a patch of colour, for example, I see it as having borders that somehow belong to it and that delimit it from the background against which it appears. The patch is thus given as a unity that coheres; all the points within it are given as points of the same patch, which is set off from what the patch is not. This demonstrates that sensation, the supposedly most basic element of perception, 'is already charged with a *sense*' or a meaning.[7] We cannot understand sensible sense as originary, then, because it is contaminated by another kind of sense – intelligible sense – always already.

Since we cannot make sense of our experience of the world on the basis of the empiricist commitment to the priority of undifferentiated, meaningless sense data, we might conclude that our most basic access to the world is given by intelligible sense. According to this intellectualist thesis, our apparent receptivity to the sensibly given world is better understood as an act of judgement about the world. This, of course, is Descartes's position: when he looks outside his window, he is inclined to say that he sees men crossing the square. But this, he decides, cannot be right, since the only images imprinted on his retina are the patches of colour that correspond to their hats and coats. He does not literally see that they are men, since the very same sense data would be compatible with his seeing automata dressed in hats and coats. Instead, he *judges* that they are men. 'And so something which I thought I was seeing with my eyes is in fact grasped solely by the faculty of judgement which is in my mind.'[8] Merleau-Ponty rejects this position on the grounds that it too accounts badly for our actual experience of the world. We experience sensing as something sharply distinct from judging: when we judge, we strive to know something in a way that is inter-subjectively valid, whereas when we sense, we give ourselves over to the object without attempting to know it. The intellectualist thesis collapses this distinction, treating all of our relations to the meaning-ful world as judgements.[9] This makes it difficult to account, among other things, for perceptual ambiguity and for optical illusions. For example, if, fully aware of what I am doing, I draw a cube on a piece of paper, I will find that the drawn figure presents itself ambigu-ously: it appears sometimes as if seen from the side and sometimes as if seen from above. According to the intellectualist thesis, this can only be because I alternate between two different judgements about the cube. But why would I do that? I myself drew the cube knowing in advance its geometrical properties, which represent a kind of view from nowhere. Why can I not avoid seeing the cube from somewhere? Of course the answer is that the sensibly given cube motivates the ways I direct my consciousness to it, and thus motivates the ways I judge it.[10] The judgement, in short, is respon-sive to sensible sense. If this kind of responsiveness to the sensible given manifests itself in cases in which I have explicitly constructed the given, we can be certain that the contribution of sensible sense to intelligibility is irreducible in experience generally.

The sense that constitutes the most originary dimension of our being-in-the-world, then, is given neither in sensation, as this is understood in the empiricist tradition, nor in acts of pure intellec-tion. It is given rather in perception, which Merleau-Ponty charac-terises as a 'nascent *logos*', as an immediate presence to the world as 'cradle of significations, as the sense of all senses, and as the ground of all thoughts'.[11] The originary sense given at the level of percep-tion is irreducibly ambiguous. It is certainly sensible, but it does not have the kind of immediate, full presence that characterises pure sense qualia. A quale is completely unambiguous; it is no more than it gives itself to be. The sense given in perception, on the other hand, points beyond itself to what is not present, adumbrating more sense. It is this fact about perceptual sense that accounts for the ambiguous presentation of the drawn cube. Likewise, originary sense is certainly intelligible, significant sense. When I recognise the supposedly primitive patch of colour, for example, I recognise it immediately *as* a patch distinct from its background and *as* having the determinate colour green. But my judgement that I am seeing a green patch is not a cognitive act completely separate from my initial reception of meaningless sense data. Rather, it is the sensibly given itself that motivates my seeing-as. The originary sense given at the level of perception, then, is ambiguous between sensible and intelligible sense. Importantly, though, we must not understand this ambiguity, as Hegel put it, 'simply by running together what thought has put asunder'.[12] It is not merely a mixture of sensible and intelligible sense, but rather a phenomenon in its own right, characterised by its own dynamic.[13] Much of the present chapter will be devoted to describing this dynamic of originary sense and to showing how that dynamic can be understood as grounding the bindingness of obligation.

The most basic features of the dynamic of originary sense are captured nicely in a passage from the Introduction to *Phenomenology of Perception*:

If I am walking on a beach toward a boat that has run aground, and if the funnel or the mast merges with the forest that borders the dune, then there will be a moment in which these details suddenly reunite with the boat and become welded to it. As I approached, I did not perceive the resemblances or the proximities that were, in the end, about to reunite with the superstructure of the ship in an unbroken picture. I merely felt that the appearance of the object was about to change, that something was imminent in this tension, as the storm is imminent in the clouds.[14]

What the perceiving subject is confronted with here is a nascent sense: the determinate sense of the spectacle is given as intimated and as in the midst of being brought forth. This moment of 'vague uneasiness' or of sense-in-process brings to light the irreducibility of ambiguity.[15] To bring out the latent sense of the spectacle, the subject must do more than merely open her eyes. She must not only see the spectacle, but must see according to it, orienting herself toward it in the manner called for by the thing itself. Eventually, after the subject changes her position relative to the vaguely given spectacle, moving perhaps to the left or to the right, forward or backward, and after she adjusts the focus of her eyes, the sense will all of a sudden crystallise. The semi-determinate colours and shapes take on the Gestalt of the superstructure of a ship set against the background of a forest.

Once the sense of the spectacle has stabilised, though, the perceiving subject is likely to forget about the condition of ambiguous nascency from which the stability emerged. She will thus be inclined to conceive the act of perception not on its own terms, but rather on the basis of its results. She will believe that she determined the meaning of the spectacle by comparing different sensations – the various colours – and their locations in objective space: similar colours appear together in one region of space, and so they must be the colours of one thing, namely the superstructure of the ship. This interpretation of the experience is confirmed by the contiguity of the superstructure with the ship itself. But this account of the act of perception cannot be right. As Merleau-Ponty showed in the '"Sensation"' chapter, there are determinate patches of colour in determinate points of space only within a scene that is already gestalted; the points are given only as points *of* some coherent thing. The Gestalt itself emerges at the level of perception, and not of sensation or of intellection. Nascent sense and its specific dynamic of tension and orientation are thus originary. Intelligible and sensible sense must be understood on the basis of these, and not vice versa.

Already we can recognise here a kind of normativity originating in our condemnation to the nascent sense given in perception. To have perceptual experience at all is to be called upon to orient oneself toward the object in just the right way. Individual perceiving subjects are not at liberty to decide for themselves what the right way is. The meaning of 'the right way' is determined rather by the nature of perceptual experience itself. Specifically, to perceive is to be drawn toward that point of view from which the object appears with 'the maximum of visibility'.[16] It is this draw that accounts for the tension the subject experiences when she first comes upon the scene of the ship that has run aground. The subject perceives a vaguely given *something*, and experiences the vagueness as something to be overcome in favour of greater determination. She adjusts her perspective on the *something* until the spectacle is suddenly reorganised and her vague expectation of meaning is satisfied.[17] If this were not the case – if the subject were not drawn toward greater perceptual determinacy – then the subject would have before herself only nongestalted scenes, and not objects. But merely to behold nongestalted scenes is not to have experience at all.[18] Thus, as Sean D. Kelly has argued, 'it is a necessary fact about our experiences of objects that in themselves they eschew lack of clarity'.[19] The imperative of perceptual clarity that weighs on the experiencing subject is simply a fact whose legitimacy cannot be justified by any deduction. To be a perceiving subject at all is to have already accepted its bindingness.

Importantly, the subject to whom this demand for perceptual clarity is addressed is not the subject present to himself in reflection. Merleau-Ponty writes:

Each time that I experience a sensation, I experience that it does not concern my own being – the one for which I am responsible and upon which I decide – but rather another self that has already sided with the world, that is already open to certain of its aspects and synchronized with them.[20]

The demand weighs on what Merleau-Ponty calls *'l'on primordial'*, a pre-subjective, pre-personal dimension of anonymity and generality.[21] To have an experience even as simple as perceiving a colour as blue, for example, the subject must orient himself toward the vaguely given object in precisely the way necessary to allow it to become present as the determinate colour it is. If the subject adopts toward the blue object a bodily attitude appropriate to seeing red, 'an inner battle ensues, a sort of spasm, which ceases as soon as he adopts the bodily attitude that corresponds to blue'.[22] But to say that the perceiver adopts a bodily attitude toward the coloured object is to run the risk of suggesting a too subject-centred account of what actually happens in perception. When faced with the vaguely given sense of the situation, the subject does not think to himself, 'I shall comport myself bodily toward these puzzling sensory givens in such a manner as to see them as blue.' If one were to ask the subject how to adopt the bodily attitude necessary to see a colour as blue, he would almost certainly be unable to explain. Indeed, he would probably not be aware that he was *doing* anything at all beyond merely opening his eyes and turning his head toward the blue object. And in a sense his perspective would be correct: it is not he, the self-conscious subject with his own projects, his own personal history and his own values who orients himself toward the vaguely given spectacle. It is rather his body that knows prior to all reflection how to respond appropriately to the nascent sense intimated in the perceptual world. Between this pre-reflective, embodied subject and the world there exists a kind of communication 'more ancient than thought'.[23] The normativity internal to the very happening of perceptual experience has its origin in this pre-subjective communication between the knowing body and the intimated sense of the world.[24]

The normative demand to which the pre-subjective, knowing body finds itself responsive always already gives rise to what could be called the imperative of the world. In chapter 4 of *Phenomenology of Perception*, Merleau-Ponty articulates this imperative in terms of what he calls the silent thesis of perception, which is a pre-reflective commitment to the idea that

experience, at each moment, can be coordinated with the experience of the preceding moment and with that of the following one, that my perspective can be coordinated with the perspectives of other consciousnesses – that all contradictions can be removed, that monadic and intersubjective experience is a single continuous text – and that what is indeterminate for me at this moment could become determinate for a more complete knowledge, which is seemingly realized in advance in the thing, or rather which is the thing itself.[25]

It belongs to the dynamic of perceptual experience that we encounter individual objects as gesturing beyond themselves toward a world that gives itself as an 'open and indefinite unity'.[26] Our perception of asphalt mirages provides a good example of what Merleau-Ponty has in mind. When I drive on hot summer days, I often perceive sheets of water on the road approximately 150 yards ahead of me. This gives rise to a perceptual tension similar in some ways to the kind that Merleau-Ponty described in the case of the ship that had run aground. Unlike the spectacle of the ship, the spectacle of the sheet of water is gestalted from the beginning: the *something* that I see is given straightaway *as* a sheet of water. But in both cases, the spectacle is given as unsettled and as falling short of the perceptual ideal of maximum visibility. Something registers as not being right with the scene: the sheet of water is present as the object of my perception, but it is present as somehow unreal. It can be present in this way because perceived things gesture beyond themselves toward the world that functions as the measure of their reality. In this case, the sheet of water seems incompatible with the world that is present along with it. I perceive that it is a hot, dry day, and I recall that the previous few days have been hot and dry as well. Moreover, nothing else in my field of vision seems to be wet. The sheet of water is thus incompatible with the silent thesis of perception: my experience of it cannot be coordinated with my other experiences of the same world. Because of this, it comes to take on the sense of an optical illusion.

The world that is projected in accordance with the silent thesis of perception, though, is not merely a world of things to be perceived more or less clearly. The pre-subjective communication that takes place at the level of the knowing body also extends practical worlds. Things in the world are not given as simply there, standing over and against the perceiving subject. Rather, they are given more basically as imperatives addressed to the sensory-motor powers of the body that knows prior to all reflection how to gear into the nascent sense that they present. Hilary Putnam gives a striking expression of this idea in his *Realism with a Human Face*:

> If I dared to be a metaphysician, I think I would create a system in which there were nothing but obligations . . . Instead of saying with Mill that the chair is a 'permanent possibility of sensations', I would say that it is a *permanent possibility of obligations* . . . What I do think, even outside my fantasies, is that fact and obligations are thoroughly interdependent; there are no facts without obligations, just as there are no obligations without facts.[27]

Perception encounters things in their maximum of visibility when those things play a role in the practical world of the embodied subject. This becomes especially manifest in our spatial perception. To perceive things in space is to perceive them as having orientations that are proper to them, as having their own tops and bottoms.[28] For example, I perceive a chair standing upright differently from the way I perceive the same chair placed upside down on top of a table. Of course I am able in each case to recognise what I perceive as a chair, but the modes of givenness are importantly different. When I encounter the chair in its proper, upright position, I find it to be present straightforwardly and unproblematically as a chair. But when I perceive it upside down on top of the table, I find there to be something unnatural about it. The materiality of the object – the thickness and softness of the chair's padding, the texture of its fabric, the rigidity of its metal legs – stands out more prominently. In short, the sensible qualities of the chair do not recede as readily to make way for the meaning they sustain. The reason the upright chair appears as more solid and more real is that my body knows how to engage with such a thing. The upright chair, unlike the one that is upside down, is the concretion of a fundamentally practical situation.

The things that we encounter as correlates of our knowing bodies extend coherent, determinate practical worlds in which we take our bearings as fundamentally practical subjects. It is not the case, in other words, that subjects impose their intelligible projects onto a world that would be wholly indifferent to them. Rather, one becomes a practical subject in being subjected to the imperative of the world. Alphonso Lingis expresses the point nicely when he writes that the agent is 'delegated by the things'.[29] The tailor's apprentice who enters the workshop for the first time, for example, encounters a scene whose sense is unsettled. He is unable to grasp the workshop in its full determinacy because his body does not yet know how to orient its sensory-motor powers to the objects he encounters. There is a bundle of components: the cut cloth, body and collar canvases, body and sleeve linings, pocketing, sleeve head wadding, shoulder pads, buttons, and so on. Somehow these are going to become the coat of a suit, but the beginning apprentice cannot see how. There is also a set of tools: sewing machines, shears, iron, sleeve and trouser boards, L-square, curve stick, tailor's ham, and so on. Somehow these tools contribute to turning the bundle of components into a coat, but again it is not at all clear how. In order to learn the art of tailoring, the apprentice must develop the modes of perception and of muscular coordination appropriate to the tools and raw materials in the workshop. The relationship between the canvas in the bundle and the specific drape of the completed coat, for example, becomes determinately present for the apprentice as he develops the manual skill of hand padding with a needle and thimble. As the apprentice develops more of these bodily relations to the materials and tools in the workshop, the world of tailoring becomes more determinate for him. The world of tailoring becomes *his* world, the one in which he orients himself with ease. At that point he has been effectively delegated by the things. He has become a tailor.

It is important to emphasise here once again that the normativity inherent in perceptual experience weighs not on the subject present to himself in reflection but rather on *l'on primordial*. To be a practical subject of any particular kind – a tailor, a soccer player, a pianist, and so on – and to be a practical subject in general is to have already responded to the imperative of the world. The pre-subjective level of responsiveness is general and anonymous: an individual becomes a tailor by responding to the imperatives of the tailoring world in more or less the same ways any tailor would. And more generally, the imperatives inherent in the world of perceptual experience apply at the level of the practical subject's most originary opening out onto the world.

We can recognise in the imperative of the world something like Kant's Formula of Universal Law. For Kant, the law is characterised essentially by universality and necessity. This conception is evident both in nature and in political society, which serve as models for the moral imperative: 'act as if the maxim of your action were to become by your will a universal law of nature'.[30] Kant, as we have seen, believes this principle already prevails in our moral common sense; it is not merely a product of abstract moral theorising.[31] It seems, for example, that one of the most basic tenets of our moral common sense is that it is impermissible for a person to make exceptions for herself, that if an obligation legitimately binds others similarly situated, then it binds her as well. Kant's well-known example of the lying promise from the *Groundwork* illustrates the point nicely. If I find myself in financial difficulty, I might be inclined to ask a friend to lend me some money, even though I know with near perfect certainty that I will not be able to pay him back at the appointed time. Because as a practical subject I find myself responsive always already to the imperative of the world, I do not treat my desire for the money as providing me with sufficient justification to tell the lying promise. As with the sheet of water that I perceive ahead of me on the road, I experience the given inclination as only provisionally valid and as standing in need of justification within the context of the world in which it appears. As a practical subject, I take the side of the world: I step back from my perspective as a particular individual with particular interests and ask myself how the lying promise would appear to the promisee, to others who might learn of my false promise, and finally to the world of moral agents generally. If my maxim of telling the lying promise is incompatible with what we might call the silent thesis of moral experience, then I will judge it to be morally impossible, both for me and for any moral agent. The imperative, then, addresses itself not primarily to what is particular in human beings, but rather to what is impersonal and universal in them, to their humanity in general. The Merleau-Pontian account of the normativity of perceptual experience that I have been advancing suggests that the imperative of lawfulness is grounded in the dynamic proper to originary, ambiguous sense. Our embodied relations with things extend a coherent, intelligible world as the field for practical activity in general. We act correctly within this worldly context when we respond to its imperatives in the way that anyone similarly situated would do.

Two Objections to the Perception-Based Account

This account of the normativity inherent in perceptual experience captures many of the features that have traditionally been taken as definitive of the phenomenon of obligation. First, there is something like an imperative that bridles the will of the practical subject. As responsive always already to the nascent sense of the world, we find ourselves drawn toward the achievement of maximal visibility. This draw cannot be understood as a mere counsel addressed to a subject who remains free to accept or reject it based on her conception of her own interests. An object in the world, for example, does not merely recommend itself as blue for a subject who would freely decide whether or not to adopt the bodily attitude necessary to perceive it as such. To be a practical subject in the midst of the world is to have already responded to the draw toward the stabilisation of perceptual sense. That draw is pre-subjective, and it takes a special effort to resist it. In applying to the subject irrespective of her own preferences, the imperative of the world functions more like a command than like a counsel or, *a fortiori*, a petition. But second, even though this imperative orients the practical subject without her having explicitly chosen it, it does not befall her as a wholly passive being. According to Kant,

I can recognize that I am under obligation to others only insofar as I at the same time put myself under obligation, since the law by virtue of which I regard myself as being under obligation proceeds in every case from my own practical reason.[32]

Kant's point is that only subjects capable of actively taking up the law that commands them can be properly obligated. This is why we do not think of baseballs as being obligated by the laws of physics to fall back down to the earth after being hit into the air. Of course the perceiving subject does not literally represent the norms of perceptual experience to herself and then freely choose to act in accordance with them. Indeed, most perceiving subjects are probably unaware that there is a normativity inherent in perception at all. Nonetheless, the subject must actively gear into the nascent sense proposed within the perceived spectacle in order for its meaning to crystallise; it is not enough for her merely to open her eyes. And this points to the third feature of obligation that is captured by the Merleau-Pontian account of perceptual normativity, namely that there are right and wrong ways to fix the sense of situations, and that the rightness and wrongness of these ways is not determined subjectively. Modifying Samuel Clarke's well-known pronouncement, we might say that some scenes are in their own nature fit to be seen as ships that have run aground against the background of a forest. The meaning of the scene is a fact about the scene itself; if the subject does not perceive it that way, then she perceives it wrongly. Of course it is certainly possible that what seems to be a settled sense of the scene will later turn out to have been mistaken. Perhaps what the beach walker sees is really a gigantic *trompe l'oeil* painting of a ship that has run aground against the backdrop of a forest.[33] But this only strengthens the point: once the perceiving subject recognises the scene as a *trompe l'oeil*, her prior determination of the scene's meaning will come to appear as objectively false. Finally, as we have just seen, the content of the obligation suggested by the perceptual account, namely lawfulness and universality, maps fairly closely onto the content suggested by some important early modern moral theories.

But in other respects the account based on the normativity inherent in perceptual experience clearly falls short. First of all, the phenomenon of obligation has a second-personal character that is not captured here. To be obligated is to be the addressee of a legitimate demand. If I were to step on another person's toes in a crowded place, for example, that person would likely address a claim to me demanding that I pick up my foot and place it down somewhere else.[34] The person would not need to convince me, based on reasons to which I was already committed, that it would be best for me to move my foot. The moral necessitation does not derive from my commitment, say, to the idea that causing pain unnecessarily is a bad thing and from my recognition that in the present case I am causing unnecessary pain. What necessitates, in other words, is not an agent-neutral reason. Such reasons are what Stephen Darwall calls reasons of the wrong kind.[35] The ground of my obligation to

remove my foot is rather the authority that the other person possesses as what John Rawls called a self-originating source of valid
claims. I owe it *to* the person as addressor of valid claims to remove
my foot. There is nothing corresponding to this second-personal
authority in the perception-based account of obligation. It would be
very strange to suggest that I owe it to the vaguely present colour
to adopt the bodily attitude toward it necessary to make it appear as
blue. And likewise, I do not owe it to the thimble, the cloth or the
sewing machine to adjust the sensory-motor powers of my body to
them in the manner necessary to produce a coat. Of course as a tailor I respond to the demands that the tools and the materials in the
workshop address to my knowing body, but these demands seem
importantly different from the second-personal demands that give
rise to obligations.

And second, it seems clear that failure to respond in the appropriate way to norms grounded in perception does not constitute a
specifically moral kind of wrong. Failure in this case seems much
closer to simple error. To take my own case as an example, I find it
extraordinarily difficult to catch on to the sense of spatial relations.
My difficulty is especially acute when I try to make sense of the
shapes that things take as they are folded in various ways. What I
see when I witness fabric being folded is something akin to visual
nonsense. This means, of course, that I am incompetent as a tailor.
When I try to do the simplest tailoring jobs, I fail badly. I regard this
lack of ability as unfortunate, but it would seem very odd to regard
it as a moral failing. In Kantian terms, I experience the perceptual
imperatives more as hypothetical than categorical: their address
seems less like a 'you must' and more like an 'it would be good to'.
Since obligation happens as a kind of necessitation, we cannot fully
account for it by reference to the norms of perceptual experience.

Saussurian Linguistics

In the period following the publication of *Phenomenology of Perception*, Merleau-Ponty began to develop an account that treated the
dynamic proper to perceptual experience as a particular case of
the more general dynamic of expression. Simplifying somewhat,
we might say that in *Phenomenology of Perception*, Merleau-Ponty
attempted to understand sense and its expression on the basis of

a conception of the body and its specific kind of intentionality, whereas in subsequent works, including *The Prose of the World* and 'Indirect Language and the Voices of Silence', as well as in his courses at the Collège de France, Merleau-Ponty conceives expression itself as basic.[36] This later conception, I want to argue, provides us with a better understanding of what I am calling the fact of sense and thus makes possible a more adequate account of the ground of the bindingness of obligation.

The phenomenology of expression that Merleau-Ponty developed in his works of the 1950s owes a great deal to his reading, or perhaps better his creative misreading, of the linguistics of Ferdinand de Saussure.[37] In order to understand Merleau-Ponty's account and its relevance for the problem of obligation, then, it will be necessary first to examine some of the basic commitments of Saussurian linguistics, which are set forth in the *Course in General Linguistics*. Saussure's goal in this text is ambitious: he aims to establish the science of linguistics on solid ground by determining its proper object more precisely than linguists had done up to his time. Of course it might seem obvious that the proper object of linguistics is language, but that determination turns out to be unhelpful. As Saussure notes, the widely varying phenomena that fall under the umbrella term 'language' prove to be too unwieldy for a single science to capture. The linguist would need to study the mechanisms by which the ear perceives articulated sounds as well as the oral articulation of those sounds. She would also need to study the different social conditions in which linguistic signs are exchanged. And in addition to all this, she would have to examine language in its historical aspect, explaining how and why languages evolve in the ways they do.[38] No coherent science can concern itself with such a hodgepodge of different objects. The decisive innovation of Saussure's text, then, is to refound linguistics as the science of a special object that he calls the linguistic structure or *langue*, which is the necessary condition for any particular act of speaking (*parole*). The principal advantage of focusing specifically on the *langue* is that it constitutes a single, isolable object. It can be studied independently of anything external to it, including the uses that actual speakers make of it and the concrete historical and social contexts in which it is situated.

This abstraction of the linguistic structure from everything external to it finds its justification in the 'first principle' of Saussurian

linguistics, which is that 'the link between the signifier and the signified is arbitrary'.[39] To say that the link between signifier and signified is arbitrary is not at all to say that speakers are free to choose
whichever signifiers they like to refer to whichever signifieds they
like. Indeed, as we will see, it will turn out to mean almost the opposite. What the principle does mean is that the signifier is unmotivated by external reality.[40] Our use of the word *dog* to signify dogs,
for example, owes nothing at all to the properties of real dogs in
the extra-linguistic world; nothing about dogs compels us to signify
them the way we do in contemporary English. This, of course, is
obvious from the fact that different languages have different words
for the same signifieds. The signification of *dog* is rather a function
of the term's place within the system of language itself. We must
be careful here not to think of this system as a kind of treasury of
terms, each of which would stand in a one-to-one relation with its
meaning. In fact, the most essential feature of the new object of the
science of linguistics is that 'in the *langue* there are only differences.
Even more: in general a difference supposes positive terms between
which the difference is established, but in the *langue* there are only
differences, and no positive terms.'[41] The meaning of terms, or more
precisely what Saussure calls the value of terms, is a function of
their structurally fixed differential relations. The English term *sheep*
and the French term *mouton*, for example, can be used to refer to
the very same objects in extra-linguistic space, but they nonetheless have different values. This difference is attributable to the different systems of differential relations that constitute the English
and French languages. In English, the value of the term *sheep* is
determined in part by its difference from the term *mutton*, or sheep
considered as meat. Since the French *langue* does not differentiate
between a sheep considered as an animal and a sheep considered as
meat, the values of *sheep* and *mouton* are not the same.[42] The difference in the values of the two terms can thus be understood entirely
at the level of the two *langues*.

This same differential structure applies at the level of phonemes,
which are the elementary units of sound within a *langue*. Phonemes,
taken by themselves, are insignificant: it would make no sense, for
example, to ask what /ʧ/ signifies in English.[43] According to the
linguist Roman Jakobson, the value of a phoneme like /ʧ/ 'is only
its power to distinguish the word containing this phoneme from

any words which, similar in all other respects, contain some other phoneme'.[44] The value of /ʧ/, then, is to enable us to distinguish *chock* from words like *shock, sock, jock* and *Jacques*. Even if a person had never encountered the words *chock* and *hock* before, she would assume that they signify different things because of the different phonemes.[45]

It follows from this fact about phonemes that language users who want to express themselves in individual speech acts are tightly constrained by the system of differences that constitutes the *langue*. If a speaker does not respect the differences – if, for example, she treats /ʧ/, /ʃ/, /s/, /ʤ/, /ʒ/ and /h/ as having the same phonemic value – then she will fail to express a comprehensible thought. The differential structure of the *langue* is given as a kind of normative fact whose legitimacy cannot be justified by any deduction: anyone who would call it into question would by that very fact have accepted its authority. Even if a subject, for whatever reason, sought to introduce a modification into the system of phonemic differences, she could only do so in language that accepted the constraints of the differences. Moreover, she would only ever succeed, at best, in bringing about a slightly modified linguistic system whose structural differences would still need to be respected. This explains the sharp dualism that Saussure insists upon between *langue* and *parole*, and why he believes that the former is the only proper object of the science of linguistics. Individual speech acts are merely manifestations of the linguistic structure, in something like the way an orchestra's performance of a symphony is merely a manifestation of the symphony itself. 'The symphony', according to Saussure, 'has a reality of its own, which is independent of the way in which it is performed'.[46] The performance in both cases is 'ancillary and more or less accidental'.[47]

Saussurian linguistics, then, reduces to almost nothing the role of the subject in producing linguistic meaning. 'The *langue*', he insists, 'is not a function of the speaking subject; it is the product that the individual registers passively'.[48] On Saussure's account, meaning cannot originate from a subject who gears into the nascent sense presented in perceptual experience. The perceiving subject's ability to fix the sense of what she sees as a ship that has run aground against the backdrop of a forest presupposes her ability to articulate the indeterminate totality of the world's signifyingness, to break it up into differentiated, stable significations. This segmentation of indeterminate signifyingness is the work of the *langue*. In no way can it be conceived phenomenologically as the product of subjective acts of sense-bestowal, even if those acts are understood in a Merleau-Pontian way as involving an irreducible moment of passivity and responsiveness.[49]

Merleau-Ponty's Reinterpretation of Saussure

Despite all of this, when Merleau-Ponty begins to write and to lecture about Saussure in the late 1940s and early 1950s, he consistently credits him with having 'inaugurated a linguistics of *speech*'.[50] Considered strictly as an interpretation of Saussurian linguistics, this seems plainly false. Indeed, Merleau-Ponty seems to attribute to Saussure exactly the position that the *Course in General Linguistics* was meant to refute.[51] Whether Merleau-Ponty's reading is mistaken as an exegesis of Saussure's work is an open question. What is clear, on the other hand, is that his reading is philosophically fruitful.[52] Specifically, his understanding of the role of speech in the total phenomenon of language provides new resources for thinking through an especially thorny problem in Saussurian linguistics that results from the strict dualism of *langue* and *parole* and from the priority assigned to the former. On the one hand, the *langue* must be a closed system; this follows from Saussure's foundational commitment to the idea that the signifier is unmotivated by factors outside the *langue* itself. And as Paul Ricoeur has argued, the closure of the system is necessary as a defence against the return of psychologism, or the idea that meaning has its origin in the acts of speaking subjects. It is the rejection of the psychologistic position on meaning that constitutes one of the most important innovations of Saussurian linguistics.[53] On the other hand, though, it is an undeniable fact that linguistic structures do change over time. Moreover, this change is certainly attributable, at least in part, to speaking subjects making use of the *langue* in novel ways. This suggests that the *langue* is not quite as closed off from extra-linguistic events as the theory seems to require. Of course Saussure is aware that languages change over time and that some account needs to be given of these changes. For the most part, he treats linguistic change as accidental and as the product of an evolution that takes place without the members of the linguistic community even recognising it. In Old High German, for example, the plural of *hant* (hand) was made by adding an *i* to the end of the word, but over time this *i* produced an effect on the vowel of the preceding syllable, changing it to an *e*. Eventually, the final *i* weakened into an *e*, leading to the current German *Hände* as the plural for *Hand*. Exactly the same pattern characterised the change of similar German words such as *gasti* (guests), which evolved into *Gäste*.[54] Clearly, these changes, which developed over the course of centuries, were not intended by the linguistic community. Nobody reflected on the expressive possibilities available within Old High German and concluded that the true meaning of *hands* would be captured better by *Hände* than by *hanti*. But even this account, which attempts to limit the role of speaking subjects, ends up compromising the strict dualism of *langue* and *parole*: intentional or not, the acts of speaking subjects play some role in shaping the linguistic structure. *Parole* must be something more than 'ancillary and more or less accidental'. Merleau-Ponty's idiosyncratic reading of Saussure presses on this point, reconceptualising the interdependence of *langue* and *parole* in a way that accounts for the stability of language while still doing justice to the facts of linguistic change.

When Merleau-Ponty invokes the distinction between *langue* and *parole*, he typically substitutes his own preferred terminology. In some places he distinguishes between the empirical and the creative uses of language respectively[55] and in others he marks the distinction as one between spoken language and speaking language (*langage parlé* and *langage parlante*).[56] This terminology suggests a rejection of Saussurian dualism: in both ways of marking the distinction, Merleau-Ponty treats *langue* and *parole* as two different manifestations of the same thing, and not as ontologically distinct realities.[57] On his account, the two sides of the phenomenon of language stand in a quasi-dialectical relation, such that spoken language envelops the speaking subject while at the same time being enveloped by it.[58] The first part of the relation – the envelopment of the speaking subject by the already existing system of language – is the one that Saussure's work emphasises, almost to the exclusion of the second part. In any attempt to express himself, the speaking subject finds himself given over to a sedimented system of meanings. He can never situate himself anterior to this system, reducing it to the status of a correlate of his intentional, constituting consciousness:

to intend the sedimented system of meanings at all presupposes the resources of that very system. Even when the speaking subject strives to express a meaning that has never been expressed before, he can do so only by calling upon the expressive resources already present in the *langue*. Merleau-Ponty's description of the dependence of *parole* on the *langue* is clearly inspired by the Saussurian account, but his own development of the point leads his philosophy of expression in an importantly different direction. For Saussure, as we have seen, the *langue* is a 'product that the individual registers passively'. This conception, which treats the system of language as a kind of natural object, is entirely incompatible with our experience of language.[59] On Merleau-Ponty's account, as we will see in more detail in what follows, the speaking subject is dependent on the *langue* in something like the way the perceiving subject is dependent on the nascent perceptual sense within which he finds himself embedded always already. In both cases, the subject is best described as actively passive, and not merely as passive.

This point leads directly to the idea, underemphasised in Saussure, that the system of language is enveloped by the *parole* of the subject. As Émile Benveniste has argued, it is a fundamental property of language 'to imply that something corresponds to what is uttered, some thing and not "nothing"'.[60] It is essential to language, in other words, that it signify and that it refer to something other than itself. It is not and can never be a purely formal, closed system, even if it is sometimes helpful to view it that way for methodological reasons. Now a language can signify and refer only if there is a subject to animate it with his expressive intention. The subject means to say something and the language is present to him as a means of doing so. Importantly, the subject who strives to express himself alters the system of language as it exists at the moment he takes it up, inflecting it in such a way as to make it say something that has not already been said. If the *langue* were not open to being inflected by the expressive intentions of speaking subjects in this way, then it would be reduced to the status of a mere code in which signifiers would stand in static, one-to-one relations with their signifieds, similar to the relations that obtain between house numbers and the houses they refer to.[61] But the *langue* is not like a code. Speaking subjects are able to put terms to nonstandard uses without throwing the linguistic system completely out of equilibrium. For example, subjects can express affirmation by using conventionally accepted signs for negation. If I have a guest in my home and he asks if it is all right if he uses my restroom, I might tell him no. But in saying no, I mean to express to him that yes, it is indeed all right if he uses my restroom. More specifically, I mean to convey that allowing him to use my restroom is such a basic courtesy that I would not seriously think to deny it. I draw attention to the unthinkability of denying the courtesy by playfully denying it. When I do this, my friend has no difficulty whatever catching on to the intended sense.[62] Any adequate account of how language works must be able to account for possibilities like this. That I can express myself successfully while violating one of the most fundamental differential relations within the *langue* – that yes is not no and no is not yes – demonstrates that the linguistic system is not a mere code and that particular speech acts do not 'perform' the *langue* in the way that a particular orchestra performs the symphony. Cases like this suggest that it is the speaking subject's expressive intention, along with the capacity of other speaking subjects to catch on to that intention, that carries the sense. Terms can take on new and even contradictory significations without in the least endangering the stability of the *langue*. Since the speaking subject has this power to modify the equilibrium of the system, and since the system is what it is only as enabling this subjective power of novel expression, it is legitimate to say that the *langue* is enveloped by *parole*.

The Dynamic of Communication

Merleau-Ponty's reconceptualisation of the relation between *langue* and *parole* calls into question our common-sense understanding of what we are doing when we communicate with each other, and more specifically, when we make second-personal, moral claims against each other.[63] Our everyday experience suggests to us that communication happens when one person (the sender) possesses a piece of information (the message) and conveys that message via some medium (the channel) to another person (the receiver). According to this model of communication, the sender encodes her thoughts by putting them into the form of language and the receiver decodes the message, translating the sender's words back into the thoughts they stand in for. Communication is successful when the sender's thoughts reach the receiver's mind undistorted. That this 'transmission model' accords with our intuitions is suggested by many of the idioms we use when we talk about communication: we are concerned to 'convey' our meaning and to 'get our points across'. And in the educational context, instructors at all levels are tasked with 'delivering the course content'.[64] Signs, according to this common-sense, transmission model of communication, are 'no more than monitors which notify the hearer that he must consider such and such of his thoughts'.[65] When I say 'tall coffee' to the barista, for example, I am advising him to consult the ideas in his mind that match up with the sign *tall* and the sign *coffee*. Communication is possible, then, only for interlocutors who have the same ideas in their minds and who connect those ideas with the same words.

This common-sense account of communication cannot be correct, according to Merleau-Ponty. If it were true, then it would be impossible for communication ever to bring interlocutors to understand the topics they discussed any differently from the ways they already did. Receivers would understand senders' messages simply by decoding the signs that conveyed them, translating them into thoughts they already possessed. These codings of thoughts into linguistic formulations and decodings of the linguistic formulations back into thoughts would leave no remainder; the formulations would be perfectly sufficient vehicles of thought. If they were not, then the attempted communication would simply fail. But, as suggested above, communication certainly can give rise to new and unforeseen meanings. Literature provides some of the most compelling examples of this phenomenon. 'Before I read Stendhal', Merleau-Ponty writes, 'I know what a rogue is. Thus I can understand what he means when he says that Rassi the revenue man is a rogue.'[66] If the reader did not understand the meaning of the term *rogue* at all, then he would necessarily fail to make sense of an important part of Stendhal's *The Charterhouse of Parma*. In this, at least, the transmission model of communication is certainly correct. But merely having the concept *rogue* within one's treasury of significations is not sufficient. To understand the character Rassi within the context of the novel requires much more than simply recognising that he is a token of the type *rogue*. (Indeed, it would not be sufficient even to know the established significations of every one of the predicates that Stendhal attributes to Rassi.) As the reader makes his way through the text, catching on more and more to Stendhal's unique style of literary expression, he comes to acquire an understanding of the signification *rogue* that is genuinely new. The general idea *rogue* becomes incarnated and thus fulfilled in the unique man Rassi. All of the situations in which the character is described, along with all the other qualities he is presented as having, contribute toward drawing out of the idea *rogue* meanings that are richer and more nuanced than the ones the reader brought with him to his encounter with the text. In Stendhal's work, stock significations 'are given a new twist. The cross references multiply. More and more arrows point in the direction of a thought [the reader has] never encountered before and perhaps never would have met without Stendhal.'[67] The same is true for any successful work of literature; if it were not, then literature would not continue to hold our interest.

Genuine communication, which goes beyond the exchange of messages that are understood in advance, is rendered possible by a dynamic of sense that emerges with the mutual envelopment of *langue* and *parole*, of spoken language and speaking language. Speakers (and by extension writers, painters, musicians, etc.) find themselves responsive always already to a sense that pre-exists them. But as we have seen, this sense cannot be understood as a treasury of fully formed significations at the disposal of speaking subjects. Just as in the case of strictly perceptual experience, the sense to which subjects find themselves responsive is experienced as nascent and as soliciting them to bring it to greater determinacy. When the writer begins working on his novel, then, he does not conceive the meaning of the whole with perfect clarity, such that he would only need to put down on paper the thoughts that were already fully present in his mind. He knows he has *something* to say, but that something is 'as yet no more than a precise uneasiness in the world of things-said'.[68] In response to this uneasiness, the writer will strive for the right words, trying out different formulations. Many of these he will experience as failing to capture the sense that solicits him, but eventually, if things go well, he will hit upon just the right expression. At that point, the sense is no longer nascent; it becomes a settled signification. The crystallisation of the sense of Rassi's specific style of roguishness was no doubt the result of this kind of process. But the quasi-dialectic of spoken language and speaking language does not come to a halt at this point. *The Charterhouse of Parma* does not express the sense of rogue so completely that nothing more remains to be said. What happens instead is that Stendhal's successful expression is integrated into the spoken language, where it will form once again a part of the nascent sense that other subjects will take up and crystallise in different ways. And of course we can describe the same process from the side of the reader: at first, the sense of *rogue* that Stendhal is developing is given as less than fully determinate. The reader knows that Rassi is being presented as a rogue, but she does not yet have a clear sense of his specific mode of roguishness. The sense is nascent, soliciting her to work out the more determinate sense that Stendhal is developing. She reads the text attentively, trying out this interpretation and that until eventually the sense crystallises. At that point the Stendhalian rogue becomes part of her stock of sedimented significations. Once again, the reader's sense of *rogue* will not be frozen from that point forward; it will be developed in unforeseeable ways in her future communicative encounters.

Merleau-Ponty characterised the dynamic that emerges in the mutual envelopment of spoken and speaking language as a 'moving equilibrium'.[69] His account makes sense of the two features of language that appeared contradictory within Saussurian linguistics, namely its stability and its capacity to undergo changes as a result of the choices of speaking subjects. On the one hand, the system of language is quite stable. When Stendhal writes *The Charterhouse of Parma*, his expressive possibilities are strongly constrained by the *langue*. He cannot make *rogue* mean whatever he wants it to mean. If he tries to do that, his expression will fail. But his constraint is not so total that he is condemned merely to repeat well-worn significations. The terms of the language are given as adumbrating new sense; speaking subjects gear into that adumbrated sense and crystallise it in new significations. The new significations do not destroy the equilibrium of the *langue*, reducing it to non-signifying chaos. Rather, they effect a slightly modified equilibrium that will continue to constrain the expressions of speaking subjects, but that will also continue to adumbrate new and unforeseen meanings.

In his book, *Merleau-Ponty and the Paradoxes of Expression*, Donald A. Landes fleshes this out in terms of what Gilbert Simondon calls a metastable equilibrium. A metastable state is one that is 'precariously stable', that is, one in which there is some degree of tension between the sense that is expressible and the sense that has already been expressed.[70] In contrast to this, a state of sense would be in a stable equilibrium just in case all the sense that is expressible has already been expressed. Such a state would contain the lowest possible degree of potential sense. Communication in that case really would amount to nothing more than the transmission of signs that functioned merely as monitors for significations that the interlocutors already possessed. Finally, if the state of sense were in an unstable equilibrium, meanings would not be fixed into established significations at all, so that genuine expression would be impossible.[71] There can be genuine expression, then, only because the sense to which we find ourselves given over always already is metastable, because there is an excess of determinable sense over the sense that has already been determined. This excess not only makes possible, but also calls for, the production of new determinations of sense.

Obligation and the Claim of the Other

In his book *Antwortregister* and in later works that have expanded on its main thesis, Bernhard Waldenfels developed an account of obligation based in part on this dynamic of metastable sense. Waldenfels's account emphasises the element of responsiveness that belongs irreducibly to any kind of expression. To be an expressive subject is to find oneself responsive to a world of sense that is in a metastable equilibrium, with an excess of potential, determinable sense over determinate sense. The subject experiences the nascently meaningful situations she finds herself in as calling for her to do something, but without knowing for certain what that something is. This is where Waldenfels locates the necessitation that is essential to the phenomenon of obligation: 'We cannot not respond. The double "not" points to a *must* in the sense of a practical necessity.'[72] Waldenfels's argument here is similar in structure, though not in its conclusion, to the one advanced by Korsgaard in *The Sources of Normativity*. As we have seen, Korsgaard believes the problem of normativity arises with reflection, or with the capacity to step back from our beliefs, desires and values and to question their legitimacy. To solve the problem of normativity is to discover the point from which it is impossible to step back and reflect further. For Korsgaard, that point is the value of humanity: 'it is simply the truth' about us that we are the kinds of beings who require reasons to act.[73] All such reasons, she believes, are grounded in humanity as a practical identity presupposed in all our action. Because all of our action presupposes humanity as a practical identity, we cannot not take it as a source of normativity. We cannot effectively step back and reflect on the value of being the sorts of beings who act for reasons, since the very act of stepping back would presuppose the value in question. Waldenfels argues similarly, insisting in a Merleau-Pontian vein on the irreducibility of responsiveness in the structure of our practical subjectivity. We cannot not respond to the nascent sense of the world, and this is simply a fact: we do not put ourselves in that condition by means of reflection and neither can we step outside it by reflection.[74]

Because the sense to which we find ourselves responsive is metastable, we cannot understand ourselves as autonomous moral agents in the Kantian sense, acting spontaneously on the basis of principles that we have always before our minds and that enable us to tell without any difficulty what we ought and ought not to do. 'As a respondent', Waldenfels writes, 'I begin elsewhere, that is, there where I am not, where I have not yet been, and where I never will be.'[75] The practical subject does not have the moral sense of situations as a secure possession, but must rather bring it into being in something like the way the attentive reader brings the sense of Rassi's roguishness into being. Thus, 'the respondent, like the lover in Lacan, gives what he does not have, but what is nonetheless demanded of him'.[76] He gives what he does not have because he must: it is impossible not to respond, since even the absence of response constitutes a kind of response.[77] If I am out for a walk in my neighbourhood, for example, and I spot a young person with a clipboard who is trying to make eye contact with me and who is wearing a t-shirt featuring the logo of a well-known charity or political campaign, I might choose to look down at the ground as I walk past her. I have good reason to believe she is going to ask me to contribute money to her cause, or that at least she will want me to listen to her pitch. My refusal to respond to her appeal constitutes a response, and that response gives expression to the ethical sense of the situation. Specifically, in looking away I treat the wide duty of beneficence as not applying to me in this case. I express the judgement that the good the young person is pursing is not weighty enough to interfere with my pursuit of my own interests. This sense of the situation is not already present in the moral law, which I would only need to apply correctly to the case. But neither do I bring the moral sense into existence *ex nihilo*. Rather, I bring the moral sense of the situation into being, as Merleau-Ponty puts it, by 'receiving and giving in the same gesture'.[78] I bring to the situation the stock of moral understandings that I have built up over the course of my life, just as I bring to my reading of *The Charterhouse of Parma* an already determinate understanding of what it means to be a rogue. But as the situation develops, I remain receptive to the ways in which the emerging sense diverges from my more or less settled moral understandings. Eventually, just as in the case of reading the novel, the sense of *this* situation crystallises. This dynamic of simultaneous giving and receiving, which is proper to metastable sense and which befalls me as a fact, obligates me.

The account of obligation grounded in Merleau-Ponty's philosophy of expression constitutes a major improvement over the perception-based account, most importantly because it does a better job of capturing the second-personal nature of the phenomenon. To find ourselves responsive always already to metastable sense is to find ourselves in relation to others to whom we are answerable. The language that Merleau-Ponty has described in broadly Saussurian terms 'is like a magic machine for transporting the "I" into the other person's perspective'.[79] Again, when I begin reading *The Charterhouse of Parma*, I do not quite grasp the sense that Stendhal is giving to the term *rogue*. But because the crystallisation of metastable sense happens not inside the space of my own mind, but rather in accordance with a dynamic in which I receive and give in the same gesture, I am able to catch on to a sense that is not already mine. The capacity of the speaking subject to be transported into the other person's perspective has obvious moral implications. It might happen, for example, that I engage with another person in a way that is condescending and disrespectful, but without recognising that I am doing so. The sense of my own act is not fully present to me as I am engaged in it; the sense crystallises for me only after the other person responds in a way that suggests he has taken offence. I experience something like a Gestalt switch as I come to see my own act from the other's perspective. I recognise that the conduct I had viewed as innocent was in fact morally problematic.

As it stands, though, this account is still not quite sufficient to capture the second-personal nature of obligation. The problem is that it looks very similar to the rationalist arguments against which Jean Barbeyrac directed his well-known objection. For the rationalists, we will recall, the necessitation proper to obligation was grounded in the supposed fact that we are unable to withhold our assent from what we perceive clearly and distinctly. According to Malebranche, for example, we perceive clearly and distinctly that coachmen have a greater degree of perfection than their horses, and so we cannot help but value them to a greater degree. Barbeyrac's criticism of such 'can't-help-but' arguments is that the mere recognition of something as having a specific moral property does not entail the obligation to act in any particular way with respect to that thing. The moral agent is conceived on the rationalist account first and foremost as a knowing subject rather than as the addressee of a demand. In Merleau-Ponty's account, as we have developed it up to this point, we find a similar problem. There is a dynamic proper to metastable sense, such that it is oriented normatively toward crystallisation. After the conversation with the other person has taken its course, I recognise the sense of my actions. Once the Gestalt switch has taken place, I cannot view my behaviour otherwise than as disrespectful. It is not obvious, though, how this recognition of the sense of my behaviour entails an obligation to act differently in the future.

But there are resources in Merleau-Ponty's philosophy of expression that are helpful toward addressing this objection. Most importantly, Merleau-Ponty writes in *The Prose of the World* that

there can be speech (and in the end personality) only for an 'I' which contains the germ of a depersonalization. Speaking and listening not only presuppose thought but – even more essential, for it is practically the foundation of thought – the capacity to allow oneself to be pulled down and rebuilt again by the other person before one, by others who may come along, and in principle by anyone.[80]

This description of the process by which the sense of a situation is determined presents the other less as a partner with whom I cooperate to discover the truth and more as an addressor of claims against me. To return to the previous example, I may bring to my encounter with another person a sense of myself as more knowledgeable or as having a higher social status than him. Acting on the basis of that sense, I might treat him condescendingly, monopolising the conversation and treating as unworthy of serious consideration the few points I allow him to get in. Because the sense of the situation is metastable, though, I never have secure possession of it; I am always vulnerable to losing it in my continued engagement with the other. In this case, the other might express his sense of what is happening with a look of annoyance on his face, or by rolling his eyes, or even by telling me straightforwardly that I am treating him with disrespect. These expressions are not just presentations of possible alternative determinations of sense. More basically, they are given as claims against me. By means of these claims, the other pulls me down from my self-appointed position as final judge of the sense of the situation, demanding that I reconsider the situation from his point of view. He does this simply by engaging in communication with me. To be condemned to sense, then, is to find oneself positioned as an addressee by others who are given, whether one likes it or not, as self-originating sources of valid claims. The permanent possibility of being pulled down by such claims is an irreducible fact of our being-in-the-world. We cannot not respond to the claims, even though it is impossible for us to know with certainty how we ought to respond. The bindingness of obligation, according to the Merleau-Pontian account I am suggesting here, lies in this double *not*.

4 Noise

In the previous chapter I proposed a Merleau-Pontian account of the genesis of moral sense and of the moral subject who at once gives and receives it. Given the broadly Kantian or Korsgaardian strategy that I pursue in this book – that of attempting to locate the source of normativity at the point where the subject can no longer step back from the contents of its consciousness and call into question the bindingness of purported reasons for action – it is essential that the genetic account be correct. Obligation, on the account suggested in the previous chapter, originates in the dynamic of metastable sense within which moral subjectivity first arises. This dynamic is a fact in the sense of the Kantian fact of reason: to be a moral subject at all is to be subjected to it always already. There can be no question, then, of the subject's getting behind this fact and putting its validity to the test.

What I want to argue in this chapter is that the Merleau-Pontian account is not quite right because it overlooks a dimension of sense that is indispensable for our understanding of obligation. Building on the work of Michel Serres, I will argue that what Merleau-Ponty misses is the dimension of noise. I will begin by developing Serres's argument that sense has its origin in noise and by demonstrating the significance of this fact for our understanding of moral experience. Next, I will argue that our exposure to noise constitutes a fact in the sense of the Kantian fact of reason. Finally, I will develop the consequences of this conception of noise for our understanding of the phenomenon of obligation.

Noise as Originary

The source of the problem in the Merleau-Pontian account of the genesis of moral sense can be stated straightforwardly: the metastable sense he takes to be originary is conceived entirely with reference to the stability toward which it tends. This is suggested by Merleau-Ponty's characterisation of this sense-in-becoming as latent sense and as nascent *logos*. At the most originary level of our opening out onto the world, we experience 'a precise uneasiness', a tension that points ahead to a determinate, crystallised sense that would resolve it. We experience a tension in the perceptual sense of the spectacle at the beach precisely because it is not yet given as what it truly is: a ship against the backdrop of a forest. And we experience a tension in the early pages of a novel because we have not yet been presented with the definitive sense of the events that are being described. To be condemned to sense in general just is to find ourselves oriented in this way always already. And as we have seen, we can understand this orientation as the source of normativity insofar as it is an originary, irreducible fact from which the moral subject cannot step back and reflect. The problem with this account is that the orientation toward determinate, fully crystallised sense is not in fact originary. This is not to deny the more general point established by Merleau-Ponty's phenomenologies of perception and expression, namely that as subjects we find ourselves responsive always already to a sense that exceeds signification. It is to deny, though, that this originary excessive sense is best understood as latency or nascence. In order to provide an adequate account of the fact of sense, then, it will be necessary to give an account of the genesis of the orientation that Merleau-Ponty treats as basic. What I want to argue, following Michel Serres, is that such a genesis must begin with the phenomenon that information theorists call noise. As Serres has demonstrated in many different works, but perhaps most explicitly in *Hermès I: La Communication*, *The Parasite* and *Genesis*, noise is originary; meaning, whether this be understood as accomplished signification or as orientation within and toward sense in general, emerges from it.

In order to show how this is so, we must begin with a provisional characterisation of the phenomenon of noise. In the essay 'Platonic Dialogue and the Intersubjective Genesis of Abstraction' from *Hermès I: La Communication*, Serres offers a definition that is taken directly from information theory: noise is 'the set of these phenomena of interference that hinder communication'.[1] Communication is understood here on the basis of the 'transmission model' described in the previous chapter: a sender conveys a message to a receiver through a channel. The communication is successful when the message that the sender meant to convey reaches the receiver in a form that is sufficiently undistorted. What gives rise to the science of information theory is that the message never arrives at its destination completely undistorted; there is always noise in the channel. In a telegraph, for example, the discrete pulses of current – the dots and dashes – that are emitted by the sender tend to become smoothed out and indistinct by the time they reach the receiver, sometimes to the point where the message becomes indecipherable. This is an unavoidable consequence of having to send the current through a telegraph wire that conducts less than perfectly. Likewise, the analogue signal transmitted by a television station at a particular frequency can be affected by electromagnetic emissions from the environment, producing static that distorts or even drowns out the message. The basic concepts of information theory – sender, receiver, message, channel, noise – were developed with these kinds of communication systems in mind, but they can help us to understand many other forms of communication as well. A face-to-face conversation, for example, can be understood as an exchange of messages between a sender who encodes his message in natural language and a receiver who decodes the language, transforming it into thoughts that are identical, ideally at least, to those intended by the sender. In this case, the channel of communication is natural language. If the sender has a strong accent or a speech impediment, then the receiver will have to struggle to separate the message from the noise. The same kind of analysis can be given for an exchange of handwritten letters: to write badly, or merely idiosyncratically, is to 'plunge the graphic message into this noise' and thus to endanger the success of the communication.[2]

In all of these examples, noise appears as something bad, something that we should want to eliminate to the greatest extent possible. This is the point of view of anyone who is engaged in everyday acts of communication, whether as the sender or as the receiver of messages. If I order a pizza by telephone, for example, I want to be sure that my message cuts through the background noise coming from the kitchen. If I am not confident that my order has been correctly received, I will try to allay my concerns by asking for confirmation. But I would be happier not having to worry about the noise at all. That is why, given the option, I would prefer to order online. And of course if I am in the business of selling pizza, I have a strong interest in receiving my customers' messages exactly as they intended to send them. This common-sense perspective is also the perspective of information theory, which has been concerned from the beginning with 'the technical problem of accuracy of transference of various types of signals from sender to receiver'.[3] In 'Platonic Dialogue and the Intersubjective Genesis of Abstraction', Serres suggests that we can understand philosophical reflection itself as responding to this 'technical problem'. For example, although we typically think of the interlocutors within the Platonic dialogues as antagonists, he argues that we can understand them more basically as allies struggling together against the noise that threatens to engulf them all. The interlocutors 'battle together for the sake of producing a truth on which they can agree, that is, for the sake of successful communication. In a certain sense, they struggle together against interference, against the demon, against the third man.'[4] In Book X of *The Republic*, to take just one example, Plato presents Socrates and Glaucon as doing battle together against the noise of the sensible for the sake of producing an idea whose sense could be agreed to in principle by anyone. In order to help Glaucon to conceive the idea of a bed, Socrates emphasises its difference from the beds that are given in perceptual experience: particular beds with their particular colours, sizes and shapes, which are seen from particular points of view. The sensibly given beds are best understood as channels through which the abstract idea of a bed in general is made manifest. But the channel is noisy: the particularities of the particular beds obscure the ideality of the intelligible bed. Just, then, as the geometer must be able to disregard the perceived qualities of particular triangles – their being drawn in chalk or in pencil, their being drawn more or less precisely, and so on – and to direct her thought to the properties of intelligible triangles, so more generally the philosopher must take a stand against the noise, turning away from the sensible and toward the intelligible.[5]

Although Serres himself does not extend his argument in this way, we can also recognise in Immanuel Kant's moral philosophy, and specifically in his conception of obligation, an overriding concern to eliminate noise. As we have seen, for Kant the experience of obligation is only possible for a being whose faculty of desire is split between higher and lower faculties. The lower faculty of desire, on Kant's account, is determined entirely pathologically, that is, by the feelings of pleasure and pain. The principle that governs this faculty is that of 'self-love or one's own happiness'.[6] For beings that have only a lower faculty of desire – cats, for example – the fact that some state of affairs appears pleasurable constitutes by itself a sufficient reason to try to bring it about. In any particular case, then, their wills are equivalent to their contingent desires. The question of obligation, or unconditional necessitation of the will, can never even arise for such beings. The higher faculty of desire, on the other hand, is pure practical reason itself and is thus determined 'by the mere form of a practical rule without presupposing any feeling and hence without any representation of the agreeable or disagreeable as the matter of the faculty of desire, which is always an empirical condition of principles'.[7] A being with only a higher faculty of desire, such as God, would act in accordance with the moral law simply as a matter of course. Such a being could have no experience of necessitation, and thus of obligation: 'the "ought" is out of place here, because volition is of itself necessarily in accord with the law'.[8] The experience of unconditional necessitation is only possible for beings like us for whom 'the will stands between its a priori principle, which is formal, and its a posteriori incentive, which is material, as at a crossroads'.[9] Our wills are pulled in two different directions at once, toward the satisfaction of our inclinations and toward conformity with the law. The experience of constraint is the experience of the authoritativeness of the higher faculty over the lower. It is the recognition that our inclinations cannot give us sufficient reason to pursue particular courses of action and that we must refuse to let them determine our wills, even at the cost of our happiness.[10] Returning to the vocabulary of information theory, we can say that the pure moral law is the message and that the inclinations are the noise. For a being like God, who has no pathologically determined inclinations, there is no moral noise at all, and hence no moral struggle. And for beings with only a lower faculty of desire, there is no specifically moral message; the only relevant, action-guiding messages come from the inclinations themselves. Genuinely moral experience is only possible for finite rational beings like us, that is, for beings who are constitutively oriented toward a moral message that is constantly obscured by the noise of the inclinations. To be a moral agent, on this account, is to do battle against the noise.[11]

This reconstruction of Kant's account of moral experience in terms of information theory presents noise as a kind of interference, as an obstacle to the moral subject's reception of the pure moral law. Ideally, our moral experience would be as free of noise as possible. Kant argues explicitly in *The Metaphysics of Morals* that we have a duty to strive continually toward such moral perfection, which

consists subjectively in the *purity (puritas moralis)* of one's disposition to duty, namely, in the law being by itself alone the incentive, even without the admixture of aims derived from sensibility, and in actions being done not only in conformity with duty but also *from duty*.[12]

Of course we do not have a duty actually to achieve such purity of will, as that would be impossible for beings like us whose wills are pathologically affected. We must remain committed, however, to the ideal of eliminating as much moral noise as we can, as noise is the implacable enemy of morality.

But this reconstruction of Kant's position is insufficiently radical, in that it begins at a point where moral sense has already been constituted. It reflects the point of view of someone whose being-in-the-world is already oriented, albeit imperfectly, by the moral law. To be a moral subject at all, on the standard Kantian account, is to have this law constantly in mind, using it as the sole standard by which to judge the difference between acts that are in conformity with duty and those that are contrary to duty.[13] All rival action-guiding principles, that is, all those that have their origin in the lower faculty of desire, are experienced as interference. Moral virtue, for such a subject, manifests itself as the strength to resist this interference, to exclude the noise of the inclinations in favour of the message of the law.[14] But if it is true that noise is the enemy of moral sense, it is equally true that there can be no moral sense without the noise. It is not the case, in other words, that noise appears within moral experience merely as a dangerous intruder and that morality would be well served by its complete elimination. Noise, rather, is the *conditio sine qua non* of moral experience. It is the presence of noise that accounts for the imperatival form in which the moral law is given, and thus for the phenomenon of obligation. Without it, our practical experience would be either non-moral like a cat's or automatically moral like God's.

What is common to the Serresian account of the genesis of abstraction presented in *La Communication* and the account of the genesis of obligation suggested above is the idea that sense emerges only within the space of an oriented relation that is prior to the terms related. The sensible and the intelligible, the inclinations and the moral law, are what they are only in their relations. The sensible is what it is only as oriented *toward* the intelligible, and conversely, the intelligible is what it is only as the intelligible *of* the sensible. Likewise, the inclinations are what they are only as standing *under* the judgement of the law. Pre-position, as its name suggests, is prior to position. Or, returning explicitly to the language of information theory, the channel is prior to the terms whose communication it makes possible. And this channel is noisy, always already. There is no position, no matter how foundational an account we might try to give, where we can discover sense in a pure state, completely undistorted by noise. Not even God can occupy such a position. As Serres argues in *Angels: A Modern Myth*, God is only God insofar as he manifests himself, and this manifestation presupposes the angels as channels of communication between him and human beings. ('Angel' comes from the ancient Greek *angelos*, messenger.) In order to convey God's word with perfect fidelity, the angels must disappear entirely. If they manifest themselves along with the messages they transmit to even the slightest degree, they will introduce noise into the communication. But the angels cannot disappear entirely. In order to perform their function as mediators, they must be both different from and the same as the parties to the communication. They must be different from God in such a way as to enable them to communicate with human beings in a way that God himself presumably cannot, and they must be different from human beings in such a way as to enable them to receive God's messages unmediated, as human beings presumably cannot. The angels are thus a third, distinct from the sender and the receiver. In short, they are *something*. As such, they introduce noise that ought, for the sake of perfect communication, to be excluded. But the noise cannot be excluded from the system even in principle, since it is the noise, the included third, that makes the system.[15]

Noise, then, is originary. It is very easy to overlook this fact, though, because the conditions of the possibility for undertaking an investigation into the genesis of sense are the very same conditions that conceal the foundational role that noise plays. More specifically, in order even to be able to think about investigating the genesis of sense, one must inhabit a world of meaning from which noise has already been largely excluded. This, of course, is because the question of the genesis of sense makes sense; it is meaningful. It would not be meaningful within a world inundated with noise. The subject who undertakes the genesis of sense, then, is necessarily one who, in Merleau-Ponty's words, 'has already sided with the world, [and who] is already open to certain of its aspects and synchronized with them'.[16] To be in the world (from which noise has been sufficiently excluded) just is to find oneself oriented, seemingly always already, toward meaning. This is what Merleau-Ponty meant when he wrote that 'because we are in the world, we are condemned to sense'.[17] Merleau-Ponty's account of the genesis of this sense is actually similar to Serres's in three important respects. First, Merleau-Ponty is committed to the idea that sense emerges only within a relation. Perceptual sense, for example, emerges only in the relation between a sensible given and a perceiving subject who is herself of the sensible and who therefore knows, prior to all reflection, how to gear into the sense it adumbrates. And the sense of a novel emerges in the relation between an established, sedimented system of language and a speaking subject who breathes new life into that system with her meaning-bestowing intentions. Second, for both Merleau-Ponty and Serres, a sense that is excessive to crystallised, constituted sense manifests itself within the space of the relation. And third, both thinkers emphasise the way in which this excessive sense tends to disappear from view, receding in favour of the constituted sense that it makes possible. But for Merleau-Ponty, the excessive sense is understood entirely on the basis of the constituted sense. The tension within the metastable perceptual or fictional sense is resolved in the crystallised, relatively stabilised sense. Oriented within an already established world of meaning, Merleau-Ponty misses the phenomenon of noise, which cannot be conceived as any kind of nascent *logos*. If noise were to appear at all for Merleau-Ponty, it would appear only as an interference that must be excluded. There is no room in Merleau-Ponty's phenomenological account for a conception of noise as originary, as a third that cannot be excluded even in principle.

Noise and Moral Sense

Let us suppose that Serres's account of the genesis of sense is correct, that there is indeed a dimension of sense that is prior to the latent, metastable sense that Merleau-Ponty had treated as basic. Let us suppose, further, that Serres is correct in arguing that we tend to overlook or misunderstand the dimension of noise because of our orientation within a world whose meaningfulness depends precisely on the exclusion of that dimension. What would any of this have to do with our understanding of moral experience, and specifically our understanding of the experience of obligation? Moral experience, it seems, is only possible within a meaningful world, that is, one from which noise has been sufficiently excluded. The question 'what ought I to do?' can arise only for a subject who can contemplate different possible courses of action, all of which must be in some sense meaningful. Why should such a subject concern himself with noise, except perhaps to take care that it continue to be excluded?

Serres's answer to questions like these is developed most explicitly in *The Parasite*. His point, broadly stated, is this: the noise that we exclude *might* have a moral significance that we fail to recognise. We would fail to recognise this moral significance precisely because the sense of the world in which we find our moral orientation would depend on the exclusion of the noise. But how is it possible that noise, which Serres has defined as the 'phenomena of interference that hinder communication', could have some kind of unrecognised moral significance? How could noise do anything other than *undermine* moral signification? The key to Serres's response to these questions is that message and noise are irreducibly relative terms: what counts as message and what counts as noise depends on one's point of view. Serres presents a helpful illustration of this relativity in *The Parasite*. He asks the reader to imagine herself engaged in conversation at a party she is hosting. Within this context, the messages are obviously the things that the participants in the conversation say to each other. The noise would be anything in the environment – the conversations of other groups, the music that is playing in the background, the sirens of an ambulance passing through the neighbourhood, and so on – that would interfere with the exchange of messages. If the noise increased to a sufficient degree – for example, if someone turned the music up to a very loud volume – then the small world of meaning that came into being with the conversation would collapse. But as long as the noise is kept below a certain threshold, the conversation can continue. Now suppose that the telephone rings. For most of the participants in the conversation, the ringing is noise: it is an obstacle to the exchange of messages. But for the host, the ringing is a message, which she is able to decode without any difficulty: she is being called upon to participate in a new conversation. Once the host picks up the telephone and begins talking with the caller, she will experience the conversation she had just left as noise. And the participants in the original conversation will experience the telephone conversation as noise. The members of both groups are oriented by the meanings that are emerging within the contexts of their conversations, and in both cases, that orientation presupposes the exclusion, at least to a degree, of the noise.[18] What the example brings out is that noise is the bearer of a potential significance, even though the participants in the conversations tend not to experience it that way.

The shared effort of the participants to exclude the noise that would interfere with their communication contributes toward the consolidation of a *we* whose members are all oriented toward a common sense. The persistence of this determinate *we* depends on the continued effort to exclude the noise that is produced by *them*. If we look at groups with better established, more persistent identities than the kinds that develop from the flow of conversation at parties, we can see how these groups take advantage of the relativity of message and noise to secure their boundaries. Specifically, groups can keep others at a distance by producing messages that the others are sure to perceive as noise. Among relatively informal groups of friends, in-jokes and frequent reference to a shared history perform this function. The use of unnecessarily obscure technical jargon can perform the same function among professional associations. Exchanges of these sorts of messages exclude the outsider, who does not understand them. They also serve to reinforce the bonds of recognition within the group: *we* are the ones who can make sense of this noise.[19] And once a group's identity has been consolidated in this way, its members, whose lives are oriented by the meanings that emerge within the group, have a strong incentive to remain closed off from other groups. If the noise that consolidates my identity as belonging to a particular community of meaning comes to be experienced by outsiders as a message, then I become much less secure in my group-based identity: I am no longer so different from *them*. I run the same risk if I make the effort to understand the noise that other groups make.[20]

A number of moral philosophers, particularly those whose thought could be characterised as broadly communitarian, have argued that these practices of consolidating group identity are necessary for the development and sustenance of moral experience. Alasdair MacIntyre, for example, has argued that 'it is an essential characteristic of the morality which each of us acquires that it is learned from, in and through the way of life of some particular community'.[21] The youngest members of the community develop a specifically moral orientation as they come to recognise determinate ways of life as worthy of being pursued and others as worthy of censure. These ways of life are necessarily connected to social roles that are understood differently in different communities. To be a good friend, a good father or a good employee, for example, is to pattern one's conduct on the model of those who are recognised within one's own community as good friends, fathers or employees. Education in the expectations associated with these roles presupposes the community as a relatively noise-free system for the communication of moral information. As MacIntyre notes, acting in accordance with 'the rules of morality is characteristically and generally a hard task for human beings . . . We are continually liable to be blinded by immediate desire, to be distracted from our responsibilities, [and] to lapse into backsliding.'[22] If the moral messages that circulate within a community are distorted too much by noise, such that the members of the community cannot form clear conceptions of what kind of behaviour is expected of them, then backsliding and distraction will become more common. If this is right, then it seems as if communities can secure the necessary conditions of moral life only by consolidating their own identities, excluding moral noise to the greatest extent possible.

In constituting itself as a 'city of communication maximally purged of noise',[23] the communitarian community presents itself to itself as 'the good, the just, the true, the natural, the normal'.[24] If moral messages circulate within this community with a minimum of interference, then Kant's description of the experience of rational moral agents generally will apply to its members: they will experience themselves as knowing 'quite easily and without hesitation' what they ought to do in any situation they find themselves in.[25] And because of this, moral necessitation will appear to them as unconditional: they will experience courses of action other than those endorsed by the community as morally impossible. The question is, *should* they experience moral necessitation this way? Is it possible that there is some morally relevant sense in the noise, such that the moral subject risks doing wrong by excluding it? From the point of view of the subject whose moral understanding is made possible by her community's work of excluding the noise, the answer seems to be no. If there is some value in terms of which she might think to question the validity of her moral understanding, then presumably this value would itself be thinkable only on the basis of her community's exclusion of the noise. The noise itself, it seems, cannot be the source of any morally relevant sense.

The problem with this communitarian account is that it under-emphasises the fact that moral sense emerges most originarily from encounters. As Stephen Darwall argues in *The Second-Person Standpoint*, obligation is first and foremost obligation *to* others, and not *about* them.[26] That is to say, obligation does not have its origin in a shared moral understanding. Rather, we are answerable directly to other persons who make purportedly valid claims against us. We take these others' claims seriously not because we already agree with the moral sense they invoke, but because we regard them as 'self-originating sources of valid claims'.[27] The authority we recognise in others, then, is not epistemic: it is not the case that we are obligated by others' claims against us because we judge those others to be sufficiently knowledgeable on matters of the moral good. Returning to an example of Darwall's that we discussed briefly in the previous chapter, if someone steps on my toe, there are two ways I can try to convince him to pick up his foot and to put it down elsewhere. First, I can appeal to moral principles to which I know he is committed. For example, if I know he is a utilitarian, I might argue that his stepping on my foot causes me pain, that the quantity of pleasure he takes from having his foot on mine is less than the quantity of pain I am experiencing, and that therefore he ought to remove his foot. In this case I am not addressing a claim against him, but rather pointing to reasons for action that he already has. In other words, I am counselling him to act in a way that is consistent with his own principles. The fact that it is I who am counselling him is irrelevant; anyone with similar background knowledge could have done the same.[28] This kind of counselling, if successful, would provide the other person with convincing reasons to believe that stepping on my foot has the property of being wrong. But as Jean Barbeyrac demonstrated in his 'Jugement d'un Anonyme', recognising the validity of a moral principle is not the same as being obligated to act in accordance with it.[29] The first strategy, then, cannot yield an obligation.

The second kind of strategy I can employ is to insist on my right not to have my foot stepped on.[30] In doing so, I would not be merely advising the other person, referring him to the authority of reasons to which he was already committed. Nor would I be coercing him. Instead, I would address my claim to the other as a rational being, whom I take to be capable of representing to himself the rule of conduct I propose to him, of recognising that the rule justly applies to him, and of judging himself 'worthy of some censure' if he fails to act accordingly.[31] It is here, in the encounter between an addressor and an addressee, each of whom regards the other with respect, that is, as a self-originating source of valid claims, that obligation arises.

But one might plausibly argue here that Darwall's example fails to show how noise can be the source of any morally relevant sense. After all, anyone who has even a little moral maturity can easily understand that one ought not, under normal circumstances, to step on others' toes. If the person stepping on the other's toe is able to recognise the legitimacy of the demand that he remove his foot, and if he is able to judge himself worthy of censure for failing to do so, this, one might argue, is simply because he comes to the encounter with a sufficiently well-formed moral understanding. And his having this understanding in the first place presupposes his having been brought up within a culture from which moral noise has been excluded to a sufficient degree. If this is right, then it is not the case that obligation originates in the encounter between addressor and addressee; the encounter is merely the occasion for the offender to be reminded of what he surely already understands. Indeed, if the person really were not already committed to the principle that he ought not to step on others' toes – if he experienced the very idea as so much moral noise – then it is highly unlikely that he would experience himself as obligated by the other's demand that he remove his foot.

In order to answer this objection, it will be necessary to present an example in which the encounter between addressor and addressee is undeniably noisy and in which the addressee more clearly runs the risk of doing a moral wrong to the addressor by trying to exclude the noise. Such an example, I believe, can be found in the life of Simone Weil. From her earliest childhood, Weil felt an extraordinary degree of compassion for those whose lives were filled with suffering. Already as a five-year-old child during World War I, for example, she refused to eat sugar, having been told that the French soldiers were deprived of it.[32] In 1934, hoping to gain a better understanding of the sufferings of the working class, she took a leave of absence from her teaching position and began working as a manual labourer in various factories. This work was very hard for Weil, given her physical clumsiness and the extreme fragility of her health. And throughout her life, Weil always refused to eat any more or any better food than the least fortunate were able to eat, a practice that played an important part in her death at the young age of thirty-four. Even as her health rapidly deteriorated during a stay at a London hospital, Weil refused the nutrition that her doctors insisted was necessary for her recovery. The reason she gave for this refusal was that 'she couldn't eat when she thought of the French people starving in France'.[33]

Now I ask myself what I would have done if I had been a friend of Weil's, especially near the end of her life. I feel reasonably certain I know the answer: I would have tried to convince her to follow her doctors' orders and to give up, at least temporarily, her ascetic way of life. At the very least I think I would have tried to convince her to moderate her asceticism somewhat. I would have done this on the basis of a perceived duty to beneficence, understood in the broadly Kantian sense as the duty 'of making others' happiness one's end'.[34] Given my life experience, it seems obvious to me that a person would be better off not wasting away in a hospital from self-imposed malnutrition. And if I merely stood by as she destroyed her own health, never even trying to convince her to change her ways, I am reasonably certain I would feel that I had failed to fulfil a basic duty as a friend. But suppose Weil had said to me, 'Please stop trying to convince me to change my ways. You need to understand that this way of life is morally important to me and that it overrides my concern for my own well-being. If you are my friend, you need to respect my decisions.' How would I respond to this claim made against me? What makes the case so much more difficult than the one presented by Darwall is that I experience Weil's commitments as moral noise. I simply cannot comprehend the moral sense of her behaviour. Specifically, I cannot understand what morally significant purpose was served by Weil's acts of self-sacrifice. Although concern for the well-being of others is no doubt morally praiseworthy, the fact of the matter is that Weil's self-imposed suffering contributed almost nothing to the betterment of those for whom she professed concern. And so in stating her claim against me, Weil would not be merely reminding me of values to which I was already committed, either explicitly or implicitly.

In my imagined dealings with Weil, then, should I try to exclude the moral noise? Ought I to insist upon engaging with her in terms of the moral sense that I bring with me to the encounter and that seems so clearly appropriate to the circumstances? In short, ought I to take her claim against me seriously only on the condition that it make sense to me? Or, on the other hand, would I risk doing her a moral wrong in excluding what I perceive as noise? These questions point to more abstract questions of moral epistemology: if there were some potential moral sense in the noise, how would I know it? If I could recognise a possible moral sense that ought to be taken seriously, would I not do so on the basis of the relatively clear, noise-free moral understanding I already have? And if so, would it not be the case once again that I respect her claim against me only on the condition that I already understand it, albeit obscurely?

In order to get a handle on these questions, it will be best to begin with a close description of the experience I had when I first learned about Weil's life, being careful of course not to presume that my experience would be shared by everyone. The experience I had corresponds quite closely to the description of the feeling of respect that Kant gives in a well-known passage from the *Critique of Practical Reason*: respect, he says, 'is a *tribute* that we cannot refuse to pay to merit, whether we want to or not'. Whenever I perceive in someone an 'uprightness of character in a higher degree than I am aware of in myself *my spirit bows*, whether I want it or whether I do not'.[35] When I first read about Weil's life, I had a strong sense that there was something admirable in her adherence to the way of life she had chosen for herself, and that in my own life I fell somewhat short of the example given by her conduct. My spirit bowed. But to what, exactly? Here my experience becomes crucially different from the one described by Kant. The object of the feeling of respect, he thinks, is necessarily the moral law. The example provided by another's conduct 'holds before me a law that strikes down my self-conceit when I compare it with my conduct, and I see observance of that law and hence its *practicability* proved before me in fact'.[36] On Kant's account, then, the moral sense against which I measure my conduct is one that I already possess, and one that I understand with

perfect clarity.[37] It is only because the law is so clearly present to me
that I can recognise another's living up to it better than I do. But
in the case of Weil, I find myself respecting moral conduct whose
sense is very noisy to me; there is *something* I respect, but I cannot
articulate what it is. Respect, in this case, is not the singular, a priori
feeling whose object is the moral law,[38] but rather the intimation of a
potential moral value in the noise. If this account both of the feeling
of respect and of its object is correct, then I would unavoidably run
the risk of wronging Weil by trying to exclude the moral noise in my
imagined dealings with her.

But it is certainly possible that the account I have given here is
mistaken. It might be the case, for example, that the intimation of
moral sense that I discerned in her conduct is based on a misun-
derstanding, and that the feeling of respect would disappear if I had
more information at my disposal. Perhaps further investigation would
reveal that Weil's conduct was not as altruistic as it had seemed, and
that her acts of self-sacrifice were in fact motivated by self-serving
considerations. Kant addresses exactly this kind of possibility in his
Anthropology from a Pragmatic Point of View:

From the day that the human being begins to speak by means of 'I', he
brings his beloved self to light wherever he is permitted to, and egoism
progresses unchecked. If he does not do so openly (for then the egoism of
others opposes him), nevertheless he does so covertly and with seeming
self-abnegation and pretended modesty, in order all the more reliably to
give himself a superior worth in the judgment of others.[39]

Some of Weil's closest friends were inclined to interpret her behaviour in this way. Gustave Thibon, for example, suggested that Weil's
'aim was self-forgetfulness, and she came upon herself in this very
forgetfulness'.[40] Perhaps I would have viewed Weil's conduct in a
similar light if I had known her in real life. It seems highly unlikely
to me that such an interpretation would adequately capture the
sense of her behaviour, especially given the extreme degree of suffering she imposed on herself throughout the whole course of her
life, but I cannot rule out the possibility that it does. A second possibility is that the feeling I have described as respect would be better
described as something like admiration for the discipline she was
able to impose on herself. This would not necessarily entail any kind
of moral judgement at all; it could be similar to the admiration I feel

for elite athletes who work extraordinarily hard to develop their talents to their full potential. Given these possibilities, then, how can I know that what I feel really is respect and that what it makes manifest is a genuine possibility of moral sense within the noise? The answer is that I cannot know. But that, it turns out, is not what is most important here. What is most important is that I cannot know that her way of life, and her insistence that I respect it, *lacks* moral sense. To return to Kant's language, I do not in fact know 'quite easily and without hesitation' what duty would require of me in a case like the one I have described. And not knowing, I would take Weil's claim against me seriously, even without understanding its sense. Of course this would not commit me to agreeing ultimately with her conception of the moral sense of her acts or to judging myself 'worthy of some censure' if I did not act in accordance with the rule proposed in her claim against me. I would certainly retain the right to conclude, upon reflection, that her behaviour really was pointlessly self-destructive and that duty required me to do what I could to convince her to treat herself better. But taking her claim seriously would commit me at least to acknowledging the possibility that my obligation to her was quite different from what I had thought. I would find myself responsible *to her*, second personally, whether I liked it or not. What this example brings out is that obligation happens in encounters, that these encounters are noisy, and that the noise matters from a moral point of view.[41]

Exposure to Noise as the Fact of Sense

In the previous chapter, I developed a Merleau-Pontian account of the fact of sense, demonstrating that our condemnation to sense – our finding ourselves always already in the midst of metastable sense and thus oriented toward an intimated, crystallised sense – could be understood as the origin of the phenomenon of obligation. What I want to argue now, building on some of the points I have just developed, is that this condemnation to sense presupposes a more basic exposure to noise and that this exposure can be understood as a fact in the sense of the Kantian fact of reason. To show how this is the case, I would like to begin with an insight that was central to Merleau-Ponty's reconceptualisation of Saussurian linguistics: when we communicate with each other, we do not merely exchange tokens

of already fully established significations. That is, when my interlocutor speaks to me, it is not the case that she encodes her thoughts
into the words that stand for them and that I subsequently decode
them, translating them back into the thoughts they represent. If this
transmission model were correct, it would follow that communication could never bring us to understand the world any differently
from the ways we already do. My interlocutor's words would only
ever remind me of significations I already possessed. But as Merleau-
Ponty's discussion of *The Charterhouse of Parma* demonstrated in
detail, communication does effect changes in our sense of the world.
And this means that we must understand ourselves as exposed to a
sense that exceeds the stock of significations we have at our disposal
at any given point. As we have seen, Merleau-Ponty interprets this
excessive sense as nascent or latent sense. I am able to catch on to the
sense that my interlocutor communicates, and she is able to catch on
to the sense that I communicate to her, because beneath the stocks
of significations that each of us brings to our encounter there is an
undetermined signifyingness that mediates the relation between us.
Both of us are oriented toward a common, intimated sense.

What Serres emphasises, though, is that this transition from a
sense I already possess to another that is given at first only nascently
requires me to pass through a point where I lose my orientation. In
The Troubadour of Knowledge, Serres develops this point by means of
a description of what it means to learn how to swim:

No one really knows how to swim until he has crossed a large and impetu-
ous river or a rough strait, an arm of the sea, alone. In a pool there is only
the ground – a territory for a crowd of pedestrians.

Depart, take the plunge. After having left the shore behind, for awhile
you stay much closer to it than to the one on the other side, at least just
enough so that the body starts reckoning and says to itself, silently, that
it can always go back. Up to a certain threshold, you hold on to this feeling of security: in other words, you have not really left. On this side of
the adventure, your foot, once it has crossed a second threshold, waits
expectantly for the approach: you find yourself close enough to the steep
bank to say you have arrived. Right bank or left bank, what does it matter, in both cases it is land or ground. You do not swim, you wait to walk,
like someone who jumps, takes off, and then lands, but does not remain
in flight.

The swimmer, on the contrary, knows that a second river runs in the
one that everyone sees, a river between the two thresholds, after or before
which all security has vanished: there he abandons all reference points.[42]

To see how this pertains to the question of sense, we can look at the experience of learning a new language. Let us say that I am a monolingual English speaker and that I am learning to speak Dutch. How do I make the transition from being someone who makes sense of the world entirely in English to someone who can make sense of the world in English and in Dutch? No doubt Merleau-Ponty is right, to some extent at least: I am able to learn Dutch because it gives expression to the very same world that English gives expression to. That is not to say, of course, that the two languages give expression to the world in exactly the same way, except for the fact that Dutch uses different words. There are certainly nuances of expression that I would not think of in English that would be obvious to a Dutch speaker. The extensive use of the diminutive suffix in Dutch is an example: it is used to express an extraordinary variety of senses, including physical smallness, endearment, disparagement and euphemism. As a native English speaker, I find the use of diminutives to express physical smallness and endearment quite natural, but their use to express euphemism is much less obvious. In the early stages of learning Dutch, I would most likely misjudge the cases in which the diminutive was appropriate. But I would be able to catch on eventually because I am already oriented within a world in which euphemism, and politeness more generally, is called for.

But this Merleau-Pontian account misses something essential, something that is brought out nicely in Serres's description of the process of learning to swim. To see how this is the case, let us begin again by describing my earliest efforts to read, pronounce and listen to sentences in Dutch. At first, I proceed timidly, remaining close to the shore: I read the sentences in Dutch, but I translate each of the words into its English equivalent as I go. I see the sentence 'Ik hou van katten' and I say to myself 'I hold from cats.'[43] In pronouncing Dutch words, I confine myself to the sounds I am familiar with from my native language: I pronounce the consonant cluster *sch* as I would pronounce it in the English 'school' and I pronounce the diphthong *ui* as I would pronounce it in 'altruism'. At this stage in my journey, I am obviously not yet a Dutch speaker. Even when I do get the sense of a Dutch sentence right, I do so from the perspective of an English speaker. I am still holding onto the feeling of security provided by my familiarity with my native language, and so I have not really left the shore. In order genuinely to understand the sense of the world as expressed in the Dutch language, I must swim out into the middle, abandoning the security of the first shore without any guarantee of security on the other shore. In the middle I give up translating each Dutch word into English as I go, but without yet knowing how to read Dutch on its own terms, with its own idioms and its own characteristic syntax. I give up my expectation that spoken Dutch will have a cadence similar to that of the Midwestern American English I am familiar with, but without having yet geared into its actual cadence. I try to form my mouth into the shapes necessary to pronounce Dutch correctly, knowing that I am getting it wrong and fearing that a more competent speaker would laugh at my efforts. In the middle, I am no longer oriented by English and not yet oriented by Dutch. I am exposed, disoriented; the 'reference points lie equally far'.[44] There can be no genuine transition from a familiar to an unfamiliar sense without this passage through the disorienting middle.

This experience of being in the middle is importantly different from the experience of standing before the spectacle at the beach or of reading a novel. I do not find myself oriented toward a sense that is given as being on the verge of crystallising, but rather exposed to noise. On the one hand, this noise is manifest negatively as a hindrance to my ability to pick out a message. Having ventured out into the middle, I do not understand Dutch on its own terms and I have refrained from trying to understand it in terms of English. Exposed to the noise, I am keenly aware of sense as lacking. But the noise is also manifest positively as white noise. When we hear white noise, such as the sound of static on an old television set, we do not find ourselves attuned to any determinate sense, either fully present or on the way to full presence. As the noise that contains all frequencies equally, white noise is rather 'the epitome of the various and unexpected. It is the least predictable, the most original of sounds.'[45] According to Serres, white noise 'is possibility itself. It is a set of possible things, it may be *the* set of possible things. It is not potential, it is the very reverse of power, rather it is capaciousness. This noise is the opening.'[46] Understood in this way, white noise is not the absence of sense but rather the pure, wide-open possibility of sense. This possible sense is not given in the way suggested by Merleau-Ponty's phenomenology of expression, namely as adumbrated by the stock of familiar, sedimented sense. Noise, Serres insists, 'is not a matter of phenomenology'.[47] A phenomenon, to appear as such, must be

> separated from it, a silhouette on a backdrop, like a beacon against the fog, as every message, every cry, every call, every signal must be separated from the hubbub that occupies silence, in order to be, to be perceived, to be known, to be exchanged.[48]

Unlike phenomena, white noise is indeterminate. It is like the blank domino or the joker, having all meanings because of its having none.[49] And the I who is attuned to this noise, who does not attempt to exclude it, 'is nobody in particular, it is not a singularity, it has no contours, it is the blankness of all colors and all nuances, an open and translucent welcome of a multiplicity of thoughts, it is therefore the possible'.[50]

It is this welcoming I that is open to the possible moral sense in the life of Simone Weil. The moral subject who is made manifest in the feeling of respect is nobody in particular. I do not make sense of Weil's conduct with reference to the stock of sedimented moral significations that help shape my own self-understanding. I find myself rather in the middle, exposed to a possible moral sense that I can understand neither on my own terms nor on Weil's. To be condemned to sense is to be condemned to this disorienting passage through the middle.

But if this is truly the case, then why is exposure to pure, indeterminate possibility not a more salient feature of our experience generally and of our moral experience in particular? My encounter with the case of Simone Weil is very much not the norm; indeed, the reason I chose it as an example is that it stands out so prominently against the background of my everyday moral experience. It is in fact very rare that I find myself disoriented in this way, open to possibilities of moral sense that I cannot make head nor tail of based on my accumulated moral experience. In the vast majority of cases, I pick up the moral sense of the situation I find myself in relatively unproblematically. The reason for this, Serres argues, is that we do eventually catch on to the message, and the message obscures the noise. At some point in the process of my learning Dutch, I will come to understand it on its own terms, even if only imperfectly. I will read and listen to Dutch sentences and I will understand them without simultaneously translating them back into English. Once I can recognise the message more or less straightforwardly, I no longer experience the disorientation that I felt at a given stage of my journey. Indeed, I cannot recreate that experience even if I try: I hear the Dutch sentence and the sense is there immediately and relatively transparently. The case of moral experience is similar. Even if I do find myself exposed to possibilities of moral sense that I cannot understand in terms of my accumulated moral experience, I cannot remain in that condition indefinitely. As a practical subject I must eventually decide what to do. If I persisted in the state of being 'the blankness of all colors and all nuances', I would simply fail as a moral agent. That means that I must perform an act of moral sense-bestowal. And once I do so, I will unavoidably lose some of my sensitivity to the noise.

Harlequin Emperor of the Moon

As he so often does, Serres provides a compelling illustration of his point in the form of a story.[51] In *The Troubadour of Knowledge*, he offers a variation on Nolant de Fatouville's seventeenth-century farce *Arlequin empereur dans la lune*. Harlequin, of course, is a stock character in the commedia dell'arte tradition, recognisable by his multicoloured patchwork costume. He is usually depicted as a comically unintelligent and unscrupulous servant in love with Columbine, a maid whom he attempts incompetently to court. In *Arlequin empereur dans la lune* Columbine is depicted as a servant to Dr Balouard, who is obsessed by the idea that there is a civilisation on the moon that resembles the civilisation here on earth. In the opening scene Harlequin overhears Dr Balouard telling Pierrot that three men – an apothecary, a baker and a farmer – have asked him for Columbine's hand in marriage. Recognising that his opportunity to win the heart of his beloved is slipping away, Harlequin adopts a succession of disguises, hoping to gain access to Dr Balouard's home and thus to Columbine. In one scene Harlequin disguises himself as a woman, trying to convince the doctor's wife to take him in as her chambermaid. Later he attempts unsuccessfully to impersonate the apothecary, the baker, and the farmer who had requested Columbine's hand in marriage. And most comically, Harlequin presents himself to Dr Balouard as an ambassador from the Emperor of the Moon, on whose behalf he requests permission to marry the doctor's daughter, Isabelle. In the final scene, Harlequin arrives in the guise of the Emperor of the Moon himself.

In Serres's retelling, Harlequin is presented at a press conference, where he is giving a report on his most recent inspection of his lunar territories.[52] The press are all excited to hear about how life on the moon differs from life on earth. But Harlequin's presentation leaves everyone disappointed: everything on the moon, he insists, is just as it is here. The press cannot believe that this is true; surely there must be *some* differences to report. But Harlequin continues to insist that everything is the same. This scene corresponds to the well-known final scene of *Arlequin empereur dans la lune*, where Harlequin presents himself to Dr Balouard and his household as the Emperor of the Moon. Dr Balouard happily grants the Emperor permission to marry his daughter. Since his advanced age will prevent him from accompanying Isabelle to her new home, however, the doctor takes advantage of the Emperor's presence to ask as many questions as he can about life on the moon. In response to each question the Emperor gives a description of lunar life that could pass just as well for a description, albeit satirical, of life on earth. On the moon people are governed by self-interest and ambition, wives spend too much of their husbands' money, and the treatments that doctors give their patients are worse than the original illnesses.[53] In response to each of these descriptions, the various members of the household declare 'c'est tout comme icy', 'it's just like here'.

In the original play, the other characters were excited to learn that the lunar world was just like their own. In Serres's retelling, however, the press remain incredulous. Although Harlequin continues to insist that everything is exactly the same, the press observe that his own appearance belies that claim. 'You who say that everywhere everything is just as it is here, can you also make us believe that your cape is the same in every part, for example in front as it is on the back?'[54] Harlequin's patchwork costume evidences his multiplicity and his exposure to alterity while his words bespeak nothing but unity and sameness. Caught in this embarrassing contradiction, Harlequin's only solution is to remove his costume, showing thereby that his multiplicity is only apparent. It turns out, though, that under each layer of clothing there lies yet another patchwork. Eventually we learn that even Harlequin's skin is a patchwork: he is multiplicity and exposure all the way down.

Harlequin is full of possibility, very little in himself and poten-tially almost anything at all. This is reflected in his patchwork cos-tume, but also in his presenting himself in so many different guises. Harlequin appears as everything from a chambermaid to a farmer to the Emperor of the Moon. Indeed, it is not at all obvious how we could answer the question, who is Harlequin *himself?* There does not seem to be any 'true' Harlequin standing under his multiform appearances. Rather, Harlequin's defining characteristic just is his holding himself back, his not fixing himself in any determinate posi-tion. Serres expresses this understanding in his retelling of the story by showing how, at the conclusion of his undressing, Harlequin becomes Pierrot:

Now then, when everybody had his back turned, and the oil lamps were giving signs of flickering out, and it seemed that this evening the improvisa-tion had ended up being a flop, someone suddenly called out, as if some-thing new were playing in a place where everything had, that evening, been a repetition, so that the public as a whole, turned back as one, all looking toward the stage, violently illuminated by the dying fires of the floodlights:
    'Pierrot! Pierrot!' the audience cried, *'Pierrot Lunaire!'*[55]

Pierrot is another of the stock characters of the commedia dell'arte tradition, recognisable most readily by his all-white costume. His whiteness represents, at least in Serres's version of the story, pure indetermination, unconstrained possibility, the nothing that is also everything.[56] Harlequin's blank indeterminacy and possibility are not at all incompatible with his rigidly fixed position, his insistence that everywhere everything is the same. In fact these qualities are two sides of the same coin. As we have seen, exposition and preposition are the necessary conditions for position. On the one hand, Harlequin is certainly exposed to radically different conditions of life on the moon and on the earth. Indeed, as Serres points out, the emperor is more exposed than anyone else. He owes his success, and ultimately his very life, to a finely developed sensitivity for the people's various needs and grievances.[57] But on the other hand, Harlequin assimilates these differences, integrating them into a fixed position that comes to seem entirely natural and self-evident. Having established himself in this new position, Harlequin loses some of his capacity to experi-ence genuine otherness. He encounters everything new merely as a variation of what he already knows: 'Everywhere everything is just as it is here, identical in every way to what one can see ordinarily on the terraqueous globe. Except that the degrees of grandeur and beauty change.'[58]

The Devil or the Good Lord?

Kantian moral philosophy tends for the most part to reflect Harlequin's point of view. Everywhere, in every situation, the moral sense is the same. Whether the matter is trivial or gravely important, whether one is dealing with strangers, enemies or friends, and whether one likes it or not, one ought to 'act only in accordance with that maxim through which [one] can at the same time will that it become a universal law'.[59] But as we have seen, this orientation toward unconditional, unambiguous moral sense presupposes a more basic exposure to noise, to pure, wide-open possibilities of unforeseeable sense. Harlequin is always already Pierrot. What moral conclusions can we draw from this? Ought we to adopt Pierrot's point of view rather than Harlequin's? Ought we to reverse our habits of moral evaluation, treating the noise as good and determinate sense as evil? As we have already seen, such a position would be impossible to maintain. As practical subjects, we must eventually choose, and that means that we must eventually determine the moral sense of the situations we find ourselves in. We cannot persist indefinitely as the 'open and translucent welcome of a multiplicity of thoughts'. And so we cannot simply choose between Harlequin and Pierrot; each of us is both, unavoidably. But neither can we combine their perspectives into one all-inclusive, morally adequate position. The two points of view are in tension. Insofar as I am attuned to the message, I encounter the noise as a hindrance and thus as something to be excluded. And insofar as I am attuned to the noise, I do not experience the message as clear and unambiguous. The question is, then, how ought we to negotiate this tension? Serres's answer is based on an empirical observation about the world: he thinks that on the whole we produce much more harm in our efforts to exclude the noise than we would produce by learning to live with it. And so although we cannot simply choose between the points of view of Harlequin and Pierrot, we can and ought to adopt Pierrot's point of view to a much greater extent than our moral theories have traditionally done.

Once again, Serres demonstrates the point nicely by means of a narrative. In *The Parasite*, he presents a close reading of Jean de la Fontaine's fable, 'The Gardener and His Lord'. The gardener of the story has enclosed his garden with a hedge, thereby demarcating a space that was to be wholly his own. Within this space, the gardener maintained a kind of closed economy: the vegetables that he grew were consumed within the household and the flowers were used to make bouquets for his daughter. One day, however, the gardener discovered that the closed system had been breached by a hare, which he found nibbling on his vegetables. From the perspective of the gardener's closed system, the hare is evil; it is a noise that disrupts what is proper, inserting itself between the gardener's labour and his consumption of its products. Eager to chase the hare from the enclosed garden, but unable to do so himself, the gardener called to his aid the local lord. But in attempting to chase the hare from the garden, the lord's horses trampled on the vegetables and tore a hole in the hedge far wider than the one through which the hare had originally entered. The lord and his retinue ended up doing 'more damage in an hour than all the hares of the province would have done in a hundred years'.[60] The struggle against the noise, in other words, produces far more evil than the noise itself. Clearly, it would have been better for the gardener to learn to live with the noise. Indeed, as we have seen, there is no alternative. There is no such thing as an inside – proper, pure and good – that would be wholly closed off from the noise outside.[61] 'There is always a hare in the garden. There always was a hare.'[62] Tolerance, according to Serres, begins with this insight, 'and maybe morality as well'.[63]

The moral subject who is responsive to the claim that noise makes against him cannot be understood on the Kantian model: he does not have the principle of morality 'always before [his] eyes' and he does not in fact know 'very well how to distinguish in every case that comes up what is good and what is evil, what is in conformity with duty or contrary to duty'.[64] For the Kantian moral subject, there can be no specifically moral noise. All interference with the subject's ability to receive the moral message is necessarily non-moral. Suppose, for example, that someone has accidentally left an expensive wristwatch lying on a park bench. Noticing that I am the only other person in the park, a man asks me if the watch is mine. I am an admirer of fine wristwatches, but even the lower-end models are far too expensive for me to afford, so that all I can do is admire them from afar. It would make me very happy finally to own such a wristwatch and so I am inclined to lie to the man, telling him that the watch is indeed mine. At this point, I recognise the act of lying as a practical possibility: it is one of the courses of action that make sense in the situation I find myself in. But, according to Kant, there is no point at which I conceive the act of lying as a *moral* possibility. Because I have the moral law always before my eyes, and because the requirements of the moral law are easily known by anyone capable of common rational moral cognition, I recognise immediately that telling the lie is morally impossible. I *can* do it, but I *must* not.[65] My desire for the wristwatch makes a claim on me: it purports to give me a compelling reason to pursue a certain course of action. But to be a moral subject in the Kantian sense is to recognise that the claims of the inclinations are noise and that they ought not to be taken seriously as intimating any kind of potential moral sense. All genuinely moral sense comes from the law.

On Serres's account, the moral subject is better understood on the basis of an analogy with the stem cell.[66] The most important characteristic of a stem cell is its pluripotency: it is not yet any particular kind of cell (a skin cell, blood cell, nerve cell, and so on), but it has the capacity to develop into almost any kind. The human subject is similarly pluripotent: we have the capacity to adapt to any culture, to speak any language, and to appreciate any kind of artistic expression. And most importantly in the context of the argument I am advancing here, the human subject has the capacity to make moral sense of the world in a wide variety of ways. As I attempted to demonstrate with the case of Simone Weil, these different ways of understanding really do represent different *moral* possibilities. To continue with the stem cell analogy, as moral subjects we are all differentiated to at least some degree: we make sense of the world morally in some determinate ways and not in others. For example, I tend to view Weil's acts of self-sacrifice as morally pointless and to regard myself as having a duty of beneficence to try to convince people like her to act in ways that are more conducive to their own well-being. But having determinate moral points of view does not deprive us of our pluripotency. I retain the ability to recognise the possibility of genuine moral sense in Weil's way of life, and even to be won over to her point of view. This kind of pluripotency, according to Serres, constitutes our true identity as moral subjects. To learn to identify ourselves first and foremost with it, and no longer with the differentiated and opposed forms of life that it makes possible, is to maintain our exposure to the noise that is the origin of sense.

For Serres, one of the paradigm cases of this kind of moral subjectivity is Diogenes the Cynic.[67] Asked where he came from, Diogenes refused to identify himself as belonging to any particular *polis*, insisting instead that he was *kosmopolitēs*, a citizen of the world.[68] Although we do not know a great deal about the positive content of Diogenes' ethical thought, we do know that he denied the normative force of particular customs, emphasising instead the value of living in accordance with the human nature that is common to us all. Another paradigm case is St Paul. Paul identified himself as a member of three very different communities.[69] First, he was a citizen of Rome. While others acquired that valuable status by purchase, Paul was proud to have inherited it from his father.[70] On numerous occasions, he took advantage of his citizenship and his knowledge of Roman law in order to escape danger. Second, Paul was an inheritor of the Greek intellectual tradition: he wrote and spoke in the Koine dialect of the Greek language and was well read in Greek philosophy. And finally, of course, Paul was 'a member of the people of Israel, of the tribe of Benjamin, a Hebrew born of Hebrews; as to the law, a Pharisee'.[71] But it is not this multiple belonging that renders Paul an exemplary figure of moral subjectivity for Serres; this kind of cultural mixing was in fact quite common among sailors and traders in the Mediterranean world during the period of the *pax romana*.[72] Moreover, Paul's multiple belonging did not prevent him from understanding himself and his relations to others in a strongly oppositional way. Prior to his sudden conversion on the road to Damascus, the Pharisee Saul was extremely 'zealous for the traditions of [his] ancestors'.[73] This zeal inspired him to contribute actively to the brutal persecution of the new Christian sect, including most prominently his participation in the stoning of St Stephen, whom the Sanhedrin had found guilty of blasphemy.[74] After his conversion, though, Paul renounced the exclusive point of view that had led to such evils, committing himself to the view that 'there is no longer Jew or Greek, there is no longer slave or free, there is no longer male and female; for all of you are one in Christ Jesus'.[75] It is this ethical stance that Serres finds exemplary. Instead of identifying himself and others with reference to the groups to which they belonged, Paul came to emphasise the I that is 'empty, poor, null: universal'.[76] Ethical subjectivity, Serres suggests, has its basis in this zero.[77]

This model of moral subjectivity gives rise to two problems for which there are no definitive solutions. First, although we are constitutively exposed to the noise, and although this noise makes a potentially moral claim against us, we can never know in advance whether letting the noise in will turn out to be good or bad:

Who is making this noise, this wind, these voices, these tongues? The Holy Ghost, the Paraclete, the gift-giver. The interrupter is an intercessor and a favorable one.

No. Say no to the powers of noise to be able to hear oneself, listen to oneself, understand oneself. Get thee behind me, Satan. Eliminate the parasites from the channel so the message can go through as best it can . . .

The Devil or the Good Lord? Exclusion, inclusion? I don't know.[78]

As we have seen, it is not the case that openness to the noise is necessarily good and that exclusion of the noise is necessarily bad. Sometimes there is no moral sense in the noise that deserves to be taken seriously at all. Only if moral subjectivity were constituted on the basis of an exclusion of the noise could we make confident judgements about the presence or absence of moral sense. But as I hope to have shown, this Kantian conception of moral subjectivity is mistaken.

The second problem follows from the indissociability of Harlequin, Emperor of the Moon and Pierrot described above. No matter to how great an extent I identify myself with the dimension of white noise, of the undifferentiated, wide-open possibility of sense, I cannot renounce entirely the kinds of determinate identifications that set me in relations of exclusion and opposition with others. If I understand myself in terms of the empty, poor, null, universal I, open to possibilities of moral sense in ways of life very different from my own – in the lives of mystically inspired ascetics, of Palestinians living in the occupied territories, or of the billionaire heirs to the Wal-Mart fortune – it remains the case that I am not myself an ascetic, a Palestinian or a Wal-Mart heir. My being who I am excludes the possibility of my identifying with any particular way of life. And so my identity remains one among others.

The practical consequence of this fact is brought out nicely by Serres in his book *Detachment*, where he retells the famous story of the encounter between Diogenes and Alexander the Great. Alexander figures in the story as the master of war and opposition. Diogenes, on the other hand, represents the ideal of openness: 'he has forsaken exchange, damage, gift, selling and buying, value . . . He has left comparison, from which comes all the evil of the world.'[79] In renouncing the attachments that give rise to rivalry and conflict, Diogenes attempts to create the possibility for relations of peace. Paying a visit to Diogenes, Alexander asks, 'what do you want, what do you desire? My glory and my power are capable of giving you everything.'[80] Uninterested in the kinds of goods that Alexander is capable of bestowing, Diogenes requests merely that he step aside and stop blocking the sun. This story is typically taken to exemplify Diogenes' disdain for worldly goods and for the oppositional relations to which they give rise. But Serres sees something different: in adopting the stance of openness, Diogenes sets himself up in a relation of rivalry with Alexander, competing for glory and winning:

I suspect this conceited dog to have dragged his barrel there, on the public square, in the fervent expectation of being able to provoke the king who would pass by, just as a spider stretches its sticky threads to capture flies. Playing the weak to be stronger than power.[81]

Even Diogenes, the self-proclaimed citizen of the world, establishes his particular identity through relations of opposition.

If these two problems really are unsolvable, then it seems as if the phenomenon of obligation has slipped away yet again. We will recall that the whole purpose of Kant's fact of reason strategy had been to cut off the possibility of continued reflection so that the moral agent could know with certainty both *that* she was obligated and *what* she was obligated to do. The element of necessitation was to be accounted for by the moral subject's having accepted the legitimacy of the claims of morality always already. And the content of these claims was understood to be given immediately with the subject's recognition of their legitimacy: the fact of reason, Kant argued, just is the consciousness of the moral law.[82] Since the content of the law is clear to the commonest understanding, and since its legitimacy is given as an irreducible fact, there can be no genuinely open moral questions: we are obligated unconditionally to act in accordance with the Categorical Imperative. But the fact of sense as I have articulated it in this chapter – the fact that our condemnation to sense entails an exposure to noise – has almost the opposite effect: instead of putting a stop to the process of reflection, it exposes us to problems that call for ever more reflection. Instead of orienting us morally, it disorients us.

It makes no sense, some would argue, to continue to speak of obligation here. Specifically, it makes no sense to say that a person is morally necessitated to do something when she does not, and indeed cannot, know with certainty what that something is. I want to argue, though, that this is incorrect and that the phenomenon of obligation has not in fact slipped away from us. The most important difference between the Kantian conception of obligation and the Serresian conception I have presented here is that in the latter, the element of necessitation is separated from the content of the obligation. As in the Merleau-Pontian account I presented in the previous chapter, necessitation comes from the fact that as practical subjects we cannot not respond. In the Merleau-Pontian account, it was metastable sense to which we had to respond, whereas in the Serresian account it is noise. The range of possible responses is much greater for the latter than for the former. On the one hand, it will almost inevitably seem to us as if we ought to respond by excluding the noise to the greatest extent possible. But on the other hand, there is often an intimation of moral sense in the noise, so that we are left with the problem of determining to what extent we ought to take the claims of the noise seriously. We can never know whether the noise outside is the Devil or the Good Lord, but we must respond all the same. The experience that results from the necessity of responding to the noise is not exactly the same as the phenomenon of obligation that Kant and other early modern moral philosophers describe, but it nonetheless shares many of the most essential characteristics. Most importantly, the phenomenon retains the differential relation with neighbouring ethical concepts that is definitive of obligation. First, to have to respond to the noise is not to be coerced. The one who responds to the noise is free in Pufendorf's sense: she responds to the noise on the basis of her own understanding and judges herself to be worthy of censure if she fails to do so correctly. The sanction is internal. And this leads to the second point, which is that the practical subject responding to the noise is not the addressee of a counsel.

The rightness or wrongness of the response is not determined by the subject's preferences. It is not merely a good thing for her to choose well; to fail to do so is to commit a wrong for which she is blameworthy. In short, we *must* get the sense right. The problem, on the Serresian account, is that the sense ceaselessly slips away from us. But that does not mean that the sense of obligation has slipped away from us. It means, rather, that there is a slippage that is internal to the phenomenon of obligation itself.

5 Abandonment and the Moral Law

For both the Merleau-Pontian and the Serresian accounts described in the previous chapters, the fact of sense consists in the subject's originary exposition or condemnation to a sense that she cannot fully appropriate. For both accounts, the sense to which the practical subject is constitutively exposed is given as a sense that is to be got right. The perceptual sense given in the scene at the beach, for example, is not just given as unsettled; it is given as a sense that ought to be settled. And the embodied subject knows prior to all reflection how to respond to this ought: she steps backward and forward, to the left and to the right, and focuses her eyes in different ways until the sense crystallises. Similarly, if we are so strongly inclined to exclude the noise, it is because we believe that doing so will enable us to discern the sense that it obscures. And when we do not try to exclude the noise, it is because we find in it the intimation of some sense that we ought to try to understand.

Both of these accounts attempt to make sense of the experience of necessitation that is essential to the phenomenon of obligation. As Pufendorf argued, 'obligation places a kind of bridle on our liberty'.[1] For both Merleau-Ponty and Serres, this bridling is located in our condemnation to sense: to be a practical subject at all is to have accepted always already the necessity of responding to it. As Bernhard Waldenfels put it, 'we cannot not respond. The double "not" points to a *must* in the sense of a practical necessity.'[2] There can be no question of stepping back from the experience of necessitation in order to question its legitimacy since the very act of stepping back would necessarily happen as a response to an intimated sense.

Nonetheless, I want to argue that both of these accounts fall short of presenting a fully adequate picture of obligation. Specifically, I believe that both the Merleau-Pontian and Serresian accounts resemble the kinds of 'can't-help-but' accounts that were advanced by rationalist moral theorists in the early modern period. These accounts, it will be recalled, traced the experience of necessitation back to the fact that as rational beings we cannot fail to give our assent to what we perceive clearly and distinctly. According to Nicolas Malebranche, clear and distinct perceptions 'oblige the will to give its consent'.[3] We cannot refrain from giving our consent to these perceptions 'without feeling an inward pain and the secret reproaches of reason'.[4] This certainly describes a kind of bridling of our liberty. Even if I want to believe that a stone has a greater degree of perfection than a neighbour who annoys me by playing bad music at a loud volume at all hours of the night, I cannot do it. This 'can't-help-but' account treats moral necessitation as analogous to epistemic necessitation: my commitment to the idea that my neighbour has a greater degree of perfection than a stone is just like my commitment to the idea that four is greater than two. I am committed to both simply because of the nature of human reason. But the kind of necessitation we experience when we do mathematics seems importantly different from the kind we experience when we find ourselves morally obligated. It is not merely the case that I cannot not think of my neighbour as having greater moral standing than a stone; it is more accurate to say that I *must* view my neighbour as having greater moral standing than a stone. The voluntarist critics of the rationalist position argued that we must understand specifically moral necessitation not epistemically but rather in terms of a law addressed to us by a superior and backed with sanctions. If we do not, then we fail to capture the uniquely moral sense of 'must'.

Of course neither the Merleau-Pontian nor the Serresian account grounds obligation in our inability not to give our consent to clear and distinct perceptions. But they do treat necessitation as having its basis in the nature of human experience, and specifically in the fact that we are constitutively exposed to a dynamic of sense whose legitimacy we can't help but accept. Like the rationalist account, they treat moral experience in broadly the same way they treat non-moral experience, thereby eliding features that are unique to obligation.

To exemplify the point, I would like to describe a series of experiences I had when I was first learning how to listen to forms of music to which I had not had any prior exposure. In my first year as an undergraduate student, I took an introductory level class on music appreciation. Toward the end of the semester the professor introduced us to classical music of the post-World War II period, including the music of the Darmstadt School. As I recall, we did not spend more than a day or two on this music. The professor had very little appreciation for it, and I think he included it only for the sake of completeness. When he first played recordings of the Darmstadt School compositions in class, I could not comprehend their musical sense at all. Nonetheless, I became very curious about this strange kind of music and so I sought out opportunities to hear more of it. Eventually I acquired a recording of Karlheinz Stockhausen's *Hymnen*. This is a work that is noisy in the most straightforward sense of the term: throughout the majority of the two-hour long piece, the most prominent sounds are background noises associated with short-wave radio transmissions. Here is Stockhausen's own description of the work:

With these short-wave events, I created a situation which one experiences time and again when driving in a car at night and listening to the car radio, or when at home at night searching for a programme on a short-wave receiver. Especially around midnight one hears many fragments of national anthems, which mark the end of the day. I have left the short-wave sounds as they are, with all the crackling and interference and intermodulation, shreds of Morse code, etc. After choosing a recording of a short-wave setting, I copied a fragment of a national anthem onto it, and as soon as such a connection was impressed on the memory, I switched to another station.[5]

Given the background musical knowledge I brought with me to my encounter with this music, the only elements that made any musical sense to me were the national anthems. But these appeared only intermittently and were almost always obscured by the noise. And so it seemed to me that whatever musical sense the piece contained would be better presented in proper recordings of the various anthems.

And yet for some reason I felt compelled to keep listening. I could not understand the musical sense of the piece, but I had a strong feeling that there was some sense to be made of it. Specifically, I had a feeling that what I was hearing as noise in fact contained a kind of musical sense, even though I could not articulate at all what that musical sense might be. In order to catch on to the unfamiliar musical sense, I had to give up trying to hear the piece in terms of the musical logic that I was already comfortable with, but without having any idea how to understand the music on its own terms. I had to make myself responsive to a sense that was given only as intimated within the noise. Despite being unsure that it would ever produce any results, I continued to listen in that way, and eventually the sense of that piece, and of music written in that style more generally, became clearer to me. And so now, having been listening to this kind of music regularly for more than twenty years, I am tempted to adopt Harlequin's point of view: I can pick up easily and without hesitation the musical sense of the Darmstadt School compositions I listen to and I am genuinely surprised when other people perceive those same compositions as noise.

I mention this experience because it resembles closely the more specifically moral experience I had when I learned about the life of Simone Weil. The close resemblance between the two cases, I believe, points to an important shortcoming in the account of obligation that I have been developing over the previous two chapters. In both the Weil and the Stockhausen cases, I found myself responsive to an intimated sense that I could not comprehend very clearly on the basis of the understanding I brought with me to the encounter. And in both cases, this intimation of a sense that deserved to be taken seriously manifested itself in something like the feeling of respect that Kant had described in the *Critique of Practical Reason*. In the case of Weil, I felt that her life expressed some kind of moral sense that I had fallen short of, even though I could not articulate what that moral sense was. And in the case of Stockhausen's *Hymnen*, I felt that the work expressed a musical sensibility that was not only different from my own but better. That is to say, it seemed to me that I was a less good musician for not understanding Stockhausen's musical sensibility. In Kant's terms, my spirit bowed even though I could not articulate precisely what it bowed to. In both cases, I could not not respond to the noise. I could have responded either by trying to exclude the noise, judging that it contained no genuine potential sense, or by venturing out from the shore of my own understanding and making myself receptive to the potentially new sense. But in the case of Stockhausen's *Hymnen*, it seems plainly wrong to characterise this 'can't help but' as an experience of obligation. It does seem right to say that I would be better off responding to the noisy sense of Stockhausen's music in the right way, but this does not entail that I *must* do it, at least in the specifically moral sense of 'must'. Now if the Stockhausen and Weil cases really are analogous, then the 'must' that is characteristic of obligation should be lacking in the latter as well. But the Weil case seems obviously to involve obligation. If this is right, then there must be some relevant difference between the two cases. I do not believe that we can account for the difference within the framework of the Merleau-Pontian or Serresian philosophies of sense, both of which present the practical subject as originarily responsive to a sense that is given as something to be got right. The 'must' of obligation demands something more of us than simply getting the sense right. To understand that something more, I believe it will be necessary to look beyond Merleau-Ponty and Serres to another account of sense.

Sense as Shared

In what follows, I will argue that the work of Jean-Luc Nancy provides us with the resources for a more adequate account of necessitation in its specifically moral sense. I will begin by describing the ways in which Nancy's account of sense resembles those of Merleau-Ponty and Serres. I will then describe the ways in which Nancy's account differs from these, focusing especially on his commitment to the idea that sense is not a milieu and that it is better understood in terms of what he calls sharing (*partage*). This will lead to an investigation of Nancy's ontology of abandonment, which provides the background for all of his thinking about obligation. I will show how abandonment is always abandonment to the law, whose unconditional command is the source of an obligation whose sense cannot be captured in any formula. Finally, I will argue that what the law commands is respect for dignity, that is, for the singular and incommensurable value that happens in the event of our exposure to each other.

In explicating a Nancian account of the fact of sense, I would like to begin by describing three closely related commitments it shares with the Merleau-Pontian and Serresian accounts. First, Nancy agrees that to be a practical subject at all is to be in sense always already. Nancy expresses this idea most explicitly in *The Sense of the World*, where he writes that 'there is no *epokhe* of sense, no "suspension" of a "naïve thesis" of sense, no "placing in parentheses"'.[6] This is not to say, of course, that Nancy believes we ought to accept the point of view of the natural attitude with regard to sense. The sense of a novel or of an object given in perception is not 'out there' among the things that make up the world, present to a subject understood as another one of those things. But rejecting the point of view of the natural attitude does not require us to accept Husserl's transcendental idealist account of sense-bestowal, according to which 'every imaginable sense, every imaginable being, whether the latter is called immanent or transcendent, falls within the domain of transcendental subjectivity, as the subjectivity that constitutes sense and being'.[7] The epoché that leads to this subject-centred account of the origin of sense happens unavoidably as a response to a philosophical problem that already makes sense. The epoché, in other words, arrives on the scene too late, presupposing the very sense that it is supposed to bracket.

Nancy's point in denying the possibility of an epoché of sense is somewhat similar to the idea expressed by Merleau-Ponty when he writes that 'the most important lesson of the reduction is the impossibility of a complete reduction'.[8] Reflection on the world, in other words, cannot lead us all the way back to a constituting consciousness that would be the origin of the world's sense. (Reduction, in the Husserlian sense of the term, is to be understood in the sense suggested by its Latin etymology: *re-ducere*, to lead back.) What reflection can help us do, though, is to 'rupture our familiarity' with the world, bringing to light 'the unmotivated springing forth of the world', which is covered over in the natural attitude.[9] Philosophy, according to Merleau-Ponty, is thus a perpetual beginning, a refusal to 'take itself as established in the truths it has managed to utter'.[10]

Like Merleau-Ponty, Nancy is concerned to think that which 'precedes consciousness and the signifying appropriation of sense' and which 'precedes and surprises the phenomenon in the phenomenon itself, its coming or its coming up'.[11] But he goes further than Merleau-Ponty – or at least the Merleau-Ponty of *Phenomenology of Perception* and *The Prose of the World* – in his criticism of the basic conceptual apparatus of phenomenology. Merleau-Ponty's conception of a perpetually incomplete reduction helps to undermine the

Husserlian conception of the subject whose activity grounds 'every imaginable sense', but it nonetheless preserves an essential role for subjectivity as the site of 'presentation, placing-in-view, exhibition, and manifestation'.[12] Even for the Merleau-Pontian subject who is of the world and who has always already sided with it, the advent of sense takes place within the bounds of the structure of intentionality. Significant sense becomes manifest for a subject who knows how to gear into the latent sense of the world. The de-familiarisation of the world that is made possible by the incompleteness of the reduction is thus insufficiently radical: 'All types of phenomenology, indeed all types of beyond-phenomenology, do not open up sufficiently to the coming of sense, to sense as a coming that is neither immanent nor transcendent.'[13] For Nancy, the coming of sense – what Merleau-Ponty called 'the unmotivated springing forth of the world' – not only precedes constituting subjectivity, but precedes it infinitely. To be in the world is to be condemned to this infinitely precedent sense that no epoché can reach.

A second idea that the Nancian account of the fact of sense shares with the Merleau-Pontian and Serresian accounts is that to be in the world is to be responsive to a sense that exceeds determinate sense. This excessive dimension of sense was understood in the Merleau-Pontian account as metastability and in the Serresian account as noise. For both, there is always an excess of moral sense given along with the determinate, relatively noise-free moral sense with reference to which we orient our conduct in the world. The fact of our originary exposure to this excessive sense undermines the possibility of our capturing moral sense in a rule or set of rules that would enable us always to know 'quite easily and without hesitation' what we ought to do. Nancy is committed to a similar idea. One of the most persistent themes in his work concerns the experience of the loss of an orienting sense that had supposedly been present to us at one point in a straightforward and unproblematic way. According to Nancy, 'the enterprise of sense always begins by signifying the anterior or transcendent presence of a *sense* that has been lost, forgotten, or altered, one that is, by definition, to be recovered, restored, or revived'.[14] One of the most common responses to this experience of loss has been to call on philosophers to produce 'an ethics', which would take the form of a theory of duty, a set of true propositions that would tell us definitively what our obligations were.[15] But Nancy is sceptical of calls for an ethics of this sort. The loss of a moral sense fully sufficient to orient our conduct, he suggests, is not a historical accident whose effects could be reversed by ethical thinkers working with sufficient care and good will. We misunderstand our experience when we characterise it as one of lost presence. According to Nancy, 'we have never forgotten, lost, muddled, or masked signification in such a way that we would have to retrieve or reconstitute it. We are always already in it.'[16] Our sense of disorientation, of the lack of an ethical North Star, is better understood in terms of an originary exposure not to *a* sense or to the lack of sense, but rather to a sense 'that preexists signification and exceeds it'.[17]

A third and final commonality between the three accounts of the fact of sense is the idea of the subject as originarily exposed. For all three accounts, it is not merely the case that the practical subject finds herself always already in the midst of a sense that exceeds signification; the subject is also constitutively ex-posed, opened out to this sense. The subject, in other words, is not in a sense that exceeds her in the way that a bottle of water is in a lake. The subject's sense – the sense that is the subject's own, that she identifies with and that orients her conduct – is not sealed off from a world of sense 'outside' her. It follows from this that the subject is not autonomous in the Kantian sense of the term: she is not the source of the moral sense that obligates her. As a subject *of* sense, she is more basically subjected *to* sense, and specifically to a dynamic of sense whose legitimacy she cannot step back from and attempt to confirm. This exposure, as we have seen, is the ground of the necessitation that is essential to the phenomenon of obligation.

Nancy's account of this exposure, though, is importantly different from the Merleau-Pontian and Serresian accounts. To show how this is so, I would like to begin with a passage from *Being Singular Plural*, where Nancy argues that 'sense is not a milieu in which we are immersed. There is no *mi-lieu* [between place].'[18] We must not conceive of sense, in other words, as the medium within which we encounter each other or as any kind of bridge or connective tissue that would bring us together.[19] But that, it seems, is precisely how both Merleau-Ponty and Serres understand sense. This can be seen especially clearly in Merleau-Ponty's account of expression in *The Prose of the World*. I am able to catch on to the sense presented in *The Charterhouse of Parma* despite the fact that my day-to-day experience is wildly different from the experiences of Stendhal's characters.

I am able to do so because neither Stendhal's world of meaning nor my own is hermetically sealed. What mediates the relation between Stendhal and me is a general signifyingness, a dimension of latent, metastable sense that subtends our very different worlds of established significations. Serres expresses a very similar understanding of sense as milieu with his conception of white noise as pure possibility of sense. Even though I make moral sense of the world in terms of principles that are familiar to me, I am able to recognise the possibility of very different moral understandings that deserve to be taken seriously. I am Harlequin, Emperor of the Moon, but I am also Pierrot. And so once again, different worlds of established significations are mediated by a dimension of possible sense that subtends them.

It is this treatment of sense as a kind of milieu, I want to argue, that explains the failure of these two accounts to capture the specific 'must' of obligation. For both, the world is present to the practical subject as mediated by a latent sense that is given as something to be got right. But as I argued above, this orientation toward getting the sense right is characteristic of many forms of experience that have nothing to do with obligation as it is typically understood. My relation to a promisee or to a dependent child is mediated by a sense that I experience myself as capable of getting right or wrong, and as the very names 'right' and 'wrong' suggest, I experience the right sense as the better one. But the same is true of my relation to a painting or a pair of scissors or a sentence in a foreign language. It seems strongly counterintuitive to suggest that I have an obligation to get the sense right in these latter cases, and so it is unclear why I would have one in the former cases.

If we should not think of sense as a kind of milieu, then how should we think of it? A more adequate account of the characteristic 'must' of obligation will depend to a great degree on our answer to this question. In *Being Singular Plural*, Nancy argues that we should understand sense as 'the sharing [*partage*] of being'.[20] This must not be taken to mean that sense is the parcelling out of the whole of being, such that each particular being-in-the-world would receive its share. According to Nancy, there is no being that pre-exists its sharing out among plural beings that are exposed, posited outside themselves and thus present *to* each other. Being is irreducibly being-with.[21] To begin to unpack what Nancy means with these somewhat dense formulations, it will be helpful to refer to a passage from his *Hegel: The Restlessness of the Negative*. Commenting on Hegel's conception of sense as mediation, he asserts that 'the given always gives itself as something other than simply given. This way of "giving itself" is mediation – and this mediation is therefore that of being itself and not exterior to it.'[22] There is, in other words, no brute givenness of being. The given never gives itself as what Hegel in his *Science of Logic* calls 'the indeterminate *immediate*'.[23] Rather whenever being is given, it is given *as*. The perfume I am wearing as I type these words, for example, is present to me *as* smelling like rose. When I smell the perfume, I do not have two discrete experiences: first, an experience of unqualified, brute givenness and second, an experience of the scent of rose. This thing that I smell is given right from the outset as rose. Likewise, other persons are present to me as family members or colleagues, or more distantly as persons unknown to me who are suffering and whom I could conceivably benefit. They are never present in an unqualified way. And the same kind of analysis applies to the case of my presence to myself: I am given to myself as someone with a particular life history, as someone who occupies various social roles and who is committed to different projects. And most generally, being is given *as* being. To think of the given as something distinct from its 'as' is to think an abstraction that has no place whatsoever in our experience.

To say that being is necessarily given *as* is to say that being is inseparable from its sense. As Nancy puts it in *The Sense of the World*, 'sense does not add itself to being, does not supervene upon being', as if being somehow pre-existed its sense.[24] It is this ontological commitment that grounds Nancy's claim that there can be no epoché of sense: our opening out onto being just is an opening out onto sense. This, of course, looks very similar to Merleau-Ponty's claim that 'because we are in the world, we are condemned to sense'.[25] And indeed it is similar. But an essential difference between the two accounts emerges from Nancy's answer to the question, how is this sense given? What are the conditions of possibility for being's being given *as*? Nancy addresses these questions most straightforwardly in a passage from *Being Singular Plural*:

Sense begins where presence is not pure presence but where presence comes apart [*se disjoint*] in order to be itself *as* such. This 'as' presupposes the distancing, spacing, and division of presence . . . Pure unshared presence – presence to nothing, of nothing, for nothing – is neither present nor absent. It is the simple implosion of a being that could never have *been* – an implosion without any trace.[26]

Sense, or the presence of being *as*, presupposes being's exposure to an outside. Pure, undivided presence – presence *simpliciter*, without a *to* or an *of* – is unexperienceable and unthinkable. Such a thing would be completely impenetrable to sense, a kind of black hole of meaning. This idea develops Hegel's thesis about mediation, which Nancy summarises as follows: 'What is thus "of being" – proper to being itself – is to negate itself as being so as to become sense.'[27] Being *is* only in negating its unshared immediacy, only in exposing itself to an outside that gives it to be what it is in truth, namely being. But how precisely is this exposure to be understood? How ought we to characterise the dynamic of sense that happens in and as this exposure? Hegel's own conception of this dynamic is nicely expressed in a passage from the *Aesthetics* that we discussed briefly in the Introduction:

'Sense' is this wonderful word that is used in two opposite meanings. On the one hand it means the organ of immediate apprehension, but on the other hand we mean by it the sense, the meaning, the thought, the universal underlying the thing.[28]

The word 'sense' refers both to the sensible intuition of the given and to the universal, the intelligible meaning of the given. We speak, for example, of the five senses, but also of the sense of a proposition. Hegel's point is that 'sense' names the givenness of the sensible and its intelligible meaning as a single, unified phenomenon. The sensible is given as more than the sensible given, as pointing beyond itself toward the sense or meaning that is its own. In short, 'ideality is ideality *of* sensibility, and sensibility is sensibility of ideality'.[29]

Nancy expands on this conception of mediation but also disrupts it, emphasising a third sense of 'sense' that is passed over in Hegel's account. In *The Sense of the World* Nancy notes that

although the etymology of the word *sense* is not clear, one constant is that the word is attached to a semantic family in which one finds, first of all, in Irish, Gothic, or High German, the values of movement, oriented displacement, voyage, 'tending toward'.[30]

This third element is captured in the French word *sens*, which in addition to naming the organ of immediate apprehension and ideal meaning or signification, can also be used to mean 'direction'. To focus only on sense as sensible and as ideal is to suggest a circular dynamic in which a being's sense is appropriated: the sensibly given being becomes what it truly is in the journey outside itself and back. Nancy, on the contrary, insists that '*all* sense resides in the nonappropriation of "being"'.[31] The *to* of being – its exposure to an outside – makes sense, in the most literal sense of the idiom. It is the originary spacing or *différance* without which being could not be, but which itself *is not*. The exteriority onto which being opens in its spacing is not transformed into an interiority:

To exist does not mean simply 'to be'. On the contrary: to exist means *not* to be in the immediate presence or in the immanency of a 'being thing'. To exist is not to be immanent, or not to be present to oneself, and not to be sent forth *by* oneself. To exist, therefore, is to hold one's 'selfness' as an 'otherness', and in such a way that no essence, no subject, no place can present *this otherness in itself* – either as the proper selfness of an other, or an 'Other,' or a common being (life or substance).[32]

The otherness of the self that Nancy refers to here is not another self, but rather the inappropriable limit to which each being is necessarily exposed and which is itself neither inside nor outside.[33] Sense happens right at this limit where beings are exposed to each other.

This idea of sense as arising in the *to* of exposition is exemplified nicely in the case of people meeting each other for the first time:

When you introduce yourself [*te présentes*], when you name yourself, this has no signification; it is not a concept joined to an intuition; there is neither distance nor immediacy; it is not a representation, nor is it sheer indetermination, since you stand out from both the world and significations.[34]

Our presentation to each other takes place as an exposition that is never reducible to the significant context within which the presentation happens or to the significant meaning that results from it.[35] These significations are appropriable. When I introduce myself to my students on the first day of class, for example, I do so as a professor, as someone with fairly well-defined expectations about how our student–professor relationship will proceed. The signification 'professor' is mine; I identify myself with it and orient my conduct with reference to it. But what I cannot appropriate is the *to* of my exposure. This exposure happens neither inside me nor outside me, but rather right at the limit at which I am opened out onto the world. As an experience of the limit, it is best described as a kind of touching, a contact that both presupposes and preserves separation.

To touch is necessarily to touch at the limit, such that the touched resists appropriation. Sense happens most originarily as a touch, as a relation not between signifier, signified and referent, but rather between us.[36] For Nancy, then, 'we' names 'the sense of sense, the very opening of sense, and sense as opening'.[37] This is what accounts for the experience that is captured in the common saying, 'people are strange', and for our relating to each other on the basis of what could be called a '"transcendental" curiosity':[38]

The other origin is incomparable or inassimilable, not because it is simply 'other' but because it is an origin and touch of sense. Or rather, the alterity of the other is its originary contiguity with the 'proper' origin. You are absolutely strange because the world begins its turn with you.[39]

The origin of sense happens nowhere else than at the limit where beings touch.

The beings at whose limits sense most originarily emerges are conceived by Nancy as singularities. A singular *qua* singular cannot be understood as a particular, which is always an instance of a general signification, a particular *something*: a particular stone, a particular lamb, and so on. Nor can we understand a singular as a self-enclosed, self-identical atom. The singular, rather, is only singular as exposed to other singularities: 'The concept of the singular implies its singularization and, therefore, its distinction from other singularities.' As a result, 'singularity is indissociable from a plurality'.[40] Nancy compares singularities in this regard to the concept of the atom as it was developed specifically within the context of ancient atomism. In the hypothesised initial condition of laminar flow, the atoms, which pursue their own courses independent of all the others, do not form any kind of meaningful world. It is only with the clinamen – the completely inexplicable deviation of one of the atoms from its parallel fall – that a world comes into existence. In Nancy's terms, the clinamen is the inappropriable being-to, the exposure that is the *conditio sine qua non* of sense. A singularity, then, is the atom plus the clinamen. 'But the clinamen is not something else, another element outside of the atoms; it is not in addition to them; it is the "more" of their exposition.'[41] There is no singular, in other words, that would pre-exist its exposition. To be a singular just is to be exposed at the limit to other singularities.

As the comparison to ancient atomism helps to makes clear, the exposure of singularities to each other is an event. As Nancy uses the term, event names 'the "it happens" as distinct from all that precedes it and from everything according to which it is codetermined. It is the pure present of the "it happens"'.[42] François Raffoul expresses the point nicely when he describes the event as what happens 'outside the conditions of possibility offered in advance by a sub-ject of representation'.[43] Neither a pond's freezing at 32° Fahrenheit nor a baseball team's winning the World Series is an event in this sense of the term: both of these happen within a context of mean-ing that renders them predictable to greater or lesser degrees. The event, on the contrary, is always a radical surprise.[44] The clinamen, the originary *to* of singularities' exposure to each other, is a pure 'it happens' whose possibility is not established in advance. The sense of the world happens in and as this clinamen, as an event. It happens, incommensurably and each time uniquely, at the limits of singulari-ties that do not pre-exist their being-to. This is why Nancy insists that sense is not a milieu. Sense happens rather as absolute origin, as creation of the world *ex nihilo*, where the *nihil* is not a nothing that would be somehow prior to the world, but rather the very spacing or dis-position in which the world first comes to presence.[45] This spac-ing thus constitutes 'an unprecedented kind of "fact of reason"':[46] as an event of sense – an event in and as which sense is given – it cannot be deduced 'from antecedent data of reason' and it 'is not based on any intuition, either pure or empirical'.[47] To be, on Nancy's account, just is to be exposed to this fact always already.

Abandonment and Obligation

The condition of beings exposed at their limits to the fact of sense – to the fact of the event of originary spacing – is characterised by Nancy as one of abandonment. This characterisation is most basi-cally ontological: it is a claim about the meaning of being. But as we will see, it is also irreducibly ethical. In 'Abandoned Being', Nancy argues that 'abandoned being has already begun to constitute an inevitable condition for our thought, perhaps its only condition. From now on, the ontology that summons us will be an ontology in which abandonment remains the sole predicament of being.'[48] Abandoned being constitutes the condition for our thought now because of our situation within the history of metaphysics, a situation characterised by 'the exhaustion of transcendentals'.[49] This, broadly speaking, is the situation that Nietzsche had described in terms of the death of God and that Heidegger had described as the end of metaphysics: we are no longer convinced by those principles – God, Nature, History, Subject – whose function has been to gather the multiplicity of being together in a unity, thereby grounding its sense.[50] If Aristotle is correct that being is *pollakōs legomenon*, the spoken-in-multiple-ways, then we must not understand this to mean that there is being on the one hand and its being-spoken on the other. The *pollakōs legetai* must not be understood as ordered by a *monōs legetai*, by a univocal *logos*. Rather, being simply is the *pollakōs*, without identity:

What is left is an irremediable scattering, a dissemination of ontological specks. As a result, this scattering itself is not left – at least not as the remainder of a subtraction or as the remains of a fragmentation, which leave something to keep hold of.[51]

There is no being, in other words, whose prior unity has come apart, such that being would have fallen into abandonment; being has never been anything other than *pollakōs legomenon*.[52]

We can express the same idea, this time in a way that emphasises the point of view of the agent, by characterising abandonment as the withdrawal of essence. As François Raffoul has shown, this conception of abandonment is best understood as a development of Jean-Paul Sartre's understanding of the relation between essence and existence.[53] In 'The Humanism of Existentialism', Sartre suggests that what all existentialists have in common is a commitment to the idea 'that existence precedes essence'.[54] Beings, according to Sartre, are given first simply as existing and not as meaningful, as being instances of a general kind. *That* something is, in other words, is prior to its being *what* it is. This ontological conception is important from an ethical point of view because it deprives us of the kinds of identity-based norms that we often rely on as guides to action. For example, if I am a son – if that is *what* I am – then I can orient myself relatively unproblematically with reference to that concept, choosing to do the things that a good son does and refraining from doing the things that a good son does not do. The problem, though, is that my existence exceeds my concept; I am more than a son, and indeed I am more than any list of qualities that could be truly predicated of me. The result of this fact, according to Sartre, is that

I am *abandoned* in the world, not in the sense that I might remain abandoned and passive in a hostile universe like a board floating on the water, but rather in the sense that I find myself suddenly alone and without help, engaged in a world for which I bear the whole responsibility without being able, whatever I do, to tear myself away from this responsibility for an instant.[55]

I am condemned to responsibility precisely because my existence precedes my essence. My being what I am – a son, a professor, a neighbour, a human being, and so on – does not suffice to determine my will. If I act as a son or a professor typically does, it is because I have freely chosen to do so. To be abandoned, on this Sartrean account, is to be abandoned to a responsibility without measure. Faced with a difficult moral decision, I cannot rely on any existing norms, values or role requirements for guidance. As Sartre argues in 'The Humanism of Existentialism', there is nothing for the abandoned, and thus free, moral subject to do but 'choose, that is, invent'.[56]

Nancy's account of abandonment takes up and develops Sartre's ideas that the meaning of our being-in-the-world is not given in advance and that this non-givenness imposes certain demands on our praxis. But Nancy's account is importantly different from Sartre's in its deprioritising of subjectivity. In 'The Humanism of Existentialism', Sartre suggests that existentialism in all of its different forms is committed to the idea that 'subjectivity must be the starting point'.[57] Nancy rejects this idea. For reasons we have already touched on, the happening of the sense of the world cannot be understood starting from the subject. Sense begins rather with exposure, which is not the exposure of a subject who would pre-exist it, but rather the exposure that first gives there to be subjects who are present to themselves. What we must begin with, then, is the simple fact that 'this exposure takes place'. [58] This exposure takes place not within the subject but rather at the limit where beings are exposed to each other. This, once again, is the meaning of Nancy's claim that 'we are sense':

Before all produced or disclosed sense, and before all exchanges of sense, our existence presents itself to us as sense – and when I say 'we' in this sentence, I designate equally and indissociably each of our singular existences, whose singularity is each time the place of such a presentation . . .

Our existence presents itself as sense . . . and simultaneously, we present ourselves *to ourselves*. That is to say, at once to one another, through one another, and each one to him or herself. We *co-appear* [*comparaissons*], and this appearing [*parution*] is sense.[59]

To be abandoned, in Nancy's sense, is to be exposed to the inappropriable sense that is at stake in this co-appearing.

It is the ontological structure of abandonment, understood in the Nancian sense, that gives rise to the experience of obligation.[60] What I want to argue more specifically is that this structure enables us to account for many of the elements that have traditionally been included in our conception of obligation, but that we could not make sense of on the Merleau-Pontian or Serresian accounts. As we have seen, both of these accounts make sense of the experience of necessitation by treating the subject as responsive always already to a sense that is given as something to be got right. But in neither of these accounts is the practical subject presented as the addressee of a law, promulgated by a superior, that *commands* the subject to get the sense right. As the early modern voluntarists argued, without the elements of law and command we cannot make sense of the distinction between what we are obligated to do and what would be good in a more general sense for us to do. Of course Nancy's account of obligation will be importantly different from Pufendorf's or Barbeyrac's. As we will see, the law that commands is not addressed by an authority, be it God or a political superior, who has both the power and the right to enforce his commands with sanctions. Indeed, the law that is given in abandonment is not backed by sanctions of any sort. Rather, to be abandoned, to find oneself exposed to the fact of sense, just is to be singled out as the addressee of an imperative that is given immediately as authoritative.

In order to see how this works, it will be helpful to begin by unpacking the etymology of 'abandonment':

The origin of 'abandonment' is putting at *bandon*. *Bandon* (*bandum, band, bannen*) is an order, a prescription, a decree, a permission, and the power that holds these freely at its disposal. To *abandon* is to remit, entrust, or turn over to such a sovereign power, and to remit, entrust, or turn over to its *ban*, that is, to its proclaiming, to its convening, and to its sentencing.[61]

It is important here to recall that this is most basically an ontological thesis. The etymology, of course, refers to a political context in which a human being is turned over to the rule of another, the sovereign, who issues legitimate imperatives. But this must not be taken to suggest that there is some being who would function as the ground of abandonment, as the being by whom or to whom we are abandoned. Being *is*, rather, only as abandoned. As Nancy writes in *Being Singular Plural*, 'Being absolutely does not *preexist*; nothing preexists; only what exists exists.'[62] What exists exists as abandoned, as remitted or turned over *to*, where the *to* is to be thought on its own terms, and not with reference to that by which it has been remitted. To be, more precisely, is to be exposed at the limit to an exterior where sense is at stake. As Nancy argues in the essay 'Originary Ethics', abandoned being is itself the fact of sense: the fact of the withdrawal of given, fully established sense and the fact of sense's givenness as an unconditional demand on our praxis.[63] It is not the case, in other words, that first there is a fact of being and then second, the demand to confer some sense on this fact. Returning to Sartre's language, it is not the case that existence precedes essence. To exist, rather, just is to be turned over or remitted always already to the demand to *make* the sense that is never given to us fully formed.[64]

To be abandoned, then, is necessarily to be abandoned to the law.[65] But this law is not any particular law. There is no formula that could adequately express its sense and that we could refer to as a guide to right conduct. It is not the law that commands me 'never to act except in such a way that I could also will that my maxim should become a universal law' or to will in such a way that my maxims would 'harmonize with a possible kingdom of ends as with a kingdom of nature'.[66] The sense of the law cannot be captured in these or any other formulas precisely because it is sense itself that is at stake in our abandonment. To be abandoned is to be exposed to the groundlessness of our origins, to the *nihil* of originary spacing where sense does not pre-exist as a kind of milieu but rather happens as an event right at our limits. Given over to this *nihil* absolutely and without reserve, we find ourselves thrown into our having-to-be. François Raffoul expresses the point perspicuously when he writes that the abandoned being 'is thrown in such a way that, each time, it *has to be* this being-thrown, that is, *it has to be this not-being-itself-the-basis-for its being*'.[67] Exposed to the groundlessness of our origins, we find ourselves enjoined 'to take absolute responsibility for making-sense of the world'.[68] This is just to say that the law given in abandonment 'prescribes nothing but abandonment'.[69]

There is no point at which we can have succeeded in satisfying this demand, at which we can have fully lived up to our condition as abandoned. To be, rather, is to be turned over to the *demand* to be, unremittingly.

But how is it, precisely, that this law commands or enjoins us? As exposed ineluctably to the groundlessness of our origins, we *have to* make sense. We have no choice but to be the not-being-ourselves-the-basis-for our being. But how does this not amount to another 'can't-help-but' account of necessitation? How does the ontology of abandonment give rise to the kind of 'must' that is unique to obligation? Nancy's answer to this question involves an explicit rejection of one of the elements that the voluntarist moral theorists had considered essential to the phenomenon of obligation, namely the credible threat of sanctions. In 'The *Katagorein* of Excess', Nancy insists that 'the imperative contains neither threat nor promise. Indeed, its essence lies in the fact that it contains neither.'[70] As Kant recognised at the time he wrote the *Groundwork*, but seemed not to have recognised a year earlier when he gave the Collins lectures on ethics, an imperative whose force is derived from any kind of threat is necessarily a hypothetical imperative, which can never be the source of genuine obligation. The force of the 'must' in a hypothetical imperative is conditional, as it depends on the moral subject's desire to avoid the sanction. But the necessitation proper to obligation is unconditional.[71]

As we have seen, Kant attempted in the *Critique of Practical Reason* to account for the unconditional necessitation of obligation in terms of the fact of reason: it is just a fact, unexplainable in terms of any antecedent data of reason, that we experience ourselves as obligated to act in accordance with the moral law. In 'The *Katagorein* of Excess' and in 'Abandoned Being' Nancy offers a similar account, interpreting the fact of reason in terms of abandonment and locating the force of the unconditional 'must' in the *to* of our originary exposure. Specifically, Nancy argues that the law that obligates us is given to us most basically as an authoritative address and in the experience of respect. Following Kant, Nancy treats respect as 'the very relation to the law'.[72] It is not the case, in other words, that we have a theoretical cognition of the law and then in addition to that a feeling of respect for it. The law, rather, is given only in respect. And the relation of respect, in turn, is given in the ontological structure of abandonment, which just is abandonment to respect for the law.[73] Respect is to be understood here, in accordance with its etymology, as a kind of gaze or regard. But it is not at all an ideational regard, a contemplation that would take the law as its object. If the law were given as the object of a theoretical or knowing regard, then Barbeyrac's objection would once again apply: we cannot make the leap from our merely recognising the moral law to our being unconditionally necessitated to act in accordance with it. This problem does not arise for Nancy, who conceives of respect in the precise manner suggested by its etymology: *re-spicere*, to look behind or to look back at. In respect we are 'turned toward the *before* of abandonment, where there is nothing to see, which is not to be seen'.[74] We are turned back toward the groundlessness of our being, toward the exposure that first presents us to ourselves as having to be our being-there. The before of abandonment is a fact in the sense of the Kantian fact of reason, one that is utterly incommensurable with the world of sense that it opens up. It constitutes an alterity that is unassignable and inassimilable. This alterity, the groundless ground of our practical being, does not *have* a sense that the subject could appropriate, taking it as the principle of its autonomous willing. This is why 'respect is the very alteration of the position and structure of the subject; that is, the latter faces up – but without being able to fix its gaze upon – or responds – but without *responding* – to the alterity of the law'.[75] The subject, in other words, is given to itself as the addressee of an injunction whose sense is not given. The subject cannot back up from this injunction in order to verify its legitimacy since the subject is given to itself most basically *as* its addressee. What is enjoined in the address to the practical subject is praxis itself: not action directed toward producing a result, nor even action for the sake of action, but rather the action that is necessary simply because sense is not given and must thus be made.[76] The fact of sense is thus a demand for sense, and any attempt to verify this demand's legitimacy would unavoidably presuppose it.[77]

Dignity

Does this account of obligation in terms of abandonment to respect for the law constitute a genuine improvement over the Merleau-Pontian and Serresian accounts? There is at least some reason to doubt that it does. Specifically, it seems as if the Nancian account has solved a problem in the other two accounts – namely that they could not make sense of the 'must' proper to obligation – only at the price of introducing an even greater problem. For Nancy, as we have just seen, sense is given most basically as an interpellation, as a demand for sense. The practical subject is given to himself in the experience of respect as the addressee of this unconditional demand, and not as immersed in a nascent sense that presents itself as something to be got right. The experience of necessitation that arises in this address is specifically moral. It is clearly distinct from the non-moral necessitation that arises in perceptual experience or in the experience of reading a novel. But if obligation has its source in the inappropriable, unassignable alterity of a law whose sense is never given, then how can the practical subject know *what* he is obligated to do? On Nancy's account, the obligating force of the law seems completely divorced from the content of obligation. This problem does not arise in the Merleau-Pontian and Serresian accounts, which present the practical subject as immersed in a milieu of sense. Even though these accounts differ from Kant's in denying that the unambiguous sense of the law is given immediately with the experience of necessitation, both retain some link between the 'must' and its content. Nancy, on the other hand, insists that the law to which we are abandoned 'prescribes nothing but abandonment', nothing but the demand actively to be the there.[78] But *how* ought we to be the there? *What* is the sense that we ought to make? On Nancy's account, the law that obligates us cannot authorise any definitive answers to these questions. What follows, it seems, is the idea that any activity of sense making is just as good as any other.[79] But this seems so far removed from both from our common-sense conception of obligation and from the conception that was worked out over the course of the early modern period that it cannot possibly be right. There must be at least some connection between the experience of unconditional necessitation and the content of that necessitation.

What I want to argue in the remainder of the chapter is that this weakness in the Nancian account of obligation is only apparent. It is true that the sense of the law cannot be expressed in a formula that we could refer to as a guide for our conduct; it can never function as anything like a protocol. The law, rather, is present as what haunts us. As Nancy argues in 'The *Katagorein* of Excess',

what haunts [*hante*] is, according to its accepted etymological origins, what inhabits or occupies [*habite*] or, on a more knowing etymological reading, what returns to the stable, to the hearth, to the home. *Haunt* is from the same family as *Heim*. The proximity of the imperative might well be the *Un-heimlichkeit* that haunts our thinking, a disturbing peculiarity that disturbs only because it is so close, so immediate in its estrangement.[80]

It cannot be the task of ethics to domesticate the law, to bring it about that it no longer haunts us. A law that did not haunt would function like the rules and regulations familiar to us from social, political and religious life. These rules apply only conditionally: they presuppose the parcelling out of distinct spheres of life in which their legitimacy is generally recognised. The rules that require fasting on Ash Wednesday and Good Friday, for example, apply to Roman Catholics. As a non-Catholic, I am aware of the rule and I am capable of applying it more or less accurately to a variety of possible cases. I know, for example, that eating a filet mignon on Ash Wednesday would violate the rule. But my recognition of the rule and of its application to particular cases is not sufficient to give me the experience of being obligated to refrain from eating filet mignon on Ash Wednesday. Such familiar, domesticated rules, then, cannot open up the space of obligation. They do not command us immediately and unconditionally to act, as the imperative does, but rather call on us to subsume possible actions under the rule and to act accordingly, supposing that we recognise ourselves as properly addressed by it.[81]

The moral law can only open the space of obligation if it haunts us, resisting all appropriation by the practical subject. The law is given as radically other, but as nonetheless closer to me than any determinate sense I might identify with. It is not given as any particular sense, but rather as the unconditional, unassignable command to make sense. As we have seen, the validity of the law does not depend on my antecedently recognising myself as someone who falls under its jurisdiction: I am a practical subject, a being-there, only as enjoined to act. And as the addressee of this command, I am given to myself as singular, as incommensurable. Insofar as I orient my life with reference to determinate identifications, on the other hand, I am commensurable. As a teacher, for example, my conduct can be judged by standards that are public and at least reasonably well defined. I can be evaluated – and can evaluate myself – relative both to other teachers and to the ends that the activity of teaching is supposed to promote. The same applies to me as a son, a citizen, a friend and a guitar player. But as haunted by the law, which is applied only in its withdrawal, I am incomparable.[82] My being-there, which I am commanded actively to be, is the space of the event of sense, and not one sense among others. I am, as Nancy writes in *Being Singular Plural*, 'an origin and touch of sense'. I am 'absolutely strange because the world begins its turn with [me]'.[83]

My being the site of the event of sense forecloses the possibility of a general rule that could succeed in fixing the ethical sense of the world and of my conduct within it. But it is precisely this foreclosure that gives rise to a phenomenon that will provide some content to our being obligated, namely the phenomenon of dignity.[84] Ethical subjectivity, according to Nancy, originates in our being 'entirely responsible for sense, and for [our] own existence as making-sense, without prior subjection to any fixed sense'.[85] As abandoned, we find ourselves exposed always already to a sense that is given as withdrawn and that 'doesn't let itself be incorporated, appropriated, and fixed as an acquisition'.[86] Our dignity lies in this exposure and this responsibility. Although Nancy makes use of a very different vocabulary to unpack the meaning of dignity, his conception is ultimately quite Kantian. For Kant, dignity is to be understood on the basis of its distinction from price, which names a relative, and thus comparable, value. If something has a price, it 'can be replaced by something else as its *equivalent*'.[87] It is possible for the thing to have an equivalent because it and its potential replacements are all instances of the same kind: they have the same sense. If I own two clean copies of the same book, for example, then it makes no difference which one I take off the shelf to read. I do not encounter each of them as having a unique, incomparable value. For practical purposes, one is just as good as the other. Or if one is not just as good as the other, then the difference in their value can be measured on the same scale. If some of the pages in one of my two books are uncut, for example, then I might judge it to be less good than the other. The value of both books derives from their being instances of the kind 'book' and in their being what a book should be. The value of a being with dignity, Kant thinks, is qualitatively different from that of a being whose whole value consists in its price. Specifically, a being with dignity has a value that is absolute and incommensurable, 'raised above all price'.[88] A being with dignity is something more than an instance of a general kind of value. But this 'something more' is not to be understood as another kind of which it would be the instance. A book, for example, does not acquire dignity from its being both a functional book and a rare collector's item. *Qua* collector's item, the book's value is commensurable with that of other collector's items and *qua* book, its value is commensurable with that of other books. The 'something more' that constitutes the dignity of persons consists rather in their rationality, in their being origins of value through their activity of setting ends. Persons do not have dignity merely as instances of the species *Homo sapiens*, or insofar as they are good specimens of *Homo sapiens*, but, returning to Nancy's language, because of their lack of 'prior subjection to any fixed sense'. As abandoned to sense in withdrawal, we find ourselves addressed by a law that commands us to '*respect existence*', that is, to respect our own and others' being origins and touches of sense.

A second way in which Nancy's account of dignity resembles Kant's is in its commitment to the idea that the value of dignity is given by the law. It is not the case, in other words, that dignity is a kind of intrinsic value that certain beings have and that the law commands respect for those beings *because* they have it. To be sure, there are certain passages in Kant that do seem to present dignity as a property that is given independently of the law. In Section 11 of the Doctrine of Virtue, for example, Kant writes that each person 'possesses a dignity (an absolute inner worth) by which he exacts respect for himself from all other rational beings in the world'.[89] This makes it seem as if the property of dignity gives the law to our practical reason, exacting a respect that it would not freely grant. But this understanding is entirely incompatible with one of the most basic commitments of Kantian ethics, namely the priority of the right over the good. In the second *Critique*, Kant argues explicitly that it is 'the moral law that first determines and makes possible the concept of the good, insofar as it deserves this name absolutely'.[90] This rules out the possibility that the moral law could be grounded in any kind of good at all, including that of dignity: 'For, nothing can have a worth other than that which the law determines for it.'[91] Although Nancy does not refer explicitly to the priority of right over the good, he does advance a similar claim. We experience ourselves as having a kind of value incommensurable with all others precisely because we are abandoned to the law, which does not refer us to a determinate sense as a model for our conduct but rather commands us to *make* sense.

Kant characterises this value that the law commands us to respect as an 'inner worth'.[92] It is a property possessed by all rational beings just in virtue of their 'capacity to give universal law'.[93] Our dignity does not consist in our being subject to laws that are already given, but rather in our capacity actively to make the law. Insofar as we have this capacity, we are all equal to one another. Our dignity, Kant insists, is innate and inalienable: we do not need to do anything to earn it and there is nothing we could do that would result in our forfeiting it.[94] Kant gives his clearest expression to this idea in Section 39 of the Doctrine of Virtue, where he argues that we must never treat others with contempt, even when they have acted in ways that render them unworthy of their dignity. We must never subject criminals, for example, to 'disgraceful punishments that dishonor humanity itself (such as quartering a man, having him torn by dogs, cutting off his nose and ears)'.[95] No matter how badly he has acted, the criminal retains a dignity that imposes limits on others in their dealings with him. He can do nothing that would reduce him to the status of a moral non-entity, undeserving of the basic respect we owe to human beings in general.

But in other passages Kant suggests that we have only a tenuous hold on our dignity and that we must take great care not to forfeit it. In the Doctrine of Virtue, for example, Kant argues that we disavow our dignity when we make ourselves lackeys, parasites, flatterers or beggars and when we accept favours we could do without.[96] He states the point even more strongly when he argues that a person who tells a lie

throws away and, as it were, annihilates his dignity as a human being. A human being who does not himself believe what he tells another (even if the other is a merely ideal person) has even less worth than if he were a mere thing . . . [He is] a mere deceptive appearance of a human being, not a human being himself.[97]

And in the *Lectures on Ethics*, Kant insists that what he calls the bestial vices deprive those who commit them of their dignity

in that partly they make him equal to the beast, e.g. drunkenness and gluttony, so that he becomes incapable of using his reason; and partly they bring him even lower than the beast, e.g., the *crimina carnis contra naturam*, which are called unmentionable vices, because they so demean humanity that even to name them already produces horror.[98]

And in another passage from the *Lectures*, Kant argues that a person who disposes of himself as if he were a being without freedom – for example, by selling parts of his own body or by allowing himself to be used as an object of another's sexual enjoyment – thereby disposes of his humanity. Having become for practical purposes a mere thing, he has put himself into a position in which 'anyone may treat him as they please'.[99]

Nancy's account resolves this tension by denying that dignity is any kind of inner worth. A person does not have dignity on the basis of any of her properties, such as her being a member of a particular political community, religious group or socioeconomic class, or on the basis of her being intelligent, athletic or beautiful. And more generally, she does not have dignity in virtue of her personhood. Instead, dignity is given as an event right at the person. The locution 'right at' translates the French '*à même*', which Nancy uses frequently and in a wide variety of contexts. To say that dignity is right at the person is to say that it is inseparable from the person, as intimate as anything could possibly be, but that it is nonetheless inappropriable. It is to deny that dignity is something deeply internal, residing in the soul in virtue of its having been created in the image of God.[100] But it is also to deny that it is something external, residing in others who may confer it or not as they see fit. The locus of dignity, rather, is right at the limit where the person is exposed to the world. The meanings that define and orient our lives happen at this limit. My being a friend, or a brother, or a valued member of the various communities I participate in, for example, is an important part of who I am. But I can only be these things insofar as I am exposed to others who respond to me as such. And more basically, I am *somebody* – somebody whose projects and perspectives matter – only insofar as I am in touch with others, a singularity with other singularities making the sense of the world *ex nihilo*. On the one hand, this quality of being someone who matters is more intimately my own than any other; there are many people who would prefer to die rather than surrender that basic dignity. On the other hand, because my dignity, my being a somebody, happens as an event of sense right at the limit in my encounters with others, I am always vulnerable to others who might relate to me as if I were a nobody, unworthy of being treated as a self-originating source of valid claims. If we were not vulnerable in this way, then the duties of respect that are laid out in Kant's moral philosophy, and that are also important parts of our pre-philosophical moral common sense, would be superfluous. But they are clearly not superfluous; it matters to us a great deal whether or not we are treated in accordance with something like Kant's Formula of Humanity. If our dignity is not respected, we do not experience ourselves simply as having been deprived of something valuable; we experience ourselves rather as having been wronged, as having been deprived of something to which we have a rightful claim.

Nancy's account of the fact of sense enables us to explain why this claim is justified. As abandoned to respect for the law, we find ourselves turned back toward the groundless ground of our being. This ground is the clinamen, our originary inclination toward others who are given as singular. To respect the law just is to respect others' singularity, and thus their incommensurability. Once again, we cannot step back and reflect on this experience of respect, questioning whether the claim it makes on us is legitimate. One is a practical subject only as the addressee of an unconditional command to be the there, and as Nancy has argued in a number of different works but most explicitly in *Being Singular Plural*, being-there is necessarily being-with the singular others with whom we make sense. We are thus present to ourselves only as obligated to respect dignity, both our own and that of others.

Because the one whose dignity we are obligated to respect is singular, there is no general rule that can reliably guide us, such that we would know with certainty that we have done as we ought. Such a rule would fix the sense of our being-with, and in following it we would engage with each other as particulars. To respect a person's dignity, though, is precisely to refrain from treating that person merely as a particular and to treat her also as the locus of a sense that exceeds any already determinate sense. But this excess must not be understood in terms of metastability or noise, of a sense that is given as intimated and as something to be got right. In the previous chapter I suggested that respect for the other could be understood as respect for this intimated moral sense which is different, and perhaps more adequate, than my own. But as I hope to have shown in the present chapter, this conception misses the mark. Respect, understood in this way, does not open us out onto a sense that can obligate us unconditionally. The excess of sense that we are exposed to in respect is to be understood rather in terms of an event. To treat a person with dignity is to treat her neither as a case falling under a rule that I have already accepted as establishing the norm for my conduct, nor as the locus of a potentially better rule, but rather as an origin and touch of sense. The goodness of treating the other this way is qualitatively different from the goodness of understanding a complex piece of music or of learning a foreign language. It is a specifically moral good, given by the law as unconditionally obligatory.

6 Indifference

Obligation as Overriding

One of the traditional elements of obligation that the Nancian account explains especially well is its overridingness. To say that obligation is overriding is to say that whenever we find ourselves in the position of having to choose between two goods, one of which is commanded by the moral law and the other not, we must choose the former. To choose the non-obligatory good is necessarily to make oneself blameworthy. Among the early modern moral philosophers it was Immanuel Kant who put the greatest emphasis on this element of obligation. The idea of overridingness is suggested in the distinction he makes between what he calls the higher and lower faculties of desire. As we saw in Chapter 2, the lower faculty of desire posits objects and states of affairs as good or bad based on the pleasure or displeasure that the practical subject expects from them. If I see a pair of expensive shoes made by one of my favourite brands, for example, I would consider it a good thing if I could acquire it. Given the fact that the shoes are well beyond my budget, it seems to me that having a pair would bring me a great deal of happiness. But of course my expectation that the shoes would bring me happiness does not obligate me to acquire them; the goodness of having the shoes is of the kind that Kant would characterise as non-moral. Obligation, on Kant's account, has its origin rather in the higher faculty of desire, which posits objects and states of affairs as good or bad based entirely on their conformity or lack of conformity with the a priori moral law. The higher faculty of desire, in other words, is pure practical reason itself. As the names suggest, the higher faculty of desire overrides the lower. If I could only acquire the shoes I desire by violating the moral law – for example, by stealing them – then I ought to forgo the happiness that would come from acquiring them. The goodness of the state of affairs in which I have upheld the moral law trumps the goodness of the state of affairs in which I have acquired a pair of shoes that I desire. The good given by the higher faculty of desire overrides the good given by the lower faculty in every case, irrespective of the strength of the subject's desire for the latter. This is the idea behind the example that Kant used in the *Critique of Practical Reason* to establish the fact of reason: the subject who is commanded by his prince to give false testimony against an honourable man, and who is threatened with immediate execution if he fails to do so, knows perfectly well that he must not lie. The obligation given by the Categorical Imperative overrides the very great good of preserving his own life. Of course whether the subject will have sufficient moral strength to do as he ought is a separate question. But that he ought to tell the truth is never in doubt. Telling the lie is given immediately as morally impossible.

It is important that we not understand the relation of overridingness as suggesting that one good outweighs another. Moral deliberation, on Kant's account, is never a matter of placing competing goods on the balance and choosing the one with the greater weight. This model of deliberation is appropriate for cases in which we must choose between non-moral goods, since the measure of goodness is the same for all the alternatives. If I am deciding which of two cars to purchase, for example, and the only relevant difference between them is their colour, then it makes good sense to choose the colour that will bring me more happiness. Choices between obligatory and non-obligatory goods are entirely different because there is no common measure with reference to which we could compare them. The overridingness of the obligatory good does not consist in its bringing about a greater degree of happiness than the non-obligatory good. Indeed, it is often the case that the obligatory good produces less happiness, even taking into account the feeling of satisfaction that can accompany the recognition that one has done the morally right thing. The goodness of acting in accordance with the moral law, rather, is *qualitatively* different from the goodness of non-moral goods. This qualitative difference is given with the feeling of respect, which not only presents the law, but presents it as superior to the goods given by inclination. In respect for the law, we experience the thwarting of the inclinations and of their natural claim to determine what is good and bad. The law

strikes down self-conceit altogether, since all claims to esteem for oneself that precede accord with the moral law are null and quite unwarranted because certainty of a disposition in accord with this law is the first condition of any worth of a person . . . and any presumption prior to this is false and opposed to the law.[1]

For beings with both a higher and a lower faculty of desire, the goodness of the goods of the latter faculty is entirely conditional on their conformity to the law. Returning to a previous example, my acquiring the expensive shoes by theft does not reduce the goodness of having them, but rather brings it about that my having them is bad. And so I ought not to feel good about myself for having the shoes, despite the fact that I had strongly desired them.

On Kant's account, the overridingness of obligation is grounded in the incommensurability of the feeling of respect, which has no place marked out for it within the system of transcendental idealism. On the one hand, respect is a feeling. As Kant explains in the Introduction to *The Metaphysics of Morals*, feeling names what is merely subjective in our sensibility and what therefore contains 'no relation at all to an object for possible cognition of it'.[2] Sensible qualities such as redness and sweetness refer us to the objects that have them, or that seem to have them, even though they are necessarily sensed by a perceiving subject. But the feelings – pleasure and pain – do not contribute anything to our cognition of the objects with which they are associated. Instead, they express the condition of the subject, orienting its action within the sensibly given world by disclosing objects as things to be pursued or avoided. It is essential to Kant's account that respect be some kind of feeling, since otherwise it would be difficult to explain how we could be motivated to do our duty. But respect must also be a feeling of a radically different kind than the others. In the *Critique of Practical Reason* Kant characterises it as a 'singular feeling which cannot be compared to any pathological feeling'.[3] It has to be different from the other feelings because as we have seen, our inclinations can never give rise to obligation. The goods presented by the lower faculty of desire are conditional goods; their goodness depends on the subject's being constituted in such a way as to find them pleasurable. But the goodness of acting in accordance with our duty is unconditional. What differentiates respect from the other feelings, and what enables it to orient us toward an unconditional good, is that it is produced by an intellectual ground – the moral law – and that it can be cognised a priori.[4] It is a kind of pain, since it is given as striking down our self-conceit, but it is incommensurable with all the other pains. It is not given as one feeling among others to be placed on the balance as we deliberate about what to do. Rather, it presents the moral law, which is the source of the pain, as something sublime and authoritative. In presenting the moral subject to herself as pained, the feeling of respect simultaneously discloses the moral law as the objective and unconditionally valid norm for moral conduct.

Jean-Luc Nancy also accounts for the incommensurability, and thus the overridingness, of obligation in terms of respect. But he removes it from the subject-centred framework of transcendental idealism, where it never fitted very well, and thinks it instead on the basis of the ontology of abandonment. For Nancy, respect is not primarily a subjective feeling, and so he does not face the difficulty of showing how it is relevantly different from all of the other feelings. Neither does respect reveal the legislative activity of the subject's own faculty of pure practical reason. Nancy understands respect more basically as a manner of being, an orientation that is not the subject's own, but that first gives there to be practical subjectivity at all. The originary spacing that gives the practical subject to herself as the addressee of a command to make sense is radically different from any determinate sense. As Nancy argues in 'The *Katagorein* of Excess', 'the law of obligation is not a particular law; it is the law of the law, prior to any legislation and more archaic than any legislative subject'.[5] The law of the law is given as 'a factuality heterogeneous to and incommensurable with the reason from the heart of which, nonetheless, it emerges. This incommensurability measures us; it obliges us.'[6] No matter how good the sense we create together to regulate our relations with each other – sets of legally enforceable basic rights, rules for the provision of basic goods like education and medical care, social norms of etiquette and of basic decency, and so on – it will never be good enough. We will never reach a point at which we have lived up to our obligations once and for all. The law will always be there, its demand weighing on us incommensurably and authoritatively.

Is this really true, though? Do we actually find ourselves haunted constantly by an authoritative demand that we cannot possibly live up to? And is the good posited by this demand really given as over-riding every other sort of good? Or is this broadly Kantian account of the demandingness of obligation hyperbolic, overemphasising the experience of practical necessitation and underemphasising or mis-describing all the purportedly moral goods that are not given by the moral law? In his influential essay, 'Morality, the Peculiar Institu-tion', Bernard Williams argues that what he calls 'the morality sys-tem' – the specific kind of ethical theory that treats moral obligation as fundamental – is both descriptively and normatively mistaken. This system, exemplified in its purest form by Kant's moral philoso-phy, advances a Procrustean account of ethical experience, reducing the wide variety of ethical considerations familiar from everyday practical life to the sole good of acting in accordance with the moral law. Williams does not argue that the phenomenon of obligation is illusory or that ethical theory ought to jettison it entirely. Indeed, he argues that 'there is an everyday notion of obligation, as one consideration among others', that is ethically useful.[7] The problem with the morality system, he thinks, is its characteristic conception of obligation as necessarily overriding. That conception radically dis-torts our moral experience and thus ruins the viability of the moral-ity system in any form that it might take.

The overridingness of obligation is expressed in two key princi-ples of the morality system, according to Williams. The first principle is that '*only an obligation can beat an obligation*'.[8] This is the insight that is exemplified in the case of the expensive shoes. I am obli-gated by the Categorical Imperative never to steal. Given that my faculty of desire is pathologically affected, I may be tempted to treat my desire for the shoes as overriding my obligation not to steal. But I must not actually do so. If I did, then I would be deserving of blame. It is important to point out, though, that this does not entail that obligations can never be overridden in any circumstances. As the name of the principle suggests, obligations can be overridden by other obligations. To see how this is the case, let us introduce a small change to the example. Suppose that I am not particularly interested in expensive shoes, but that I know of someone else who is. Suppose, moreover, that this person has recently suffered some important setbacks in his life and that he has been mildly depressed about them. According to Kant, we all have a duty to beneficence, which amounts to the duty of making others' happiness our own end.[9] Now being alone and having easy access to a pair of expensive, unguarded shoes, I find myself in a position to fulfil that duty: I can do so by stealing the shoes and then giving them to the person whose spirits have been down. But in this particular case, my duty of beneficence is overridden by my duty not to steal. According to Kant, the duty to beneficence is an imperfect duty, one that 'leaves a playroom (*latitudo*) for free choice in following (complying with) the law', since 'the law cannot specify precisely in what way one is to act and how much one is to do'.[10] The moral law commands me to make others' happiness my own end, but it commands this as a general policy. It does not, and indeed cannot, specify all the different ways in which I may or may not do so. The duty not to steal, on the other hand, is a perfect duty, allowing of no exceptions. Whenever an imperfect duty conflicts with a perfect duty, according to Kant, the latter overrides the former.[11] But whether it is a case of duty trumping the goods of the inclinations or of a perfect duty trumping an imperfect one, the point remains the same: nothing can override an obligation except another obligation.

Although the example of the shoes seems to support the principle that only an obligation can beat an obligation, Williams argues that 'what is ordinarily called an obligation does not necessarily have to win in a conflict of moral considerations'.[12] This, he thinks, is supported by our moral common sense. Let us suppose, for example, that I have promised to meet a colleague from work at a sports bar to watch Game 7 of the World Series. My having made a promise imposes an obligation on me to keep it, so that according to the principle under consideration, only another obligation could override it. But now suppose that I have a friend who has a ticket to the game and who, because of some pressing consideration that arose at the last minute, has decided not to attend and to give his ticket to me. To attend Game 7 of a World Series, and to do so without having to pay the very high price that the ticket would ordinarily command, would be a very great good. It may even be a once-in-a-lifetime opportunity. But attending the game is not a specifically moral kind of good; I think of it as good simply because I have a desire to see the game in person. And so this should be an easy case: I ought to forgo the opportunity to attend the game in order to keep the promise I made to my colleague. But this is almost certainly not what our moral common sense would advise. Only someone committed to the morality system to an unusually strong degree would consider me blameworthy for attending the game. And it is not the case that most people would refrain from blaming me because they comprehended the greatness of my temptation and because they could envision themselves going wrong in the same way. They would probably say rather that the goodness of attending the World Series game trumped the goodness of keeping the relatively trivial promise. Of course we could add details to the example that would lead to the conclusion that I ought to keep my promise despite the rare opportunity I would have to forgo. But Williams's point is that our moral common sense is not really committed to the principle that *only* an obligation can beat an obligation.

The second and closely related principle of the morality system, according to Williams, is *'obligation-out, obligation-in'*.[13] This means that whenever we conclude that some particular act is obligatory, we must have derived that conclusion from a more general obligation. Suppose, for example, that I decide that all things considered, the best reasons support my giving the stolen shoes to the mildly depressed acquaintance or that they support my attending Game 7 of the World Series. Given the first principle of the morality system, I would have to think of myself as *obligated* to do these things. In the case of the shoes I would most likely refer to the duty of beneficence, while in the World Series case I would have to invoke some kind of duty to advance my own interests. (For reasons we have just seen, I could not make arguments like these on strictly Kantian grounds, but I could make them within the framework of other theories within the morality system, such as W. D. Ross's theory of *prima facie* duties.) This way of conceiving the goodness in question, though, is sharply at odds with our moral common sense. This is especially clear in the World Series case: it is hard to imagine anyone believing that he was under a genuine moral obligation to attend the game. Indeed, if someone did characterise his attending the game as fulfilling the unbending requirements of the moral law, we would likely think either that he was joking or that he was acting in a ridiculously self-aggrandising way. If the person was being honest, and if his habits of speech have not been excessively shaped by the morality system, he would simply say that the opportunity was too good to pass up.

Obligation would not come into it at all. Of course it may be the case that he ought to think of his act in terms of obligation and its overridingness, but that almost certainly does not represent the view of our moral common sense.

A second problem with the obligation-out, obligation-in principle is that, if taken seriously, it would disallow, or at least give us strong reason to avoid, many of the kinds of actions that we would typically characterise as morally indifferent. According to Williams,

if we have accepted general and indeterminate obligations to further various moral objectives, as the last set of thoughts encourages us to do, they will be waiting to provide work for idle hands, and the thought can gain a footing (I am not saying that it has to) that I could be better employed than in doing something I am under no obligation to do, and, if I could be, then I ought to be: I am under an obligation not to waste time in doing things I am under no obligation to do.[14]

We frequently find ourselves in situations in which obligation is and ought to be among our primary considerations. If I have made a promise, for example, and the time has come for me to keep it, I ought to keep my obligation to do so in the forefront of my mind. Or if I am meeting with a person who is thinking of buying the car I have for sale, I ought to be mindful of my obligation not to lie about its condition. But there are also many situations in which the question of obligation tends to recede into the background. After a long day of work, for example, I often relax by reading some of the websites that I enjoy. I do not think of myself as obligated to read the websites. Nor, of course, do I think of myself as obligated not to read them. Obligation does not seem to be at issue at all. But if I acknowledge and take seriously the bindingness of obligations to promote various moral goods, then there is no time at which I am justified in not attending to my obligations. There is always some duty that I could be fulfilling in some way rather than performing acts that are merely permissible. If this is right, then accepting the validity of the morality system would mean allowing obligation to completely dominate our lives, crowding out all practical considerations other than that of acting in accordance with the moral law.[15] But this idea of obligation as overriding every other practical consideration is foreign to our moral common sense. Even the sternest moralist, it seems, recognises the legitimacy of the category of the morally permissible. Obligation, in our everyday practical reasoning, counts as one consideration among others. And it is a good thing that it does. A life entirely dominated by the concern to satisfy obligations would be a dour, unpleasant life and one badly lived. And so the morality system, with its conception of obligation as overriding all other practical considerations, is mistaken both descriptively and normatively.

The Givenness of Facts

But Williams's idea of obligation as one practical consideration among others seems entirely incompatible with the line of argumentation that takes Kant's fact of reason as basic. The purpose of this line of argument, and specifically of the broadly Korsgaardian form of it that I have been advancing in this book, is to show how obligation can be given as a genuine practical necessitation and as more than a mere counsel. Now if obligation really is one moral good among others, and if practical deliberation involves evaluating its weight relative to other moral considerations, then it must be the case that the practical subject can step back and reflect on all the moral considerations, choosing case by case which is the most important. But as Korsgaard argued in *The Sources of Normativity*, as long as the subject can step back from the contents of her consciousness, which purport to give her compelling reason for acting in a certain way, and as long as she can raise the question whether the purportedly compelling reason really is compelling, her will is not necessitated and so she is not really obligated. On Korsgaard's account, we become obligated only at that point where we can no longer step back and reflect. In the previous three chapters I have been arguing that we find ourselves responsive always already to sense and its dynamic. This is simply a fact in the Kantian sense. No act of reflection can give us a point of view anterior to this fact such that we could question whether its claim on us is legitimate. To be a practical subject at all is to have accepted the legitimacy of the claim of the dynamic of sense always already. And in the Nancian form of the argument that I developed in the previous chapter, this means that the practical subject finds herself given always already as the addressee of an authoritative command that never stops haunting her. Obligation, then, is always in play as overriding; it can never be merely one consideration among others.

Despite the apparent incompatibility, though, I do believe it is possible to reconcile Williams's insights about obligation with the fact of reason strategy. I think Nancy is right to claim that there can be no epoché of sense; to be a practical subject is to find oneself exposed to sense and its dynamic always already. I also believe that this exposure takes the form of abandonment and that we are given to ourselves in this abandonment as addressees of a kind of command. We cannot take up a standpoint anterior to this command in order to evaluate its legitimacy. But I do not believe this entails that obligation is overriding or that it must be understood as crowding out all other kinds of value. Making use of the work of Charles E. Scott, and especially of his books *Living with Indifference* and *The Lives of Things*, I want to argue that in our originary exposure to excessive, inappropriable sense there is given a dimension of indifference in which the force of obligation is suspended.[16]

In making this case I would like to begin with the first chapter of *The Lives of Things*, where Scott gives an account of the givenness of facts. He is not concerned here specifically with the Kantian fact of reason or with what I have been calling the fact of sense. He is concerned rather with facts in general, with awe-inspiring facts about how galaxies 'eat' other galaxies or about the unimaginable immensity of the universe, but also with more mundane facts about the geneses of things like pimples and plastic spoons. The main point that Scott aims to establish in this chapter is that 'facts are as effective as "poetic experiences" in occasioning astonishment and a sense of wonder'.[17] He describes a conversation he once had with two friends, a poet and an artist, who, not surprisingly, disagreed: for them, emphasis on facts represents 'the very kind of objectivity and scientific rationality that we must resist in order to see things with astonished attention to their lives'.[18] The world of mere facts, from their point of view, is banal, uninspiring and utilitarian, devoid of the loftier, more ennobling dimensions of meanings to which artists and poets are supposed to be especially sensitive. Without a doubt there is at least a grain of truth in this view. I find that the students I teach often know, for example, that Nelson Mandela became president of South Africa in 1994, after having spent much of his life imprisoned for opposing apartheid and the government that enforced it. But they rarely have a genuine appreciation for the inspiring and ennobling values of solidarity, persistence and unshakeable commitment to justice that these facts represent. There is no wonder at the enormity of the accomplishment of Mandela and of black South Africans generally. The students tend to relate to these facts in a way that is primarily instrumental: they are pieces of information that the students will be rewarded for remembering and penalised for forgetting on exam day. The poet and the artist seem right in their insistence that this fact-oriented way of engaging with the world is seriously impoverished.

While I think there is indeed something importantly right about the poet's and the artist's point of view, I also think that Scott is right: facts can be as effective as poetic experience in giving rise to senses of astonishment and wonder as long as we are attuned to them in the right way. Scott provides as an example of this point the facts concerning the physiology of human hearing:

By means of a package not much larger than a sugar cube, ears hear sounds that are found by transmissions of waves of air pressure, which are transformed into waves of liquid, which in turn produce miniscule movements in tiny hair cells, which excite neurons and bio-electric energy.[19]

All of this must happen in order for me to pick out the simplest, most commonplace meanings from the world of sound. But these processes are not at all a part of the meaning I pick out. When the professor asks the students for the year of apartheid's collapse in South Africa, they do not take the transformation of air pressure into waves of liquid within their ears as part of the sense to which they must respond. All they need to do is state the year. That apparently very simple act of communication is made possible, not in the Kantian sense, but rather in the most physical way, by an occurrence that is utterly indifferent to the familiar world of meanings.

This fact is astonishing. It points to a dimension of our being-in-the-world that exceeds the familiar, sedimented meanings with reference to which we navigate the everyday world. If the poet and the artist are less sensitive than Scott to this astonishing dimension in the givenness of facts, it is probably because they are looking for something else. If there is a dimension in excess of the banal, flat givenness of facts, it seems that it ought to be something sublime or uplifting or edifying. It ought to give us a sense of transcendence, of a movement toward some kind of 'higher', 'truer' meaning that puts our everyday, worldly meanings into the right perspective.[20] Kant gives expression to this understanding of the excessiveness of specifically moral sense when he writes that we can 'never get enough of contemplating the majesty of the [moral] law, and the soul believes itself elevated in proportion as it sees the holy elevated above itself and its frail nature'.[21]

Knowledge of the intricate mechanism of the human ear or of the formation of pimples does not typically produce this kind of effect. How, then, can we understand the astonishing excess that is given with facts if not as a kind of transcendence? According to Scott, this excess is given as 'a dimension of no meaning and hence no order of meaning in ordered meanings' very happenings'.[22] This excess, in other words, is not a latent or potential sense present as something to be got right. Nor is it a higher sense or a more profound sense. It is rather a dimension of no meaning that is co-present with meaningful dimensions of our lives, but without these dimensions belonging to the same space of meaning. The excessive dimension that Scott has in mind cannot be put to use in producing a new or better meaning. It is given rather as an irreducible indifference to meaning right in the midst of ordinary meaning. In *Living with Indifference*, Scott provides close descriptions of many different ways in which this dimension of indifference becomes manifest. Perhaps the most helpful of these is his description of what happens when the body experiences trauma. As a response to a traumatic event, the body

produces a prereflective memory trace that can operate as though the past danger were present. The amygdala function apparently knows nothing of place and time and is also a center for instinctive memory. The function of the hypothalamus, on the other hand, provides spatial and temporal context for events. As long as there is cooperation between these two functions a person experiences a traumatic event as past and can remember its emotions in a spatial context as well. It was then at that place. But if there is only amygdalic impression without hypothalamic qualification, the instinctual memory in that dissociation will lack context and the traumatic stress could come to presence at any time or place.[23]

As Kant showed in the Transcendental Aesthetic of the *Critique of Pure Reason*, meaningful experience presupposes the capacity to situate things and events spatiotemporally. One could not form even the most banal judgements of experience – say the judgement that the pen is blue – if one could not first isolate the subject term of the judgement as a single, unified object in space and time. But in severe trauma, the subject finds herself haunted by an 'event' that is not submitted to these conditions of meaning. Indeed, from the sufferer's point of view, the cause of the trauma is not even *an* event, since it cannot be mapped onto the coherent order of experience that is made possible by spatiotemporal qualification. The subject tries to make sense of the trauma, integrating it into the order of worldly meaning, but she finds it extraordinarily difficult to do so. 'In this case, the body's faceless functioning comes to the fore; good sense and meaning fade away, and a physical dimension without intelligent, spatial, or temporal intention provides the traumatic presentation of a life.'[24] The dimension of indifference is just there, stubbornly present in the midst of other dimensions of the sufferer's day-to-day life, which remain just as meaningful as they had always been.

Of course we can encounter the dimension of indifference in non-traumatic experiences as well. The world itself, for example, can manifest itself indifferently. According to Merleau-Ponty, the world is given most originarily as an 'open and indefinite unity', as the locus of a nascent sense that adumbrates a fully determinate, inter-subjectively coherent totality.[25] The sense of the world is addressed to an embodied subject who knows prior to all reflection how to gear into it and thus how to bring it to more determinate expression. The subject is able to pick up the adumbrated sense of the world because she is of the world and has sided with it always already. As we have seen, the subject who gears into the adumbrated sense of the world is not the I that is present in reflection, but rather a pre-individual, anonymous 'one'. Despite this dimension of impersonality in the perceiving subject, though, the world is never given indifferently in Merleau-Ponty's account. The subject is oriented always already toward a *good* sense, toward a sense that is present as something to be got right. The sense of the world, then, is normative through and through. But in a passage that Scott quotes in *Living with Indifference*, Jerry Fodor describes a very different relation to the world:

It's very hard to get this right because of our penchant for teleology, for explaining things on the model of agents with beliefs, goals, and desires is inveterate and probably itself innate. We are forever wanting to know what things are for, and we don't like having to take Nothing for an answer . . . Still I think that sometimes out of the corner of an eye, 'at a moment which is not action or inaction', we can glimpse the true scientific fission: austere, tragic, alienated, and very beautiful. A world that isn't for anything; a world that is just there.[26]

This 'just there' quality of the world, its indifference to our projects and to our modes of knowing, does not reduce the meaning of the world to nothing. It does not refute Merleau-Ponty's account of the embodied subject and its sense-bestowal. The vaguely given object against the background of the forest really is a ship that has run aground and the subject really does come to recognise this by adjusting her perspective in various ways until the sense of the scene crystallises. The dimension of indifference does not cancel this meaning, but rather becomes manifest right at it. We must not understand this dimension as a reserve of meaning that would be somehow more profound or more elevated or truer than the ordinary meaning of the world that emerges within the structure of corporeal intentionality. It is nothing mystical or spiritual and it is not the source of edifying life lessons. Rather, just as in the case of trauma, it is present along with the world of ordered, regulated meaning, but as stubbornly resistant to being integrated into it.

Subjunctive Indeterminacy

Both trauma and Fodor's experience of the world as not *for* anything, as simply there, exemplify what Scott calls 'subjunctive indeterminacy', which he characterises as a 'withdrawal of factuality in the occurrence of facts'.[27] To unpack what Scott means by this, it will be helpful to begin with a brief discussion of the indicative and subjunctive moods in English grammar. When we form sentences in the indicative mood, we intend to express straightforwardly how the world really is. If I say 'the pen is blue', for example, I mean to say simply that in the world as it actually is, the pen that I am referring to has the property of blueness. The subjunctive mood, on the other hand, is used to express states of affairs that are contrary to fact or that are possible but unlikely. When I say 'I would not do that if I were you', I do not mean to claim that I am in fact you. I mean, rather, to present a state of affairs – my being you – precisely as contrary to fact. And when I say 'If I were to move to another country, it would be Canada', I present a state of affairs that is possible – my moving to Canada – but one that I think is unlikely to be realised. What the subjunctive mood presents, then, is a dimension in excess of the state of affairs to which it refers. As Scott puts it, 'the subjunctive mood subjoins indeterminacy with a determinate state of affairs and expresses something by reference to an elision, a "gappiness", which is said to be in the way something happens'.[28] The subjunctive mood, in other words, presents a state of affairs along with a dimension of questionability, contingency and possibility. This added dimension is not another fact. Its sense cannot be expressed by another sentence in the indicative mood. It is given, rather, as a withdrawal of present or presentable sense within a presented sense.

Scott's primary concern in introducing the idea of subjunctive indeterminacy is not grammatical, of course, but phenomenological. It is meant to describe the way in which facts of all sorts are given. The world is present to us, for example, as a set of coherent, interrelated facts whose sense can be expressed in indicative propositions. But as Fodor noted, the world is also given, or at least can be given, as exceeding this factuality. His choice of the word 'alienated' to describe the world as given in this experience is instructive: the familiar factuality of the world recedes, revealing a dimension of indetermination and of foreignness to human understanding. This dimension of indifference does not have or intimate a sense that could be reintegrated into the coherent sense of the world. It is not related to the manifest sense of the world's appearing as its ground or as its deeper truth. Its relation to the familiar, factual world is rather one of 'gappiness', of simple co-presence that is not gathered together in a unity of sense.[29] The subjunctive mood presents this kind of gappiness, exhibiting a state of affairs right along with its doubtfulness or its contrariness to fact. And in the experience of subjunctive indeterminacy, we experience the familiar factuality of the world right along with the alienation of that familiarity, without the prospect of bringing these different dimensions together under a coherent synthetic unity. The different dimensions remain stubbornly co-present.

We can relate this analysis directly to the phenomenon of obligation by describing the experience of subjunctive indeterminacy as it arises in the relation between the subject and himself. In much the same way I relate to the world, I relate to myself in terms of

familiar facts that can be stated straightforwardly in indicative propositions. When I think of myself, I think of someone who is a son
and a brother, a philosophy professor, a fan of contemporary classical
music, as someone who is committed to various political causes and
who is a member of various social and political communities. When
I act in the world, I act with reference to the norms and expectations of these different roles. Roughly speaking, I think well of myself
when I act in accordance with those norms and I think less well of
myself when I fail to do so. But of course this is not the whole story.
Even if I were to produce an exhaustive list of all the facts about
me that I regard as practically important, I would not feel as if I had
successfully expressed who I am. There is always a dimension of my
being that exceeds my familiar factuality. This account should sound
very familiar so far, as we have seen versions of it in Merleau-Ponty,
Serres, Sartre and Nancy. All of these thinkers have conceived the
excessive dimension of practical subjectivity in terms of an originary condemnation or exposure or abandonment to inappropriable
sense. On Merleau-Ponty's account, we will recall, the sense of my
being-in-the-world exceeds determinate, sedimented sense because I
am condemned to a sense that is irreducibly metastable. On Sartre's
account, I am always more than myself because existence precedes
essence. It is never entirely true that I *am* a son, or a professor, or
an American; the sense of my being is something I must continuously choose. And on Nancy's account, I am originarily abandoned
to sense, which is given as withdrawn. On all of these accounts, the
excess of sense to which I am exposed is the source of normativity:
I find myself responsive always already to a demand from which I
am unable to get any reflective distance. My being obligated, then, is
given as a fact.

If Scott is right, though, the fact of our being obligated is given, or
at least can be given within a certain sensibility, along with a dimension of indifference. This dimension would be present in the subjunctive mood, introducing a distance of questionability or contingency
between the practical subject and her being obligated. Obligation
would be present in its own eventuation, in other words, and not
primarily in its reference to the interpellated subject. Like the world
that we can sometimes catch a glimpse of out of the corner of our
eye, the phenomenon of obligation would be 'just there'. But can
obligation be given as set at a distance in this way? Can obligation

be given as questionable without losing the element of necessitation that distinguishes it from mere counsel? For Korsgaard, as we have seen, the answer seems to be no: as long as the subject can get a distance from the purported compellingness of a reason for action, she is not genuinely obligated. Modifying Hobbes's well-known formulation, we could say that obligation begins where questionability ends. It is important to note, though, that for Korsgaard questionability is a subjective phenomenon; it arises only for subjects who are capable of reflection. If we were incapable of stepping back from reasons for action that purported to be sufficient – for example, our desire to produce a certain result or the fact that a course of action was in accordance with tradition – and if we were incapable of putting those reasons to the test, then the problem of normativity simply would not arise for us. The question 'what ought I to do?' arises for the subject because she reflects, and the questionability persists up to the point at which she can no longer reflect. In Korsgaard's memorable formulation from *The Sources of Normativity*, 'if the problem springs from reflection, then the solution must do so as well'.[30] If a subject has not reached the end-point of reflection, so that the courses of action available to her still appear questionable, then she cannot regard her will as necessitated, even if she tries. Questionability and obligation, from this point of view, are simply incompatible.

But what if the questionability given in the subjunctive mood was not subjective? What if it was not present to the subject as a problem that she was called upon to solve? In sum, what if this questionability was present indifferently, alien to the concerns of the practical subject? Would such an indifferent questionability be compatible with obligation, or would it preclude the necessitation of the will that is essential to the concept? And what would our moral comportment look like if we were more attuned to the dimension of indifference given along with obligation? In the chapter from *The Lives of Things* titled 'Starlight in the Face of the Other', Scott provides some valuable resources for answering these questions. The chapter engages directly with the moral philosophy of Emmanuel Levinas, but its conclusions are just as relevant to the lineage of thinking about obligation that I have been tracing in this book. According to Levinas, 'the face opens the primordial discourse whose first word is obligation, which no "interiority" permits avoiding'.[31] In the face-to-face encounter with the Other, he thinks, there occurs an upsurge of sense that exceeds the subject's capacity for appropriation. This dis-appropriating event happens as the unconditional command, 'you shall not commit murder', which singularises the practical subject, fixing her in place and summoning her to respond.[32] The I, then, is 'by its very position, responsibility through and through'.[33] The I's subjection to the Other, on this account, is simply a fact: it is given immediately, and cannot be discovered as the conclusion to any chain of reasoning. According to Scott, though, Levinas's account of the facticity of this fact is insufficiently radical, centred as it is on a traditionally phenomenological, identity-based conception of subjectivity. He argues that there is a dimension of no meaning at all that happens right along with the fact of obligation. In the experi-ence of the face-to-face, there is revealed a kinship with a material-ity that is radically more other than Levinas's Other, something that 'seems to precede and to recede from meaningful appearances'.[34] When we look into the eye of the other, we find ourselves in the presence of minerals that

were all formed in the implosion of stars that were trillions of miles and millions of years from where we see[. The] calcium, potassium, sodium, iodine, and phosphorus – all the primary and trace minerals in our eyes – were formed in the unspeakable heat and pressure of stars that collapsed upon themselves and then exploded, sending both light energy and mineral components in an unspeakable tumult throughout the universe.[35]

The stardust that I encounter in the other does not interpellate me. It does not single me out as the addressee of the command, 'you shall not commit murder'. Indeed, the dense materiality that I encoun-ter in the other is not about me at all. I respond to it anonymously and impersonally, in something like the way that fungi or protozoa respond to light.[36]

The starlight in the face of the other is also indifferent to the lineages of meaning with reference to which we conceive our moral relations with others. As Merleau-Ponty and many others have shown, perception cannot be adequately understood as the recep-tion of meaningless sense data by the various sense organs. Bor-rowing from Gestalt psychology, Merleau-Ponty argues that even the most 'elementary perception is already charged with a *sense*'.[37] At the most originary level of our opening out onto the world, we find ourselves oriented by and responsive to this sense. And in some cases, this sense has an explicit ethical dimension. In the lineage of moral thought within which Levinas writes, for example, the Other is given with the sense of destitution and abasement, but also of height; 'he has the face of the poor, the stranger, the widow, and the orphan, and, at the same time, of the master called to invest and justify my freedom'.[38] In other traditions, a person with an upright, self-confident bearing is given as noble and as calling for a heightened degree of respect. And in other lineages of ethical sense, to perceive a person as having a certain skin colour or as being of a certain sex is to perceive him or her as being of lesser moral worth, and perhaps even as deserving of contempt. But the fact that we always perceive within the context of orders of meaning does not preclude their being a dimension of no meaning at all within perceptual experience. The stardust that we encounter in the eyes of the other is too other to human concern to be figured in the all-too-human forms of the stranger, the widow or the orphan. It is given as neither high nor low and it calls neither for solicitousness, nor compassion, nor respect, nor for anything at all.[39]

This dimension of indifference to lineages of meaning distances the practical subject from the force of obligation. According to the conception of the fact of sense that I have been developing in this book, the practical subject is constitutively condemned or exposed or abandoned to sense. To be a practical subject at all is to have accepted always already the legitimacy of the demands that originate in the dynamic proper to sense. It is to be positioned as the addressee of a demand to which it is impossible not to respond. This, as Bernhard Waldenfels argued, is the source of the necessitation that is essential to obligation. What Scott has shown, though, is that *within* this very dynamic of responsiveness to sense we encounter a dimension of indifference to sense, a dimension that does not call on us to respond to anything. Attuned to this dimension, we find that obligation does not fix us in place as addressees of an unconditional 'you must'. It is given as deprived of the force of its ineluctability and thus as questionable. The distance that the dimension of indifference gives from obligation is not the distance of reflection. It does not allow us to take up a position behind obligation's address, from which we could form a more adequate judgement concerning its legitimacy. It does not give us a perspective from which we could hope to eliminate obligation's questionability, enabling us to know with perfect certainty what we ought to do. The distance consists rather in the fact that obligation is given as simply co-present with indifference to obligation, without the promise of a higher synthesis that would establish the proper relationship between these phenomena.

To further unpack what this co-presence means, we might say that the dimension of indifference interrupts what I called in Chapter 3 the silent thesis of moral experience. This thesis is grounded in Merleau-Ponty's conception of a 'silent thesis of perception', which, once again, is our commitment prior to all reflection to the idea that

experience, at each moment, can be coordinated with the experience of the preceding moment and with that of the following one, that my perspective can be coordinated with the perspectives of other consciousnesses – that all contradictions can be removed, that monadic and intersubjective experience is a single continuous text – and that what is indeterminate for me at this moment could become determinate for a more complete knowledge, which is seemingly realized in advance in the thing, or rather which is the thing itself.[40]

The moral corollary to this thesis is just the idea that there is a coherent moral space within which inconsistencies are given as to-be-resolved. If I feel that my desire for an expensive pair of shoes gives me a good reason to acquire it by theft, for example, but I am also committed to the idea that theft is impermissible, then I will experience the situation in which I find myself as calling for resolution. The two practical principles that I am entertaining, and the two courses of action that they suggest, cannot co-exist within a coherent moral world. And so one of them will have to cancel the other: once I recognise the authority of the rule against theft, I no longer experience my desire for the shoes as making a claim on me that deserves to be taken seriously from a moral point of view. But when we are attuned to the dimension of indifference, the experience of necessitation is given along with the questionability of that experience. Neither the experience of necessitation nor that of its questionability cancels the other. And so when I am face to face with the Other, I really do experience myself as the addressee of a command not to reduce her to the status of a mere object within the field of my own constituting consciousness. I am singled out by this command, which puts me in a position of responsibility whether I like it or not. But this sense of myself and of my relation to the Other does not exhaust the moral sense of the situation. This whole sense is given in the subjunctive mood, as questionable. I am the addressee of a command, which I experience as making a legitimate claim on me, but I am also something other than such an addressee. I am given to myself as responsible, but I am not 'responsibility through and through'.

The Law of Expansion

The dimension of indifference, given in the subjunctive mood, can be understood as noise in the Serresian sense of the term, in that it presents itself as an obstacle to the addressee's reception of the message of obligation. The obligated subject, on Levinas's account, is given to himself as the addressee of a command, 'you shall not commit murder'. Or in Waldenfels's less hyperbolic account, the obligated subject is given to himself with the sense of having to respond. The dimension of indifference interrupts that sense. It is not present as the intimation of some other, perhaps better, message, but rather as rendering the message of obligation questionable. This questionability, which Scott describes in terms of subjunctive indeterminacy, establishes a distance between the practical subject and its sense of being obligated. And just as in Serres's account, the noise is not an accident that would befall an otherwise perfectly transparent message from the outside. As Scott demonstrates, questionability is given as a dimension of the phenomenon of obligation itself. The conclusion to be drawn from this fact, it seems, is the same conclusion that Serres had drawn: we ought to let the noise in, resisting the temptation to exclude it in favour of the message. Since the noise is always already internal to the message, we are likely to do more harm trying to eliminate it than we would do by simply learning to live with it. As Serres argues in *The Parasite*, this insight is the beginning of tolerance, 'and maybe morality as well'.[41]

In *The Troubadour of Knowledge*, Serres suggests an extended analogy that helps to bring out what is at stake morally in learning to live with the noise:

A single, supposedly general law results from the frenzied expansion of a local element that loses its hold, if it ever had one, that forgets its moderation, if it ever learned it, in view of making the remainder disappear . . .

By themselves, gases occupy the volume that is offered before their expansive pressure. No one has ever seen a gas show proof of restraint in order to leave a part of the space empty. Barbarism follows the single law. The law of expansion. That of gases. They propagate themselves. The barbarian spreads. Violence spreads blood, which spreads out. Pestilence, epidemics, microbes are propagated. Noise, ruckus, rumors spread. In the same way, force, power, kings spread. In the same way, ambition spreads. In the same way, advertising spreads. The rubric of all things that spread, as amply as a gas, of all the things that expand, that take up space, that occupy volume, must be named. Evil gets around, that is its definition: it exceeds its limits.[42]

For Kantians, the Categorical Imperative fills up the whole of moral space. Or more precisely, it ought to expand to fill up the whole of moral space, making the remainder of moral sense disappear. We ought never to allow any other purportedly moral considerations – concern to produce good consequences, respect for the traditions of our particular communities, the desire to maintain important relationships with others or straightforward self-interest – to compete with the Categorical Imperative as the ground for the determination of our wills. Whatever moral sense there is in the world is articulated by the Categorical Imperative; any apparent remainder is mere noise that ought to be excluded. From the Kantian point of view, then, it would be absurd to hold back the expansion of the imperative's authority 'in order to leave a part of the space empty'. To do so would be to acquiesce to immorality. But this is exactly what Serres denies: 'Morality demands this abstention first of all. First obligation: reserve. First maxim: before doing good, avoid the bad. To abstain from evil, simply hold back. Because in expanding, good itself, just like the sun, very quickly becomes evil.'[43] Without a doubt it is a good thing, generally speaking, to ask ourselves whether the maxims of our proposed actions could function at the same time as universal laws. This test does help to capture an important moral intuition about the unfairness of expecting others to act in accordance with rules from which we exempt ourselves. But if this 'local element' of our moral experience exceeds its limits, becoming the general law governing *all* of moral experience, then it yields results that are wildly discordant with our moral common sense, such as the obligation to tell the truth to a prospective murderer concerning the whereabouts of his intended victim.[44] From the point of view of the moral law, truth-telling is 'a sacred command of reason prescribing unconditionally'.[45] The person who is at risk of being murdered counts, at least from a moral point of view, only as a case falling under the rule. To take the well-being of the intended victim as the measure of our conduct, then, would be to fall back onto the paradigmatically non-moral motive of 'convenience'.[46] But this seems plainly wrong. Faced with this kind of result, of course one might choose to bite the bullet, acknowledging its counterintuitiveness while continuing to insist on the ultimate authority of the pronouncements of the moral law. But this is the sort of move one would make only if one were committed to maintaining a thesis at all costs. What cases like this really show, according to Serres, is that our obligation is to hold back: 'The sage thus disobeys the single law of expansion, does not always persevere in his being and thinks that elevating his own conduct to a universal law is the definition of evil as much as madness.'[47]

I believe Serres's insight concerning the importance of resisting the law of expansion is basically right, but that it must be pushed a little bit further. Specifically, Serres's account of holding back leaves the value of obligation itself unquestioned. Serres does not argue merely that it would be a good idea, all things considered, to resist the temptation to allow a single principle to occupy the whole of moral space. He insists, rather, that it is obligatory to do so. But if Scott's account of indifference and of subjunctive indeterminacy is correct, then the phenomenon of obligation itself is given as questionable. The appropriate way to respond to this phenomenon, it seems then, is to hold it back and thus to maintain it in the questionability that is inseparable from it. We ought, in other words, to make sure to leave some space open for other sorts of goods whose value would not be fixed in advance by the specific good of obligation. Importantly, this kind of response takes its orientation from the mode of givenness of obligation itself: obligation is given, at least within a certain sensibility, *as* not necessarily overriding all rival practical considerations. This fact helps to address some of the concerns about the morality system that Williams articulated in 'Morality, the Peculiar Institution'. Williams's criticism of the morality system is based largely on the tendency of its leading concept to fill up moral space in accordance with the law of expansion. The two major principles of the morality system – 'only an obligation can beat an obligation' and 'obligation-out, obligation-in' – express the supremacy of obligation to every other practical consideration. The latter principle, Williams thinks, even threatens to drive the category of the permissible out of our moral space, so that our sole legitimate practical concern would be to fulfil our obligations. But as Scott's arguments in *The Lives of Things* and *Living with Indifference* demonstrate, there is a dynamic internal to the morality system itself that runs counter to this expansive tendency. Obligation does not have to be understood as overriding, and indeed it should not be understood as overriding. What the phenomenon of indifference helps to make manifest is a conception of obligation endorsed by Williams himself, one that is given simply 'as one consideration among others'.[48]

But this leaves us with a very difficult problem. I have argued that in light of obligation's being given along with a dimension of indifference, we ought to hold back, that we ought to comport ourselves toward it in such a way as to maintain it in its questionability. How are we to understand this 'ought', though? Should we understand it as the 'ought' of obligation? Is it the case, in other words, that we are obligated to maintain obligation in its questionability? It seems that the answer to these questions must be either yes or no. But there are good reasons to believe that neither of these answers is right. On the one hand, the negative answer seems to be ruled out by disjunctive syllogism. The 'ought' of the claim in question does not seem to be a prudential 'ought'. The claim is not exactly that it would be in our best interest or that it would contribute to our well-being to comport ourselves to obligation in such a way as to maintain its questionability. The claim, in other words, does not appear to be a mere counsel. Of course it may very well be the case that maintaining obligation's questionability would be conducive to our well-being. But it certainly seems as if there is more to the claim than that. Moreover, the claim is obviously not an attempt to coerce: there is no threat stated or implied. And so by process of elimination, it appears that the only plausible interpretation of 'ought' left standing is that of obligation. But this result is problematic as well. If we ought to relate to obligation as something questionable, then it is hard to see why that questionability would not apply to the 'ought' itself. If we really are obligated, in any straightforward sense of the term, to maintain the questionability of obligation, then obligation functions once again as the master concept in our practical deliberations and not as merely one moral consideration among others.

The morality system would come out even stronger on this account, since to challenge it would be to reaffirm it.

And so where does this leave us? Should we understand ourselves in the final analysis as obligated to hold back, to maintain the phenomenon of obligation in its questionability? The answer seems to be both yes and no. Or perhaps better, the answer seems to be 'yes, but . . .'. Yes, we are obligated, but our being obligated is present to us with a certain gappiness, with a sense of being possibly contrary to fact. Is this even a meaningful response, though? Does the content of the 'but' clause not simply negate what is affirmed in saying that yes, we are obligated? If we think obligation – including the obligation concerning how we ought to think about obligation – as thoroughly questionable, as given at a distance from the practical subject, then do we not lose our hold on the phenomenon? Doesn't obligation slip away from us once again, just as it had slipped away from the voluntarists, rationalists, sentimentalists, egoists and Kantians, and just as it has exceeded the grasp of the Merleau-Pontian, Serresian and Nancian accounts of sense? What I want to suggest is that the argument developed over the course of the last four chapters points to a different way of understanding the slipperiness of obligation. In accordance with the broadly Kantian (and Korsgaardian) argumentative strategy that I have been following, I have tried to isolate the source of normativity at the level at which obligation is given most originarily. This, I have argued, is the level of sense, which is given as a fact in the Kantian sense of the term: to be a practical subject at all is to have been given over to the dynamic of sense always already, such that one cannot get a reflective distance from it. But what is the fact of sense? Is it the fact of our being oriented, prior to all reflection, toward the world as intersubjectively coherent totality of sense? Is it our exposure to a sense that is irreducibly metastable? Or does the fact of sense consist rather in our exposure to noise, which is present not as latent sense but rather as an interruption of sense? Or should we understand it in terms of the ontology of abandonment, as the law of the law, which commands us to make the sense that we do not have, and indeed never can have? Or is it, finally, our exposure to a dimension of indifference that is given right along with meaningful occurrences? I believe that the answer to all of these questions is yes. It is not the case, in other words, that each conception of the fact of sense has been shown to be false by the conception that followed. If it is true that we are exposed always already to noise, for example, it does not follow that we are not also committed prior to all reflection to the silent thesis of perception. And if obligation is present to us in the mode of subjunctive indeterminacy, it does not follow that we are not also interpellated by a kind of sense that haunts us in the form of an unconditional command. It is not the case, then, that we have been prevented from getting a hold on the phenomenon of obligation because our determinations of the fact of sense have been inadequate. The problem, rather, is that the sense itself to which we find ourselves condemned always already is slippery. If the most basic argument of the book is correct – that we can think the phenomenon of obligation on the basis of our exposure to the fact of sense – then we have good reason to think not that obligation has slipped away from us, but rather that obligation itself happens as a slipping away. Or perhaps better, there is no obligation 'itself'. Obligation does not have *a* sense that could provide us with a definite, unambiguous moral orientation. To be obligated, rather, is to be given over to a complex, multidimensional dynamic of sense that no subject can master.

Returning to the analogy with Alice's adventures in the Sheep's Shop, we might say that the 'large bright thing' that she pursues is simply ungraspable. If she had succeeded – if she had got hold of a doll or a workbox – then she would have failed, since the doll or the workbox would not have been the 'thing'. As it happened, though, Alice didn't get hold of anything. After the large bright thing went through the ceiling, she stopped trying to pick out an item from the shelves and started doing something entirely different. Was this a mistake? Should she have continued to pursue the large bright thing instead?

7 Conclusion

Is This Still Obligation?

Is the phenomenon we are left with here really still obligation? I have argued that obligation does not have a sense that for whatever reason tends to elude our grasp, but rather that it happens precisely as an unmasterable slipping away. In this slippage, does the phenomenon of obligation not slip away from itself? More precisely, does the subjunctive indeterminacy that establishes a distance between the practical subject and the experience of being obligated not open the space for a comportment that would be simply other than obligation? In short, has my attempt to trace the source of normativity back to the fact of sense revealed something more like a self-overcoming of obligation?

In order to begin to get a handle on these questions, I would like to return to the eight elements of the general conception of obligation that I described in the Introduction. These elements were drawn from the major theories of obligation that were developed in the early modern period: voluntarism, rationalism, egoism, sentimentalism and Kantianism. Of course not all of these theories gave equal weight to the eight elements. Indeed, some of them explicitly rejected certain elements. Nonetheless, the list does give us a reasonably determinate idea of what moral philosophers of the early modern period had in mind when they reflected on obligation. In order to determine whether the account developed over the previous four chapters is best understood as an account of obligation at all, then, it will be helpful to check it against each of the eight elements.

1. *Necessitation*. All of the early modern theories of obligation treated this element as essential. To be obligated, as Pufendorf memorably put it, is to have a kind of bridle placed on one's liberty. As we have seen, different moral philosophers conceived this necessitation in

very different ways: for the rationalists, the constraint of obligation had its source in the mind's inability to withhold its assent to truths it perceived clearly and distinctly, whereas the voluntarists understood necessitation on the basis of an explicitly political model. But what all these theorists had in common was a view of obligation as a limitation on moral agents' ability to do as they pleased. The account I have developed over the previous four chapters certainly retains the element of necessitation, but in a modified sense. The basic idea is captured best by Bernhard Waldenfels's claim that as practical subjects condemned to sense, 'we cannot not respond. The double "not" points to a *must* in the sense of a practical necessity.'[1] What makes this conception of necessitation so different from those developed by the early modern philosophers is the lack of any specific content. For all of the early modern theorists of obligation, moral necessitation was always a necessitation to perform or to refrain from performing some specified act. But as all the philosophers discussed in the previous four chapters have argued in different ways, moral sense is given as questionable. All of them would deny Kant's claim that the moral subject has the law 'always before its eyes and uses [it] as the norm for its appraisals', and thus 'knows very well how to distinguish in every case that comes up what is good and what is evil, what is in conformity with duty or contrary to duty'.[2] In the account of obligation I have developed in this book, the experience of necessitation is separated from the content of the necessitation.

2. *Law*. This element of obligation was treated as essential by Kant and by the voluntarist natural law theorists. The idea that obligation must be grounded in law was introduced by Francisco Suarez, who insisted on the distinction between law and counsel. Previous moral philosophers, including most prominently Thomas Aquinas, had elided this distinction, defining law as 'a rule and measure of acts, whereby man is induced to act or is restrained from acting'.[3] Suarez argued that this definition was too broad, including not only what we typically think of as laws but also counsels or mere recommendations. The distinction between law and counsel is important because a recommendation cannot effectively put a bridle on our liberty: even if the advisee comes to recognise that she has a very good reason to pursue the recommended course of action, she remains free to decide whether or not to do so. The constraint proper to obligation, then, must come from law. The account I have

developed over the course of the previous four chapters also treats obligation as something other than counsel: as condemned to sense, we find ourselves responsive to the demands of obligation whether we like it or not. This is brought out most forcefully by Jean-Luc Nancy, who argues that abandonment 'is a compulsion to appear absolutely under the law, under the law as such and in its totality'.[4] To be abandoned, for Nancy, just is to be given over to respect for the law. But once again, the experience of being subjected to the law is divorced from the content of the law, and this is very different from the early modern conception. What the law unconditionally commands, according to Nancy, is simply to be the there, to make the sense of the world.

3. *Promulgation by a Superior*. The reason early modern voluntarists thought that only law, and not counsel or petition, could ground obligation was that genuine laws – laws that actually functioned to determine the wills of those subject to them – are necessarily promulgated by those who are superior in power to the laws' addressees. As Suarez noted, counsels take place between equals and petitions are addressed to superiors. To Suarez and Pufendorf it was obvious that our liberty could not be effectively bridled by equals or inferiors. Immanuel Kant rejected this explicitly political understanding of the phenomenon, but nonetheless retained the idea that obligation comes to us from a superior position, which is made manifest to us in the a priori feeling of respect. As we have just seen, this Kantian conception of obligation's promulgation by a superior is one of the most prominent features of Nancy's ontology of abandonment. But this conception is rendered questionable by Charles Scott's idea that facts, including the fact of obligation, are given along with a dimension of subjunctive indeterminacy. The purpose of treating the law as being promulgated by a superior is to account for how its addressee can experience herself as obligated by its interpellation. The subject can always step back and reflect on a counsel or petition, deciding for her own reasons whether to accept or reject it, but the law is supposed to command immediately and unconditionally. This is what Scott's account denies, though. We are indeed interpellated by the law, but it is not necessarily manifest as coming from on high and it does not necessarily give us to ourselves as 'responsibility through and through'. It is given, rather, as questionable. But this questionability should not be understood as reducing the law to the

status of a counsel or a petition. It is unclear whether the phenomenon we are left with after the previous chapter is still something
we want to think of as obligation, but it is certainly something other
than merely prudential goodness.

4. *Sanctions.* For the early modern philosophers who conceived
obligation in accordance with an explicitly political model, the
superiority of the lawgiver's position consisted in his power to
impose sanctions. For Pufendorf, obligation was simply unthinkable outside the framework of reward and punishment. If someone
recognised no superior who was capable of imposing sanctions,
then he would do whatever good he did 'out of his own good pleasure', and not from obligation. But this view was rejected by all
the other early modern theories of obligation, including Kant's.
As Nancy persuasively argued in 'The *Katagorein* of Excess', 'the
imperative contains neither threat nor promise. Indeed, its essence
lies in the fact that it contains neither.'[5] Indeed, the promise of
reward or threat would be sufficient to ruin the obligation, as it
would render the imperative hypothetical. The conception of obligation that I have developed in this book follows Kant in denying
any possible role for sanctions.

5. *Addressed to a Rational Being.* To insist that the moral law is addressed
to a rational being is to deny the possibility of equating obligation
with coercion. To be obligated, the practical subject must be able to
represent the correct rule of conduct to himself and to make use of it
to govern his own behaviour. The account that I have developed in
this book has rejected the view that we fulfil our obligations by governing our conduct with reference to determinate rules, but it has
nonetheless retained the idea that obligation is different from coercion in requiring the practical subject actively to take up the sense of
the situation in which he finds himself. As Merleau-Ponty showed,
the sense of the world is not simply there, such that it would impress
itself upon us as soon as we directed our attention to it. Rather, we
can only catch on to the sense of the world, including its moral
sense, by actively gearing into it.

6. *Priority of the Good.* The idea that the good must be understood as
prior to the right was advanced by early modern rationalist moral
philosophers, who were concerned to avoid having to conceive
of the moral lawgiver as a tyrant. To treat the right as prior to the

good – that is, to treat the goodness of a particular state of affairs as grounded simply in the fact that God or some other authoritative lawgiver commanded it – would be to conceive of moral lawgiving as utterly arbitrary. Since the ultimate giver of laws is not subject to any higher authority, how can we make sense of his choosing to issue certain commands and not others? For the rationalists, the only plausible answer was that he chose to command what really was good, independently of his having commanded it, and that he forwent to command what really was not good, independently of his having not commanded it. But as Jean Barbeyrac argued, to treat the good as prior to the right in this way is to leave unexplained the most important thing, namely how the moral subject would be *obligated* by this goodness: 'That there is such and such a relation of equality and proportion, of propriety or impropriety, in the nature of things, commits us only to *recognizing* that relation.'[6] Kant's Copernican Revolution in ethics integrates this voluntarist insight, presenting the right very explicitly as prior to the good. The account of obligation developed in this book, based on a reinterpretation of the fact of reason, follows Kant on this point: goodness is given only within the dynamic proper to sense, and not prior to it.

7. *Objectivity.* All of the early modern theories treated obligation as objective. To say that a person is obligated, but only subjectively, is just to say that the person is not really obligated. It is to say merely that the person feels obligated or takes herself to be obligated. But the whole question for theories of obligation to address is whether she really is. If obligation were merely subjective, then there would be no point in raising the question at all. The account I have developed over the previous four chapters agrees in denying that obligation is subjective. As we saw especially clearly in Merleau-Ponty's phenomenologies of perception and expression, to be condemned to sense is to be given over to a dynamic of sense that orients us always already toward objectivity. But as Merleau-Ponty, Serres, Nancy and Scott all showed in different ways, this orientation is ceaselessly called into question by dimensions of sense that exceed fully determinate, objective sense. It would be misleading, then, to say that obligation is objective, even though it is decidedly not subjective. It would be more accurate to say that the phenomenon of obligation is given most originarily at a dimension of sense that precedes and exceeds the dichotomy of subjectivity and objectivity.

8. *Overriding*. All of the early modern theories conceived obligation as overriding other kinds of goods. For example, on the rationalist account, which understood the necessitation of obligation in terms of truth, that is, in terms of the mind's inability to refuse its assent to what it perceived clearly and distinctly, there was simply no room for rival moral goods. Once I recognise clearly and distinctly that 2 + 5 = 7, the thought that 2 + 5 = 6 or that 2 + 5 = 8 is no longer given as a viable claimant to truth. These possibilities are simply cancelled out, even if I would prefer that they be true. Likewise, once I perceive clearly and distinctly that lying is wrong, then the benefit I foresee from telling a lie ceases to count as a viable claimant to moral rightness. Of course the same kind of point is emphasised by Kant: to recognise oneself as falling under the moral law just is to recognise its claim as ultimately authoritative. The account of obligation I have advanced in this book, and especially in the previous chapter, rejects this idea. Obligation, I argued, is given along with a dimension of indifference that renders its authoritativeness questionable. To experience oneself as obligated, then, is not necessarily to experience all other goods as morally subordinate.

Given these major divergences from the conception developed over the course of the early modern period, does it still make sense to characterise the phenomenon I have been describing as obligation? I believe it does. My reasons for thinking so are fundamentally pragmatic. It is important that we not collapse the space, traditionally occupied by the concept of obligation, that exists between three neighbouring practical phenomena. First, the mode of practical being-in-the-world that I have been describing is obviously very different from one's simply doing as one pleases, for whatever reasons one might have. Second, it is also importantly different from what Kant calls prudence.[7] Acting on the basis of counsels of prudence is more like acting from obligation than simply doing as one pleases, since doing so does involve a kind of necessitation of the will. But the necessitation given in a counsel of prudence is subjective and contingent. As Kant puts it, whether a course of action is practically necessary depends on 'whether this or that man counts this or that in his happiness'.[8] The phenomenon I have been describing as obligation does not depend on the subject's inclinations in this way. Rather, to be a practical subject at all just is to find oneself given over always already to a dynamic of moral sense that is present as a fact and whose binding force is entirely independent of the subject's preferences. We see this most clearly in Nancy's conception of the practical subject as abandoned to the law and thus as haunted by an imperative whose demands she can never have fulfilled. Of course it may appear that the characterisation of obligation as questionable and as not necessarily overriding reduces it to a counsel of prudence. Specifically, if the practical subject is not given to herself immediately as the addressee of an unconditional command whose sense is unambiguous, then it appears as if she is free to evaluate the courses of action available to her on the basis of her inclinations. But this is not quite right. Even though the moral sense of the situations we find ourselves in cannot be captured in any particular formulation of the moral law, and even though obligation does not fix us in place, definitively foreclosing the possibility of rival moral goods, it remains the case that moral sense emerges most originarily at a level prior to the constituted practical subject and her preferences. Finally, the phenomenon I have been describing is obviously different from coercion. This follows clearly from the fifth element of obligation described above: the moral sense of the world never imposes itself on the practical subject by force. It is present only for a subject who actively gears into it.

A Deflationary Account

Our understanding of our practical being-in-the-world would be impoverished if we allowed the space between these three phenomena to be collapsed. Indeed, I would argue further that our practical being-in-the-world itself would be impoverished. Since the moral phenomenon occupying the space between prudence, coercion and simply doing as one pleases has traditionally been called obligation, it seems reasonable to retain that name for what continues to occupy that space. That said, though, it is important to emphasise that what I have advanced in this book is very much a deflationary account of obligation and of what moral philosophy can say about it. Specifically, I want to argue that moral philosophy is unable to give definitive answers to three questions that writers on obligation have typically regarded as especially important. First, the account I have put forward cannot effectively refute the sceptic. I do believe I have shown that to be a practical subject at all is to find oneself condemned to sense always already and that this sense orients the subject prior to all reflection. But the sceptic might acknowledge all this and still ask, 'so what? Why can't I disregard this sense and simply do as I please?' Christine M. Korsgaard has an answer to questions like these: practical questions arise in reflection, and reflection has its own dynamic that leads to a point where the questionability of obligation is definitively overcome. As Korsgaard put the point in *The Sources of Normativity*, 'if the problem springs from reflection then the solution must do so as well'.[9] More specifically, the process of reflection leads us to a point where further reflection on a purported reason for action becomes impossible. Once we reach that point, we are rationally compelled to accept that reason as authoritative. But this is exactly the kind of response to the sceptic that is ruled out by Scott's conceptions of indifference and subjunctive indeterminacy. Obligation is always given, or at least always can be given, as distanced from the practical subject and thus as questionable. And so the sceptic always remains free to wonder whether a purported obligation really is binding.

Second, the account I have proposed cannot tell us what we ought to do in cases when our obligations contradict each other, or at least seem to contradict each other. We cannot follow Kant in thinking that perfect duties always trump imperfect duties in cases where they conflict. If a friend of mine has suffered a great setback in his personal or professional life, for example, it seems that the duty of beneficence requires that I try to comfort him. But that is an imperfect duty. Such a duty, on Kant's account, would always be overridden by perfect duties, such as the duty never to lie. But we often tell little lies when we attempt to comfort others. For example, we often say 'everything is going to be all right', even when we don't truly believe that everything is going to be all right. For Kant, the moral sense of the situation is clear: I know easily and without hesitation that I must not lie to my friend in order to help lift his spirits. But according to the account I have developed in this book, I cannot be so certain. I can never provide a definitive, unambiguous rank ordering of duties precisely because moral sense is always open ended. Indeed, as I attempted to demonstrate in Chapter 6, we cannot even provide a definitive rank ordering between obligatory and non-obligatory goods. Moral theory cannot tell me, for example, whether I ought to keep a promise, thereby forgoing a once-in-a-lifetime opportunity, or whether I ought to break the promise in order to pursue the opportunity. These are precisely the sorts of problems that theories of obligation are typically designed to resolve. But the deflationary account I am proposing here treats them as open questions.

Finally, moral philosophy is unable to say definitively and unambiguously what the content of obligation is. Of course it has seemed to many that the primary purpose of reflecting on obligation was to discover what we were obligated to do. This is clearly the question, for example, that motivates Kant's *Groundwork*: given the experience we all have of being necessitated unconditionally, what could be the law that gives the content of that necessitation? But as I have attempted to show, moral sense is slippery; there is no formula or set of formulas that would enable us to get a handle on it. On the one hand, I do believe that the intuition captured in the first formulation of the Categorical Imperative is right: we ought to take into account how the actions we propose to carry out would fit within a world in which everyone acted in accordance with the maxim of that action. This moral perspective, I have tried to argue, can be grounded in the centrifugal orientation of sense described by Merleau-Ponty. To be condemned to sense is to be oriented toward a unified, coherent, intersubjective world that gives the measure for the validity of everything in it. But as I have also tried to show, there is always moral sense in excess of what can be accounted for in terms of this world. On Merleau-Ponty's account, there is always latent sense in excess of fully determinate sense. And in Serres's somewhat more radical account, the moral message is always accompanied by noise, which is given not merely as an excess of sense, but as an interruption. What follows from this is that we cannot know with perfect certainty what obligation requires of us at the moment when we must act, and moreover that we would not be able to know even if we had more information relevant to the choice. This, of course, is not to say that we are left with no idea at all of what we ought to do. If moral sense does not resolve itself into fully determinate, clear moral rules, it remains the case nonetheless that it is not nonsense. Moral sense does orient us, albeit ambiguously and with an irreducible dimension of questionability. But theories of obligation have typically aimed considerably higher than this.

In its minimalism, the account of obligation I am proposing resembles the one advanced by John D. Caputo in his book *Against Ethics*. Caputo also treats obligation as a fact whose objective validity we cannot reason out 'from any antecedent data of reason'.[10] Obligations simply happen, without any 'cognitive backup'.[11] The principles that we are inclined to think of as the sources of obligation are really just ways of trying to make sense of the experience after the fact. What is first is the event of obligation, which gives the subject as the addressee of a command whose source it cannot know:

Does anyone really wait for cognitive reports to come in before concluding that one is obliged? Does one really 'conclude' that one is obliged, or does one not just find oneself (*sich befinden*) obliged, without so much as having been consulted or asked for one's consent? Is obligation not a matter of finding oneself from the start, always and already, on the receiving end of commands? Is that not where we are from the start, and hence where we must begin? Is that not just a fact?[12]

The role of the moral philosopher, then, is not to produce comprehensive theories that would help us to clarify the deeper meaning of obligation or to discern in particular cases precisely what obligation requires of us and why. The task of the moral philosopher is rather to serve as a kind of 'supplementary clerk', collecting fragments of obligation just as he finds them factically given.[13] All he can do is begin where he happens to find himself: not at the level of first principles, but rather right in the midst of the various obligations he finds himself subjected to. Caputo evokes here the example of a child born with AIDS, whose life will be filled with a great deal of undeserved suffering. Such a child makes a moral claim on us. That is just a fact. We do not require a systematic theory of the Good or an account of the normative presuppositions of communicative action in order to see this. It is not even the case that our recognition of the child's claim against us depends on a rough, pre-theoretical understanding of the relevant moral principles. According to Caputo, the experience of obligation in no way depends on the application of principles to individual cases. Indeed, the reverse is true: 'we apply individuals to principles'.[14] What this means, though, is that we have nothing convincing to say to the person who simply does not recognise the child as making any sort of morally pressing claim. There is no argument we can give, starting from first principles, that can reveal to the sceptic the error of his judgement. He either experiences the claim and its bindingness or he does not.

What the moral philosopher *qua* supplementary clerk can do is to start from below, simply describing the experience of obligation from the point of view of the addressee, leaving aside questions about the source of obligations and about the objective validity of the claims they seem to make against us. Doing this, the moral philosopher will discover two things. First, as I have already mentioned, obligation is fragile; it is left to fend for itself, unsupported by any kind of cognitive backup. Caputo finds something like this insight expressed in the work of a number of very different philosophers: 'obligation happens . . . *Es gibt*: there is obligation (Heidegger). *Il arrive*: it happens (Lyotard). Obligation is a fact, as it were (Kant). Here I am (*me voici*), on the receiving end of an obligation (Levinas).'[15] And second, to be on the receiving end of an obligation is to experience oneself as fixed in place by it. We 'cannot mount it or surmount it, get a distance on it, get beyond (*jenseits*) it, overcome (*überwinden*) it, or lift it up (*aufheben*)'.[16] Obligation gets hold of us and it does not let us out of its grasp. It does not ask our permission and it does not give us justifying reasons. If it did, it would not be obligation.

But the conception of obligation, and of philosophy's role in making sense of it, that I want to argue for here is even more deflationary than Caputo's. Specifically, I want to resist the language of 'grabbing hold of' and 'fixing in place'. On the one hand, I do not believe that we philosophers can grab hold of obligation, fixing its sense in rules that will guide us safely through the various moral predicaments we find ourselves in. As I have attempted to show throughout the book, moral sense is irreducibly excessive. I believe this much is consistent with Caputo's view. But on the other hand, I also want to deny that obligation grabs hold of the moral subject, fixing her in place with its interpellation such that she can only respond with a '*me voici*'. I have attempted to show that there is a dimension of sense that exceeds the grasp of obligation, in both the subjective and objective senses of the genitive. In *The Lives of Things*, Charles Scott describes the sensibility that is attuned to this excess as one in which persons and things 'stand out in their "just-so" quality, their nonreducibility to anything else, in the simultaneous palpability and impalpability of their events'.[17] This sensibility, he suggests, can be especially acute in the time of dying, when our past accomplishments and our future prospects come to appear less significant. With the letting go that can accompany the process of dying, the lives of things 'stand out as they come to pass'. When that happens, 'their differences, their own lives, their being there as they are could well stand out as wonderful, as, just so'.[18] I believe that obligation itself sometimes stands out in its just-so quality. It is given as the presentation of a specifically moral kind of good, distinct from all those prudential goods whose goodness depends on their connections to objects of the inclinations. It is given, in Kant's terms, as an unconditional good. But as I have attempted to show, it can be given at the same time as distanced from our practical concerns. When it is given this way, in its just-so quality, its binding force recedes. It does not command categorically, leaving the subject with no legitimate practical possibility other than unconditional obedience. It is given as 'just there', with a dimension of indifference to moral sense right in the midst of moral sense. And so if we try to grasp the sense of obligation and to fix it in place – or if we try to understand ourselves as grasped and fixed in place by it – we miss it.

But if we do not try to grasp the sense of obligation and to fix it in place – or if we do not try to understand ourselves as grasped and fixed in place by it – we miss it too.

Notes

Introduction

1. Carroll, *Through the Looking Glass*, p. 185.
2. Deleuze, *Logic of Sense*, p. 41.
3. Carroll, *Through the Looking Glass*, p. 186.
4. Grotius, *Rights of War and Peace*, Book III, p. 1747.
5. Darwall, *British Moralists*, p. 6.
6. Ayer, *Language, Truth and Logic*, ch. 6.
7. Stevenson, *Language and Ethics*, p. 22.
8. Ibid. p. 100.
9. Aristotle, *Nicomachean Ethics*, p. 1732 (1096a1).
10. Hegel, *Aesthetics*, pp. 128–9.
11. Merleau-Ponty, *Phenomenology of Perception*, pp. lxxxiii–lxxxiv. Italics omitted.
12. Hobbes, *De Cive*, p. 56 [II, 10]. Numbers in brackets refer to chapter and section numbers, respectively.
13. Pufendorf, *On the Duty of Man and Citizen*, p. 27.
14. Kant, *Critique of Practical Reason*, p. 165 [5:32]. Page numbers in brackets refer to those of the Akademie Edition.
15. Kant, *Metaphysics of Morals*, p. 377 [6:222–3]. Page numbers in brackets refer to those of the Akademie Edition.
16. Aquinas, *Summa Theologica*, I–II, q. 90, a. 1.
17. Suarez, *De Legibus*, p. 21.
18. Ibid. p. 127. Cf. Grotius, *Rights of War and Peace*, Book I, pp. 147–9. Cf. also Cumberland, *Treatise of the Laws of Nature*, p. 353: 'Obligation is that act of a legislator, by which he declares, that actions conformable to his law are necessary to those, for whom the law is made.' In all quotations from *A Treatise of the Laws of Nature*, I have modernised the spelling.

19. Suarez, *De Legibus*, p. 127.
20. Ibid.
21. Ibid. pp. 127–8.
22. Pufendorf, *On the Duty of Man and Citizen*, p. 28.
23. Kant, *Critique of Practical Reason*, p. 202 [5:77]. Italics omitted.
24. Pufendorf, *De Jure Naturae et Gentium*, p. 94.
25. Cumberland, *Treatise of the Laws of Nature*, p. 353.
26. This expression appears repeatedly in *A Treatise of the Laws of Nature*, and reflects Cumberland's commitment to the idea that our obligations are to be discovered by means of the study of nature. Cf. Forsyth, 'Place of Richard Cumberland', p. 25.
27. Schneewind, *Invention of Autonomy*, pp. 111–12.
28. Cumberland, *Treatise of the Laws of Nature*, p. 255.
29. Ibid. p. 599.
30. Locke, *Essay Concerning Human Understanding*, pp. 351–2.
31. Indeed, Stephen Darwall refers to this insight as 'Pufendorf's Point'. Darwall, *Second-Person Standpoint*, pp. 22–3.
32. Pufendorf, *De Jure Naturae et Gentium*, p. 91.
33. Ibid.
34. Kant expresses a very similar insight in *The Metaphysics of Morals*: 'I can recognize that I am under obligation to others only insofar as I at the same time put myself under obligation, since the law by virtue of which I regard myself as being under obligation proceeds in every case from my own practical reason.' Kant, *Metaphysics of Morals*, p. 543 [6:417].
35. Leibniz, 'Meditation on the Common Concept of Justice', p. 46.
36. Schneewind, *Moral Philosophy*, p. xxi.
37. Cudworth, *Treatise*, p. 16.
38. Ibid. p. 17.
39. Clarke, *Discourse*, p. 611.
40. Locke, *Essays on the Law of Nature*, p. 215.

Chapter 1

1. Luther, *Bondage of the Will*, p. 168.
2. Matthew 22: 36–8. Cf. Leibniz, *Theodicy*, p. 35: 'Our end is to banish from men the false ideas that represent God to them as an absolute prince employing a despotic power, unfitted to be loved and unworthy of being loved.'

3. Luther, *Bondage of the Will*, p. 168.

4. Ibid. p. 282.

5. Korsgaard, *Sources of Normativity*, pp. 21–3.

6. Hobbes, *Leviathan*, p. 3 [Introduction, 1]. Numbers in brackets refer to chapter and section numbers, respectively.

7. Pufendorf, *De Jure Naturae et Gentium*, p. 6.

8. Ibid.

9. Ibid. p. 28.

10. Schneewind, *Invention of Autonomy*, p. 123.

11. Pufendorf, *De Jure Naturae et Gentium*, p. 114.

12. Ibid. p. 95.

13. Hobbes, *De Cive*, p. 185 [XV, 5].

14. Pufendorf, *De Jure Naturae et Gentium*, p. 101. Stephen Darwall argues for this interpretation of Pufendorf's position in Darwall, 'Pufendorf on Morality, Sociability, and Moral Powers', pp. 230–2. Cf. Schneewind, *Invention of Autonomy*, pp. 135–6.

15. Schroeder, 'Cudworth and Normative Explanations', p. 1. Korsgaard advances an argument very similar to Cudworth's in *The Sources of Normativity*, but attributes it to Samuel Clarke. Korsgaard, *Sources of Normativity*, pp. 28–9.

16. Cudworth, *Treatise*, p. 18.

17. Leibniz advances a very similar argument in his 'Opinion on the Principles of Pufendorf': 'Well, then, if the source of law is the will of a superior and, inversely, a justifying cause of law is necessary in order to have a superior, a circle is created, than which none was ever more manifest. From what will the justice of the cause derive, if there is not yet a superior, from whom, supposedly, the law may emanate?' Leibniz, *Political Writings*, pp. 73–4.

18. Hume, *Enquiry*, p. 22, n. 12.

19. Malebranche, *Treatise on Ethics*, p. 45.

20. Ibid. Translation slightly modified.

21. Malebranche, *Search after Truth*, pp. 613–14.

22. Leibniz, *Discourse*, p. 2.

23. Schneewind, *Invention of Autonomy*, p. 252.

24. Leibniz, *Political Writings*, p. 71.

25. Ibid. p. 75. Brackets in original.

26. Descartes, *Principles of Philosophy*, p. 242.

27. Descartes, *Philosophical Writings*, vol. II, p. 111.

28. Malebranche, *Treatise on Ethics*, p. 84.

29. Malebranche, *Search after Truth*, p. 10.
30. Clarke, *Discourse*, p. 609.
31. Schneewind, *Moral Philosophy*, p. 335; Wolff, *Vernünftige Gedanken*, p. 7.
32. Schneewind, *Moral Philosophy*, pp. 333, 334; Wolff, *Vernünftige Gedanken*, Vorrede zu der andern Auflage [Preface to the other edition].
33. Barbeyrac, 'Jugement d'un Anonyme', pp. 252–3. Translations from 'Jugement d'un Anonyme' are mine.
34. Ibid. p. 252. Terence Irwin emphasises the importance of Barbeyrac's assumption that obligations must be established by imposition in Irwin, *Development of Ethics*, pp. 329–30.
35. Barbeyrac, 'Jugement d'un Anonyme', p. 250. Emphasis mine.
36. Hutcheson, *Essay*, pp. 215–16.
37. Ibid. pp. 216–17; Hume, *Treatise*, pp. 293–302 [III.1.i]. Numbers in brackets refer to book, part, and section, respectively.
38. Hobbes, *Leviathan*, p. 495 [A Review and Conclusion, 13].
39. Ibid. p. 82 [xiv, 8].
40. Ibid. p. 80 [xiv, 4]. Emphasis omitted.
41. Watkins, *Hobbes's System of Ideas*, pp. 50–7.
42. Holbach, *La Morale Universelle*, p. 26. Translation mine.
43. Schneewind, *Moral Philosophy*, p. 433; Holbach, *La Morale Universelle*, p. 2.
44. Holbach, *La Morale Universelle*, pp. 102–9.
45. Hobbes, *Leviathan*, p. 90 [XV, 4].
46. Ibid. p. 84 [XIV, 18].
47. Darwall, *British Moralists*, pp. 72–6.
48. Hutcheson, *Essay*, p. 209.
49. Ibid. p. vi. Emphasis omitted. Cf. p. 209: 'Ingenious speculative Men, in their straining to support an Hypothesis, may contrive a thousand subtle selfish Motives, which a kind generous Heart never dreamed of.'
50. Hutcheson, *Inquiry*, p. 254.
51. Ibid. pp. 6–7.
52. Hutcheson, *Essay*, pp. 216–18; Hume, *Treatise*, pp. 295–6 [III.1.i].
53. Hume, *Treatise*, p. 266 [II.3.iii].
54. Ibid. p. 302 [III.1.ii].
55. Ibid. p. 309 [III.2.i].
56. Horace, *Art of Poetry*, p. 21.
57. Hume, *Enquiry*, pp. 38–40.

58. Hutcheson, *Inquiry*, p. 113.

59. Ibid. p. 160.

60. Balguy, *Foundation*, p. 9.

61. Hutcheson, *Essay*, p. 239.

62. Balguy, *Foundation*, pp. 9–10.

63. Ibid. p. 32.

64. Korsgaard, *Sources of Normativity*, pp. 92–3.

Chapter 2

1. Korsgaard, *Sources of Normativity*, p. 93.

2. Ibid.

3. Kant, *Critique of Pure Reason*, p. 110 [B xvi]. Page numbers in brackets refer to those of the Akademie Edition.

4. Ibid. p. 426 [A 369].

5. Ibid. pp. 241–2 [A 125–7]. Henry E. Allison treats the distinction between transcendental realism and transcendental idealism as essential for understanding Kant's speculative philosophy in Allison, *Kant's Transcendental Idealism*, pp. 20–49.

6. Kant, *Critique of Practical Reason*, pp. 155–6 [5:22].

7. Ibid. p. 191 [5:64].

8. Ibid. p. 202 [5:77]. Italics omitted.

9. Cudworth, *Treatise*, p. 16.

10. Kant, *Lectures on Ethics*, p. 65 [27:274]. Page numbers in brackets refer to those of the Akademie Edition.

11. Ibid.

12. Ibid. p. 66 [27:275].

13. Kant, *Critique of Pure Reason*, p. 242 [A 126].

14. Kant, *Lectures*, p. 70 [27:1426].

15. Ibid. p. 71 [27:1428].

16. Ibid.

17. Ibid. p. 72 [27:1429].

18. Kant, *Notes and Fragments*, p. 440 [19:179]. Page numbers in brackets refer to those of the Akademie Edition.

19. Malebranche, *Search after Truth*, p. 10.

20. Kant, *Groundwork*, pp. 57, 93 [4:402, 445]. Page numbers in brackets refer to those of the Akademie Edition.

21. Ibid. p. 49 [4:393].

22. Ibid. p. 50 [4:394].

23. Ibid. p. 52 [4:397].

24. Ibid. p. 55 [4:400].
25. Ibid. p. 56 [4:402].
26. Ibid. p. 57 [4:402]. Italics omitted.
27. Ibid. p. 66 [4: 412]. Emphasis omitted.
28. Ibid. p. 89 [4:440].
29. Allison, *Kant's Theory of Freedom*, p. 97.
30. Kant, *Groundwork*, p. 57 [4:402].
31. Ibid. p. 72 [4:420].
32. Timmermann, *Commentary*, p. xxiii.
33. Kant, *Groundwork*, p. 94 [4:446].
34. Ibid. p. 95 [4:447].
35. Ibid. p. 95 [4:448].
36. Ibid. pp. 97–8 [4:450].
37. Reinhold, *Briefe*, pp. 267–8. Translation mine. Henry Sidgwick advances a similar argument in Sidgwick, *Methods of Ethics*, pp. 511–16.
38. Allison, *Commentary*, pp. 359–60.
39. Kant, *Critique of Practical Reason*, pp. 178, 165 [5:47, 31].
40. Ibid. p. 164 [5:31].
41. Ibid. p. 177 [5:47].
42. Ibid. p. 164 [5:31].
43. Ibid. p. 163 [5:30].
44. Allison, *Kant's Theory of Freedom*, p. 230.
45. Hegel, *Lectures on the History of Philosophy*, p. 461.
46. Schopenhauer, *On the Basis of Morality*, p. 79.
47. Bittner, *What Reason Demands*, pp. 89–90.
48. Kant, *Critique of Practical Reason*, p. 164 [5:31]. In other passages, Kant presents the fact of reason differently. Some of these characterisations, however, plainly contradict other passages from *Critique of Practical Reason*, so that it is safe to conclude that they do not represent Kant's position. Other formulations are sufficiently similar to the one I have cited to count, at least for present purposes, as making the same basic point. Cf. Rawls, *Lectures on the History of Moral Philosophy*, pp. 259–61.
49. Beck, *Studies in the Philosophy of Kant*, p. 211.
50. This formulation is different from Beck's. Beck suggests that the fact of reason, on this second interpretation, is the fact that pure reason is practical. But as Henry E. Allison points out, this interpretation would beg the question that is at issue in *Critique of Practical Reason*,

namely whether pure reason can be practical. The formulation I have given of the second interpretation of the fact of reason is similar to Allison's suggested formulation. Allison, *Kant's Theory of Freedom*, p. 233.

51. Łuków, 'Fact of Reason', p. 210.
52. Guyer, 'Naturalistic and Transcendental Moments', p. 462.
53. Beck, *Studies in the Philosophy of Kant*, p. 203.
54. Ilting, 'Naturalistic Fallacy in Kant', p. 117.
55. Łuków, 'Fact of Reason', p. 210.
56. Ibid. p. 211.
57. Kant, *Critique of Practical Reason*, p. 178 [5:47].
58. I develop this point further in Lueck, 'Kant's Fact of Reason'.

Chapter 3

1. Merleau-Ponty, *Phenomenology of Perception*, pp. lxxxiii–lxxxiv. Italics omitted.
2. Merleau-Ponty, *The Visible and the Invisible*, p. 115.
3. Kant, *Critique of Practical Reason*, pp. 178, 164 [5:47, 31].
4. Rawls, 'Kantian Constructivism in Moral Theory', p. 543.
5. Hegel, *Aesthetics*, pp. 128–9.
6. Merleau-Ponty, *Phenomenology of Perception*, p. 3.
7. Ibid. p. 4.
8. Descartes, *Philosophical Writings*, vol. II, p. 21.
9. Merleau-Ponty, *Phenomenology of Perception*, pp. 35–6.
10. Ibid. p. 36.
11. Merleau-Ponty, *Primacy of Perception*, p. 25; Merleau-Ponty, *Phenomenology of Perception*, p. 454.
12. Hegel, *Phenomenology of Spirit*, p. 5.
13. Merleau-Ponty distinguishes between what he calls a 'bad ambiguity', which is conceived in negative terms – not sensible, but also not intelligible – and a 'good ambiguity', which is understood in accordance with its own dynamic. Merleau-Ponty, *Primacy of Perception*, p. 11. For a detailed account of the meaning of ambiguity in Merleau-Ponty's work, see Silverman, *Inscriptions*, pp. 63–9.
14. Merleau-Ponty, *Phenomenology of Perception*, pp. 17–18.
15. Ibid. p. 18.
16. Ibid. p. 316.
17. Ibid. p. 18.

18. Kelly, 'Normative Nature of Perceptual Experience', p. 158.
19. Ibid. p. 155.
20. Merleau-Ponty, *Phenomenology of Perception*, p. 224.
21. Merleau-Ponty, *Signs*, p. 175.
22. Goldstein and Rosenthal, 'Zur Problem der Wirkung der Farben auf den Organismus', p. 23. Quoted in Merleau-Ponty, *Phenomenology of Perception*, p. 222.
23. Merleau-Ponty, *Phenomenology of Perception*, p. 265.
24. Angelica Nuzzo argues that Kant also grounds normativity in a kind of pre-subjective bodily orientation. Our sense of specifically moral space is grounded in a feeling that is similar to our embodied experience of the distinction between left and right. Nuzzo, *Ideal Embodiment*, pp. 128–34.
25. Merleau-Ponty, *Phenomenology of Perception*, p. 54.
26. Ibid. p. 317.
27. Putnam, *Realism with a Human Face*, p. 115.
28. Merleau-Ponty, *Phenomenology of Perception*, pp. 262–4.
29. Lingis, *Imperative*, p. 91.
30. Kant, *Groundwork*, p. 73 [4:421].
31. Even utilitarianism, a theory opposed in so many respects to Kantian ethics, shares a commitment to the idea that it is morally impermissible for individuals to make exceptions for themselves: 'The utilitarian's ultimate moral principle, let it be remembered, expresses the sentiment not of altruism but of benevolence, the agent counting himself neither more nor less than any other person.' Smart, 'Outline of a System of Utilitarian Ethics', p. 3.
32. Kant, *Metaphysics of Morals*, p. 543 [6:417].
33. Jackson, 'Skill and the Critique of Descartes', p. 73.
34. Darwall, *Second-Person Standpoint*, pp. 5–7.
35. Ibid. p. 15.
36. Barbaras, *Being of the Phenomenon*, p. 50.
37. According to Roland Barthes, Merleau-Ponty was among the first French philosophers to take an interest in Saussurian linguistics. Barthes, *Elements of Semiology*, p. 24.
38. Saussure, *Course in General Linguistics*, pp. 8–9.
39. Ibid. p. 67. Translation modified.
40. Ibid. pp. 68–9.
41. Ibid. p. 118. Translation modified. Emphasis omitted.
42. Ibid. p. 114.

43. /ʧ/ represents the 'ch' sound as it is pronounced in 'cheese'.

44. Jakobson, *Six Lectures*, pp. 61–2.

45. Ibid. p. 66.

46. Saussure, *Course in General Linguistics*, p. 18.

47. Ibid. p. 14.

48. Ibid. Translation modified.

49. Ibid. pp. 110–11.

50. Merleau-Ponty, *Prose of the World*, p. 23. Cf. Merleau-Ponty, *Themes from the Lectures*, p. 19; Merleau-Ponty, *Sense and Non-Sense*, p. 87.

51. For accounts of the heterodoxy of Merleau-Ponty's reading of Saussure, see Lagueux, 'Merleau-Ponty et la linguistique de Saussure'; Schmidt, *Between Phenomenology and Structuralism*, pp. 105–11; Koukal, 'Merleau-Ponty's Reform of Saussure', pp. 602–6.

52. Anna Petronella Foultier provides a compelling defence of Merleau-Ponty's reading of Saussure in Foultier, 'Merleau-Ponty's Encounter with Saussure's Linguistics'.

53. Ricoeur, *Conflict of Interpretations*, p. 85.

54. Saussure, *Course in General Linguistics*, p. 83.

55. Merleau-Ponty, *Signs*, p. 44.

56. Merleau-Ponty, *Prose of the World*, p. 10.

57. Although Saussure is often read as treating *langue* and *parole* as ontologically distinct orders, it is an open question whether this reading is accurate. Paul J. Thibault, for example, argues that the distinction must be understood primarily as methodological, as necessary for establishing a distinct object for the science of linguistics. Moreover, it is not certain that the binarism Saussure institutes between these two orders is as strict as is commonly supposed. 'Saussure does not claim that *langue* and *parole* are simply opposed to each other. The distinction does not reduce to a simple dichotomy. Instead, these two theoretical notions are co-articulated in relation to each other in a theoretically much more complex and interesting way.' Thibault, *Re-reading Saussure*, p. 67.

58. Merleau-Ponty, *Prose of the World*, p. 24. Merleau-Ponty refers here to an 'envelopment of language by language', an idea he attributes to Saussure. This envelopment 'attests to a permanent affinity between my speaking and the language about which I am speaking'.

59. 'As we have seen, language is invincible to all efforts that seek to convert it into an object'. Merleau-Ponty, *Consciousness and the Acquisition of Language*, p. 7.

60. Benveniste, *Problems in General Linguistics*, p. 73.
61. Merleau-Ponty, *Phenomenology of Perception*, p. 164.
62. Merleau-Ponty, *Prose of the World*, p. 30.
63. This common-sense understanding is formalised in the influential theory of communication developed by Claude E. Shannon and Warren Weaver. Shannon and Weaver, *Mathematical Theory of Communication*.
64. Chandler, *Transmission Model of Communication*.
65. Merleau-Ponty, *Signs*, p. 42.
66. Merleau-Ponty, *Prose of the World*, p. 12. Translation slightly modified. In both the French original and in the English translation, Merleau-Ponty refers to the character from Stendhal's novel as Rossi. The correct name is in fact Rassi.
67. Ibid.
68. Merleau-Ponty, *Signs*, p. 19.
69. Ibid. p. 87.
70. Landes, *Paradoxes of Expression*, p. 25.
71. Ibid.
72. Waldenfels, 'Responsive Ethik', p. 78. All translations from this article are mine. Cf. Waldenfels, *Antwortregister*, p. 357.
73. Korsgaard, *Sources of Normativity*, p. 123.
74. Waldenfels, *Antwortregister*, p. 357.
75. Waldenfels, 'Responsive Ethik', p. 79.
76. Ibid. Cf. Waldenfels, *Antwortregister*, p. 620.
77. Waldenfels, 'Responsive Ethik', p. 71.
78. Merleau-Ponty, *Prose of the World*, p. 11.
79. Ibid. p. 19.
80. Ibid. pp. 19–20.

Chapter 4

1. Serres, *La Communication*, p. 40.
2. Ibid. p. 41.
3. Shannon and Weaver, *Mathematical Theory of Communication*, p. 6.
4. Serres, *La Communication*, p. 42.
5. Ibid. p. 44.
6. Kant, *Critique of Practical Reason*, p. 155 [5:22].
7. Ibid. p. 158 [5:24].
8. Kant, *Groundwork*, p. 67 [4:414].
9. Ibid. p. 55 [4:400].

10. Kant, *Metaphysics of Morals*, p. 512 [6:379].

11. Cf. Lueck, 'Toward a Serresian Reconceptualization', pp. 53–5.

12. Kant, *Metaphysics of Morals*, p. 566 [6:446].

13. Kant, *Groundwork*, p. 58 [4:403–4].

14. Kant, *Metaphysics of Morals*, pp. 524–5 [6:394].

15. Serres, *Angels*, pp. 99–113.

16. Merleau-Ponty, *Phenomenology of Perception*, p. 224.

17. Ibid. pp. lxxxiii–lxxxiv.

18. Serres, *Parasite*, p. 66.

19. Serres, *Malfeasance*, p. 1. 'Tigers piss on the edge of their lair. And so do lions and dogs. Like those carnivorous mammals, many animals, our cousins, *mark* their territory with their harsh, stinking urine or with their howling, while others such as finches and nightingales use sweet songs.'

20. Lueck, 'Terrifying Concupiscence of Belonging', pp. 250–2.

21. MacIntyre, 'Is Patriotism a Virtue?', p. 291.

22. Ibid. p. 292.

23. Serres, *La Communication*, p. 43.

24. Serres, *Parasite*, p. 68.

25. Kant, *Critique of Practical Reason*, p. 169 [5:36].

26. Darwall, *Second-Person Standpoint*, p. 27.

27. Rawls, 'Kantian Constructivism in Moral Theory', p. 543.

28. Darwall, *Second-Person Standpoint*, pp. 5–6.

29. Barbeyrac, 'Jugement d'un Anonyme', p. 250.

30. Darwall, *Second-Person Standpoint*, pp. 7–8.

31. Pufendorf, *De Jure Naturae et Gentium*, p. 91.

32. Coles, *Simone Weil: A Modern Pilgrimage*, p. 26.

33. Pétrement, *Simone Weil: A Life*, p. 536.

34. Kant, *Metaphysics of Morals*, p. 571 [6:452].

35. Kant, *Critique of Practical Reason*, p. 202 [5:77].

36. Ibid.

37. Catherine Chalier advances a similar criticism of Kant's account of respect. For Kant, the other's value is constituted on the basis of the subject's own reason. This kind of account misses the alterity and the singularity of the other. Chalier, *What Ought I to Do?*, pp. 67–8.

38. Kant, *Critique of Practical Reason*, pp. 199, 201 [5:73, 76].

39. Kant, *Anthropology*, p. 240 [7:128]. Page numbers in brackets refer to those of the Akademie Edition.

40. Perrin and Thibon, *Simone Weil as We Knew Her*, p. 107.

41. Lueck, 'Exposition and Obligation', pp. 189–92.

42. Serres, *Troubadour of Knowledge*, pp. 4–5.
43. This word for word reading of the Dutch sentence is a mistake. The construction 'houden van' means 'to love', and so the sentence actually means 'I love cats.'
44. Serres, *Troubadour of Knowledge*, p. 7.
45. Pierce, *Symbols, Signals, and Noise*, p. 251.
46. Serres, *Genesis*, p. 22.
47. Ibid. p. 13.
48. Ibid. p. 13.
49. Ibid. p. 32.
50. Ibid. p. 31.
51. This section draws on material from Lueck, 'Exposition and Obligation', pp. 181–4.
52. Serres, *Troubadour of Knowledge*, pp. xiii–xvii.
53. Gherardi, *Le Theatre Italien*, pp. 197–200.
54. Serres, *Troubadour of Knowledge*, p. xiii.
55. Ibid. p. xvii.
56. Serres, *Genesis*, pp. 41–8; Assad, *Reading with Michel Serres*, pp. 131–2.
57. Serres, *Troubadour of Knowledge*, p. 149.
58. Ibid. p. xviii.
59. Kant, *Groundwork*, p. 73 [4:421]. Italics omitted.
60. La Fontaine, *Fables*, p. 118. Translation mine.
61. Lueck, 'Toward a Serresian Reconceptualization', p. 56.
62. Serres, *Parasite*, p. 80.
63. Ibid. p. 89.
64. Kant, *Groundwork*, p. 58 [4:403–4].
65. Cf. Kant, *Critique of Practical Reason*, p. 168 [5:35].
66. Serres, *L'Incandescent*, pp. 77–8; Serres, *La Guerre Mondiale*, pp. 164–6.
67. Serres, *Detachment*, pp. 65–70.
68. Diogenes Laertius, *Lives of Eminent Philosophers*, p. 65.
69. Serres, *Rameaux*, p. 77.
70. Acts 22: 28 (New Revised Standard Version).
71. Philippians 3: 5.
72. Serres, *Rameaux*, p. 77.
73. Galatians 1: 14.
74. Acts 22: 1–20.
75. Galatians 3: 28.
76. Serres, *Rameaux*, p. 80.
77. Ibid. p. 96.
78. Serres, *Parasite*, p. 56.

79. Serres, *Detachment*, p. 68.
80. Ibid. p. 70.
81. Ibid. p. 81.
82. Kant, *Critique of Practical Reason*, p. 164 [5:31].

Chapter 5

1. Pufendorf, *On the Duty of Man and Citizen*, p. 27.
2. Waldenfels, 'Responsive Ethik', p. 78.
3. Malebranche, *Treatise on Ethics*, p. 84.
4. Malebranche, *Search after Truth*, p. 10.
5. Stockhausen, *Hymnen*, CD booklet, pp. 134–5.
6. Nancy, *Sense of the World*, p. 18.
7. Husserl, *Cartesian Meditations*, p. 84 (§41).
8. Merleau-Ponty, *Phenomenology of Perception*, p. lxxvii.
9. Ibid.
10. Ibid. p. lxxviii.
11. Nancy, *Sense of the World*, p. 17.
12. Ibid. p. 16.
13. Ibid. p. 17. Italics omitted.
14. Nancy, *Gravity of Thought*, p. 29. Translation slightly modified.
15. Lacoue-Labarthe and Nancy, *Retreating the Political*, pp. 32–6.
16. Nancy, *Gravity of Thought*, pp. 28–9.
17. Ibid. p. 59.
18. Nancy, *Being Singular Plural*, p. 5. Translation slightly modified. Brackets in original.
19. Ibid.
20. Ibid. p. 2.
21. Ibid. p. 30.
22. Nancy, *Hegel*, p. 52. Italics omitted.
23. Hegel, *Science of Logic*, p. 81.
24. Nancy, *Sense of the World*, p. 28.
25. Merleau-Ponty, *Phenomenology of Perception*, pp. lxxxiii–lxxxiv. Italics omitted.
26. Nancy, *Being Singular Plural*, p. 2. Translation slightly modified.
27. Nancy, *Hegel*, p. 52.
28. Hegel, *Aesthetics*, pp. 128–9.
29. Nancy, *Hegel*, p. 49.
30. Nancy, *Sense of the World*, p. 12.
31. Nancy, *Finite Thinking*, p. 9.

32. Nancy, *Birth to Presence*, pp. 154–5.

33. Morin, *Jean-Luc Nancy*, pp. 29–30.

34. Nancy, *Gravity of Thought*, p. 56.

35. Ibid. p. 57.

36. Ibid. Cf. Nancy, *Sense of the World*, p. 63: 'In a sense – but what sense – sense *is* touching.'

37. Nancy, *Gravity of Thought*, p. 61. Translation modified.

38. Nancy, *Sense of the World*, p. 73.

39. Nancy, *Being Singular Plural*, p. 6. Translation modified. Italics omitted.

40. Ibid. p. 32.

41. Ibid. pp. 39–40.

42. Ibid. p. 167.

43. Raffoul, 'Creation of the World', p. 18.

44. Nancy, *Being Singular Plural*, p. 167.

45. Ibid. p. 16. Cf. Jean-Luc Nancy, *Creation of the World*, pp. 71–3.

46. Nancy, *Gravity of Thought*, p. 60.

47. Kant, *Critique of Practical Reason*, pp. 164, 177 [5:31, 47].

48. Nancy, *Birth to Presence*, p. 36.

49. Ibid. p. 37.

50. Ibid. p. 38.

51. Ibid. p. 39.

52. Ibid. p. 36.

53. Raffoul, 'Abandonment and the Categorical Imperative of Being', pp. 69–72.

54. Sartre, *Essays in Existentialism*, p. 34.

55. Ibid. p. 67.

56. Ibid. p. 45.

57. Ibid. p. 34.

58. Nancy, *Gravity of Thought*, p. 62.

59. Ibid. Translation slightly modified.

60. Raffoul, 'Abandonment and the Categorical Imperative of Being', p. 75.

61. Nancy, *Birth to Presence*, pp. 43–4.

62. Nancy, *Being Singular Plural*, p. 29.

63. Nancy, *Finite Thinking*, p. 176.

64. Ibid. p. 175.

65. Nancy, *Birth to Presence*, p. 44.

66. Kant, *Groundwork*, pp. 57, 86 [4:402, 436].

67. Raffoul, 'Abandonment and the Categorical Imperative of Being', p. 75.

68. Nancy, *Finite Thinking*, p. 192.
69. Nancy, *Birth to Presence*, p. 44.
70. Nancy, *Finite Thinking*, p. 141.
71. The same kind of argument applies to the idea that the imperative's force is derived from the promise of some reward. If the 'must' depends on the practical subject's actually wanting the reward, then the necessitation is merely conditional.
72. Nancy, *Finite Thinking*, p. 145.
73. Nancy, *Birth to Presence*, p. 44.
74. Ibid. p. 45.
75. Nancy, *Finite Thinking*, p. 147. Translation modified.
76. Ibid. pp. 142–3, 188–9.
77. Ibid. pp. 176–7.
78. Nancy, *Birth to Presence*, p. 44.
79. Nancy, *Finite Thinking*, pp. 181–2.
80. Ibid. p. 136.
81. Ibid. p. 140.
82. Nancy, *Birth to Presence*, p. 44.
83. Nancy, *Being Singular Plural*, p. 6.
84. I develop this point in Lueck, 'Dignity at the Limit', pp. 317–22.
85. Nancy, *Finite Thinking*, p. 182.
86. Ibid. pp. 186–7.
87. Kant, *Groundwork*, p. 84 [4:434].
88. Ibid.
89. Kant, *Metaphysics of Morals*, p. 580 [6:463].
90. Kant, *Critique of Practical Reason*, p. 191 [5:64].
91. Kant, *Groundwork*, p. 85 [4:436].
92. Ibid. p. 84 [4:435]; Kant, *Metaphysics of Morals*, p. 580 [6:463].
93. Kant, *Groundwork*, p. 89 [4:440].
94. Kant, *Metaphysics of Morals*, pp. 545, 558 [6:420, 436].
95. Ibid. p. 580 [6:463].
96. Ibid. p. 558 [6:436].
97. Ibid. pp. 552–3 [6:429].
98. Kant, *Lectures on Ethics*, p. 420 [27:692–3].
99. Ibid. p. 127 [27:346].
100. This conception of dignity has a long history in western thought, beginning with Pope Leo I: 'Wake up then, o friend, and acknowledge the dignity of your nature. Recall that you have been made "according to the image of God".' Saint Leo the Great, *Sermons*, p. 114.

Chapter 6

1. Kant, *Critique of Practical Reason*, p. 199 [5:73].
2. Kant, *Metaphysics of Morals*, p. 373 [6:211–12].
3. Kant, *Critique of Practical Reason*, pp. 201–2 [5:76].
4. Ibid. pp. 199–200 [5:73].
5. Nancy, *Finite Thinking*, p. 146.
6. Ibid. p. 145.
7. Williams, 'Morality, the Peculiar Institution', p. 174.
8. Ibid. p. 180.
9. Kant, *Metaphysics of Morals*, p. 571 [6:452].
10. Ibid. p. 521 [6:390].
11. Strictly speaking, Kant would not treat this as a case of one obligation trumping another. This is because an obligation, for Kant, is defined as an objective practical necessitation, so that the idea of conflicting obligations would be contradictory. If one obligation overrides another, then it must be the case the latter was not truly an obligation, but only an apparent obligation. The kinds of cases we would naturally describe as conflicts of obligation are described by Kant rather as conflicts between *grounds* of obligation. But this does not affect Williams's point. Ibid. pp. 378–9 [6:224].
12. Williams, 'Morality, the Peculiar Institution', p. 180. Italics omitted.
13. Ibid. p. 181.
14. Ibid. pp. 181–2.
15. Ibid. p. 182.
16. I develop this line of argumentation in Lueck, 'A Fact, As It Were'.
17. Scott, *Lives of Things*, p. 3.
18. Ibid. p. 4.
19. Ibid. p. 7.
20. Ibid. pp. 11–12; Scott, *Advantages and Disadvantages.*
21. Kant, *Critique of Practical Reason*, p. 203 [5:77–8].
22. Scott, *Lives of Things*, p. 12.
23. Scott, *Living with Indifference*, p. 128.
24. Ibid. p. 129.
25. Merleau-Ponty, *Phenomenology of Perception*, p. 317.
26. Fodor, *In Critical Condition*, p. 16. Quoted in Scott, *Living with Indifference*, p. 5.
27. Scott, *Living with Indifference*, p.142.
28. Ibid. p. 141.

29. For a more detailed account of the role of 'gappiness' in Scott's conception of indifference, see Deere, 'Gappiness in Dimensional Accounts', pp. 123–42.
30. Korsgaard, *Sources of Normativity*, p. 93.
31. Levinas, *Totality and Infinity*, p. 201.
32. Ibid. p. 199.
33. Levinas, 'Transcendence and Height', p. 17.
34. Scott, *Lives of Things*, p. 101.
35. Ibid. p. 104.
36. Ibid. p. 110.
37. Merleau-Ponty, *Phenomenology of Perception*, p. 4.
38. Levinas, *Totality and Infinity*, p. 251.
39. Scott, *Lives of Things*, p. 111.
40. Merleau-Ponty, *Phenomenology of Perception*, p. 54.
41. Serres, *Parasite*, p. 89.
42. Serres, *Troubadour of Knowledge*, pp. 118–19.
43. Ibid. p. 119.
44. Kant, 'On a Supposed Right to Lie from Philanthropy', pp. 611–15 [8:425–30]. Page numbers in brackets refer to those of the Akademie Edition.
45. Ibid. p. 613 [8:427].
46. Ibid.
47. Serres, *Troubadour of Knowledge*, p. 119.
48. Williams, 'Morality, the Peculiar Institution', p. 174.

Chapter 7

1. Waldenfels, 'Responsive Ethik', p. 78.
2. Kant, *Groundwork*, p. 58 [4:403–4].
3. Aquinas, *Summa Theologica*, I–II, q. 90, a. 1.
4. Nancy, *Birth to Presence*, p. 44.
5. Nancy, *Finite Thinking*, p. 141.
6. Barbeyrac, 'Jugement d'un Anonyme', p. 250. Emphasis mine.
7. Kant, *Groundwork*, p. 69 [4:416].
8. Ibid.
9. Korsgaard, *Sources of Normativity*, p. 93.
10. Kant, *Critique of Practical Reason*, p. 164 [5:31].
11. Caputo, *Against Ethics*, p. 37.

12. Ibid. p. 22.
13. Ibid. p. 21.
14. Ibid. p. 37.
15. Ibid. pp. 6–7.
16. Ibid. pp. 26–7.
17. Scott, *Lives of Things*, p. 182.
18. Scott, *Living with Indifference*, pp. 43, 44.

Bibliography

Allison, Henry E., *Kant's Groundwork for the Metaphysics of Morals: A Commentary* (Oxford: Oxford University Press, 2011).

Allison, Henry E., *Kant's Theory of Freedom* (Cambridge: Cambridge University Press, 1990).

Allison, Henry E., *Kant's Transcendental Idealism*, revised and enlarged edn (New Haven, CT: Yale University Press, 2004).

Aquinas, Thomas, *Summa Theologica: First Part of the Second Part*, trans. The English Dominican Friars (Los Angeles: Viewforth Press, 2012).

Aristotle, *The Nicomachean Ethics*, in *The Complete Works of Aristotle*, vol. II, ed. Jonathan Barnes (Princeton, NJ: Princeton University Press, 1984).

Assad, Maria L., *Reading with Michel Serres: An Encounter with Time* (Albany, NY: State University of New York Press, 1999).

Ayer, A. J., *Language, Truth and Logic* (New York: Dover Publications, 1952).

Balguy, John, *The Foundation of Moral Goodness: Or a Further Inquiry into the Original of our Idea of Virtue* (London: John Pemberton, 1728).

Barbaras, Renaud, *The Being of the Phenomenon: Merleau-Ponty's Ontology*, trans. Ted Toadvine and Leonard Lawlor (Bloomington: Indiana University Press, 2004).

Barbeyrac, Jean, 'Jugement d'un Anonyme sur L'Original de cet Abregé, avec des Réfléxions du Traducteur', in Samuel Pufendorf, *Les Devoirs de L'Homme et du Citoyen, Tel Qu'ils lui sont Prescrits par la Loi Naturelle*, trans. Jean Barbeyrac (London: Jean Nourse, 1741), pp. 193–280.

Barthes, Roland, *Elements of Semiology*, trans. Annette Lavers and Colin Smith (New York: Hill and Wang, 1977).

Beck, Lewis White, *Studies in the Philosophy of Kant* (Indianapolis: Bobbs-Merrill, 1965).

Benveniste, Émile, *Problems in General Linguistics*, trans. Mary Elizabeth Meek (Coral Gables, FL: University of Miami Press, 1971).

Bittner, Rüdiger, *What Reason Demands*, trans. Theodore Talbot (Cambridge: Cambridge University Press, 1989).

Caputo, John D., *Against Ethics: Contributions to a Poetics of Obligation with Constant Reference to Deconstruction* (Bloomington: Indiana University Press, 1993).

Carroll, Lewis, *Through the Looking Glass*, in *The Complete Works of Lewis Carroll* (New York: Barnes and Noble Books, 2001), pp. 126–456.

Chalier, Catherine, *What Ought I to Do?: Morality in Kant and Levinas*, trans. Jane Marie Todd (Ithaca, NY: Cornell University Press, 2002).

Chandler, Daniel, *The Transmission Model of Communication*, <http://www.aber.ac.uk/media/Documents/short/trans.html> (accessed 3 July 2014).

Clarke, Samuel, *A Discourse Concerning the Unchangeable Obligations of Natural Religion and The Truth and Certainty of the Christian Revelation*, in *The Works of Samuel Clarke, Vol. II* (London: John and Paul Knapton, 1738), pp. 580–733.

Coles, Robert, *Simone Weil: A Modern Pilgrimage* (Woodstock, VT: SkyLight Paths, 2001).

Cudworth, Ralph, *A Treatise Concerning Eternal and Immutable Morality: With a Treatise of Freewill*, ed. Sarah Hutton (Cambridge: Cambridge University Press, 1996).

Cumberland, Richard, *A Treatise of the Laws of Nature*, trans. John Maxwell, ed. Jon Parkin (Indianapolis: Liberty Fund, 2005).

Darwall, Stephen, *The British Moralists and the Internal 'Ought': 1640–1740* (Cambridge: Cambridge University Press, 1995).

Darwall, Stephen, 'Pufendorf on Morality, Sociability, and Moral Powers', *Journal of the History of Philosophy*, 50: 2 (2012), pp. 213–38.

Darwall, Stephen, *The Second-Person Standpoint: Morality, Respect, and Accountability* (Cambridge, MA: Harvard University Press, 2006).

Deere, Michael A., 'Gappiness in Dimensional Accounts', *Epoché: A Journal for the History of Philosophy*, 17: 1 (2012), pp. 123–42.

Deleuze, Gilles, *The Logic of Sense*, ed. Constantin V. Boundas, trans. Mark Lester with Charles Stivale (New York: Columbia University Press, 1990).

Descartes, René, *The Philosophical Writings of Descartes*, vol. II, trans. John Cottingham, Robert Stoothoff, and Dugald Murdoch (Cambridge: Cambridge University Press, 1985).

Descartes, René, *Principles of Philosophy*, in *Philosophical Essays and Correspondence*, ed. Roger Ariew (Indianapolis: Hackett, 2000).

Diogenes Laertius, *Lives of Eminent Philosophers, Vol. II*, trans. R. D. Hicks (London: William Heinemann, 1925).

Fodor, Jerry, *In Critical Condition* (Cambridge, MA: MIT Press, 1998).

Forsyth, Murray, 'The Place of Richard Cumberland in the History of Natural Law Doctrine', *Journal of the History of Philosophy*, 20: 1 (1982), pp. 23–42.

Foultier, Anna Petronella, 'Merleau-Ponty's Encounter with Saussure's Linguistics: Misreading, Reinterpretation, or Prolongation?', *Chiasmi International*, 15 (2013), pp. 129–50.

Gherardi, Evaristo, *Le Theatre Italien de Gherardi, ou le recueil de toutes les Comedies & Scenes Françoises jouées par les Comediens Italiens du Roy, pendant tout le temps qu'ils ont été au Service. Enrichi d'Estampes en Taille-douce ... à la fin de laquelle tous les Airs qu'on y a chantez se trouvent gravez notez, avec leur Basse-continue chiffrée*, vol. 1 (Paris: Jean-Bapt. Cusson et Pierre Witte, 1700).

Goldstein, Kurt and O. Rosenthal, 'Zur Problem der Wirkung der Farben auf den Organismus', *Schweizer Archiv für Neurologie und Psychiatrie*, 26: 1 (1930), pp. 3–26.

Grotius, Hugo, *The Rights of War and Peace*, Book I, ed. Richard Tuck (Indianapolis: Liberty Fund, 2005).

Grotius, Hugo, *The Rights of War and Peace*, Book III, ed. Richard Tuck (Indianapolis: Liberty Fund, 2005).

Guyer, Paul, 'Naturalistic and Transcendental Moments in Kant's Moral Philosophy', *Inquiry*, 50: 5 (2007), pp. 444–64.

Hegel, G. W. F., *Hegel's Aesthetics: Lectures on Fine Art*, vol. 1, trans. T. M. Knox (Oxford: Oxford University Press, 1975).

Hegel, G. W. F., *Hegel's Phenomenology of Spirit*, trans. A. V. Miller (Oxford: Oxford University Press, 1977).

Hegel, G. W. F., *Hegel's Science of Logic*, trans. A. V. Miller (Atlantic Highlands, NJ: Humanities Press, 1969).

Hegel, G. W. F., *Lectures on the History of Philosophy, Vol. 3*, trans. E. S. Haldane and Frances H. Simpson (Atlantic Highlands, NJ: Humanities Press, 1974).

Hobbes, Thomas, *De Cive: The English Version*, ed. Howard Warrender (Oxford: Oxford University Press, 1984).

Hobbes, Thomas, *Leviathan*, ed. Edwin Curley (Indianapolis: Hackett, 1994).

Holbach, Paul Henri Thiry, Baron d', *La Morale Universelle, ou Les Devoirs de l'Homme Fondés sur sa Nature* (Paris: Masson et Fils, 1820).

Horace, *The Art of Poetry of Horace*, trans. Daniel Bagot (Edinburgh: William Blackwood and Sons, 1880).

Hume, David, *An Enquiry Concerning the Principles of Morals: A Critical Edition* (Oxford: Oxford University Press, 1998).

Hume, David, *A Treatise of Human Nature: A Critical Edition*, ed. David Fate Norton and Mary J. Norton (Oxford: Oxford University Press, 2007).

Husserl, Edmund, *Cartesian Meditations: An Introduction to Phenomenology*, trans. Dorion Cairns (The Hague: Martinus Nijhoff, 1960).

Hutcheson, Francis, *An Essay on the Nature and Conduct of the Passions and Affections with Illustrations on the Moral Sense* in *Collected Works of Francis Hutcheson, Vol. II* (Hildesheim: Georg Olms Verlagsbuchhandlung, 1971).

Hutcheson, Francis, *An Inquiry into the Original of our Ideas of Beauty and Virtue*, in *Collected Works of Francis Hutcheson, Vol. I* (Hildesheim: Georg Olms Verlagsbuchhandlung, 1971).

Ilting, K.-H., 'The Naturalistic Fallacy in Kant', in Lewis White Beck (ed.), *Proceedings of the Third International Kant Congress* (Dordrecht: D. Reidel, 1972), pp. 105–20.

Irwin, Terence, *The Development of Ethics: A Historical and Critical Study, Volume II: From Suarez to Rousseau* (Oxford: Oxford University Press, 2008).

Jackson, Gabrielle Bennet, 'Skill and the Critique of Descartes in Gilbert Ryle and Maurice Merleau-Ponty', in Kascha Semonovitch and Neal DeRoo (eds), *Merleau-Ponty at the Limits of Art, Religion, and Perception* (London: Continuum, 2010), pp. 63–78.

Jakobson, Roman, *Six Lectures on Sound and Meaning*, trans. John Mepham (Cambridge, MA: MIT Press, 1978).

Kant, Immanuel, *Anthropology from a Pragmatic Point of View*, in *Anthropology, History and Education*, The Cambridge Edition of the Works of Immanuel Kant, ed. Günter Zöller and Robert B. Louden (Cambridge: Cambridge University Press, 2007), pp. 227–429.

Kant, Immanuel, *Critique of Practical Reason*, in *Practical Philosophy*, The Cambridge Edition of the Works of Immanuel Kant, trans. and ed. Mary J. Gregor (Cambridge: Cambridge University Press, 1996), pp. 173–272.

Kant, Immanuel, *Critique of Pure Reason*, The Cambridge Edition of the Works of Immanuel Kant, ed. and trans. Paul Guyer and Allen W. Wood (Cambridge: Cambridge University Press, 1998).

Kant, Immanuel, *Groundwork of the Metaphysics of Morals*, in *Practical Philosophy*, The Cambridge Edition of the Works of Immanuel Kant, trans. and ed. Mary J. Gregor (Cambridge: Cambridge University Press, 1996), pp. 37–108.

Kant, Immanuel, *Lectures on Ethics*, The Cambridge Edition of the Works of Immanuel Kant, ed. Peter Heath and J. B. Schneewind, trans. Peter Heath (Cambridge: Cambridge University Press, 1997).

Kant, Immanuel, *The Metaphysics of Morals*, in *Practical Philosophy*, The Cambridge Edition of the Works of Immanuel Kant, trans. and ed. Mary J. Gregor (Cambridge: Cambridge University Press, 1996), pp. 353–604.

Kant, Immanuel, *Notes and Fragments*, The Cambridge Edition of the Works of Immanuel Kant, ed. Paul Guyer, trans. Curtis Bowman, Paul Guyer, and Frederick Rauscher (Cambridge: Cambridge University Press, 2005).

Kant, Immanuel, 'On a Supposed Right to Lie from Philanthropy', in *Practical Philosophy*, The Cambridge Edition of the Works of Immanuel Kant, trans. and ed. Mary J. Gregor (Cambridge: Cambridge University Press, 1996), pp. 605–16.

Kelly, Sean D., 'The Normative Nature of Perceptual Experience', in Bence Nanay (ed.), *Perceiving the World* (Oxford: Oxford University Press, 2010), pp. 146–59.

Korsgaard, Christine M., *The Sources of Normativity* (Cambridge: Cambridge University Press, 1996).

Koukal, D. R., 'Merleau-Ponty's Reform of Saussure: Linguistic Innovation and the Practice of Phenomenology', *The Southern Journal of Philosophy*, 38: 4 (2000), pp. 519–617.

Lacoue-Labarthe, Philippe and Jean-Luc Nancy, *Retreating the Political*, ed. Simon Sparks (London: Routledge, 1997).

La Fontaine, Jean, *Fables*, ed. Antoine Adam (Paris: Garnier-Flammarion, 1966).

Lagueux, Maurice, 'Merleau-Ponty et la linguistique de Saussure', *Dialogue: Canadian Philosophical Review*, 4: 3 (1965), pp. 351–64.

Landes, Donald A., *Merleau-Ponty and the Paradoxes of Expression* (London: Bloomsbury, 2013).

Leibniz, Gottfried Wilhelm, *Discourse on Metaphysics and Other Essays*, trans. Daniel Garber and Roger Ariew (Indianapolis: Hackett, 1991).

Leibniz, Gottfried Wilhelm, *Leibniz: Political Writings*, 2nd edn, trans. and ed. Patrick Riley (Cambridge: Cambridge University Press, 1988).

Leibniz, Gottfried Wilhelm, 'Meditation on the Common Concept of Justice', in *Leibniz: Political Writings*, 2nd edn, trans. and ed. Patrick Riley (Cambridge: Cambridge University Press, 1988), pp. 45–63.

Leibniz, Gottfried Wilhelm, *Theodicy: Essays on the Goodness of God, the Freedom of Man, and the Origin of Evil*, trans. E. M. Huggard (La Salle, IL: Open Court Press, 1985).

Levinas, Emmanuel, *Totality and Infinity: An Essay on Exteriority*, trans. Alphonso Lingis (Dordrecht: Kluwer Academic, 1991).

Levinas, Emmanuel, 'Transcendence and Height', in *Basic Philosophical Writings*, ed. Adriaan T. Peperzak, Simon Critchley, and Robert Bernasconi (Bloomington: Indiana University Press, 1996), pp. 11–32.

Lingis, Alphonso, *The Imperative* (Bloomington: Indiana University Press, 1998).

Locke, John, *An Essay Concerning Human Understanding*, ed. Peter H. Nidditch (Oxford: Oxford University Press, 1979).

Locke, John, *Essays on the Law of Nature: The Latin Text with a Translation, Introduction and Notes, Together with Transcripts of Locke's Shorthand in his Journal for 1676*, ed. W. von Leyden (Oxford: Oxford University Press, 1954).

Lueck, Bryan, 'Alterity in Merleau-Ponty's *Prose of the World*', *Epoché: A Journal for the History of Philosophy*, 16: 2 (2012), pp. 424–42.

Lueck, Bryan, 'Dignity at the Limit: Jean-Luc Nancy on the Possibility of Incommensurable Worth', *Continental Philosophy Review*, 49: 3 (2016), pp. 309–23.

Lueck, Bryan, 'Exposition and Obligation: A Serresian Account of Moral Sensitivity', *Symposium: Canadian Journal of Continental Philosophy*, 18: 1 (2014), pp. 176–93.

Lueck, Bryan, 'A Fact, As It Were: Obligation, Indifference, and the Question of Ethics', *Epoché: A Journal for the History of Philosophy*, 21: 1 (2016), pp. 219–34.

Lueck, Bryan, 'Kant's Fact of Reason as Source of Normativity', *Inquiry: An Interdisciplinary Journal of Philosophy*, 52: 6 (2009), pp. 596–608.

Lueck, Bryan, 'The Terrifying Concupiscence of Belonging: Noise and Evil in the Work of Michel Serres', *Symposium: Canadian Journal of Continental Philosophy*, 19: 1 (2015), pp. 249–67.

Lueck, Bryan, 'Toward a Serresian Reconceptualization of Kantian Respect', *Philosophy Today*, 52: 1 (2008), pp. 52–9.

Łuków, Paweł, 'The Fact of Reason: Kant's Passage to Ordinary Moral Knowledge', *Kant-Studien*, 84: 2 (1993), pp. 204–21.

Luther, Martin, *The Bondage of the Will*, trans. J. I. Packer and O. R. Johnston (Westwood, NJ: Fleming H. Revell, 1957).

MacIntyre, Alasdair, 'Is Patriotism a Virtue?', in Derek Matravers and Jon Pike (eds), *Debates in Contemporary Political Philosophy: An Anthology* (London: Routledge, 2003), pp. 286–300.

Malebranche, Nicolas, *The Search after Truth: With Elucidations of The Search after Truth*, trans. and ed. Thomas M. Lennon and Paul J. Olscamp (Cambridge: Cambridge University Press, 1997).

Malebranche, Nicolas, *Treatise on Ethics*, trans. Craig Walton (Dordrecht: Kluwer, 1992).

Merleau-Ponty, Maurice, *Consciousness and the Acquisition of Language*, trans. Hugh J. Silverman (Evanston, IL: Northwestern University Press, 1979).

Merleau-Ponty, Maurice, *Phenomenology of Perception*, trans. Donald Landes (London: Routledge, 2012).

Merleau-Ponty, Maurice, *The Primacy of Perception*, ed. James M. Edie (Evanston, IL: Northwestern University Press, 1964).

Merleau-Ponty, Maurice, *The Prose of the World*, ed. Claude Lefort, trans. John O'Neill (Evanston, IL: Northwestern University Press, 1973).

Merleau-Ponty, Maurice, *Sense and Non-Sense*, trans. Hubert L. Dreyfus and Patricia Allen Dreyfus (Evanston, IL: Northwestern University Press, 1964).

Merleau-Ponty, Maurice, *Signs*, trans. Richard C. McCleary (Evanston, IL: Northwestern University Press, 1964).

Merleau-Ponty, Maurice, *Themes from the Lectures at the Collège de France 1952–1960*, trans. John O'Neill (Evanston, IL: Northwestern University Press, 1970).

Merleau-Ponty, Maurice, *The Visible and the Invisible*, trans. Alphonso Lingis (Evanston, IL: Northwestern University Press, 1968).

Morin, Marie-Eve, *Jean-Luc Nancy* (Cambridge: Polity Press, 2012).

Nancy, Jean-Luc, *Being Singular Plural*, trans. Robert D. Richardson and Anne E. O'Byrne (Stanford, CA: Stanford University Press, 2000).

Nancy, Jean-Luc, *The Birth to Presence*, trans. Brian Holmes and others (Stanford, CA: Stanford University Press, 1993).

Nancy, Jean-Luc, *The Creation of the World or Globalization*, trans. François Raffoul and David Pettigrew (Albany, NY: State University of New York Press, 2007).

Nancy, Jean-Luc, *A Finite Thinking*, ed. Simon Sparks (Stanford, CA: Stanford University Press, 2003).

Nancy, Jean-Luc, *The Gravity of Thought*, trans. François Raffoul and Gregory Recco (Amherst, NY: Humanity Books, 1997).

Nancy, Jean-Luc, *Hegel: The Restlessness of the Negative*, trans. Jason Smith and Steven Miller (Minneapolis: University of Minnesota Press, 2002).

Nancy, Jean-Luc, *The Sense of the World*, trans. Jeffrey S. Librett (Minneapolis: University of Minnesota Press, 1997).

Nuzzo, Angelica, *Ideal Embodiment: Kant's Theory of Sensibility* (Bloomington: Indiana University Press, 2008).

Perrin, Joseph-Marie and Gustave Thibon, *Simone Weil as We Knew Her*, trans. Emma Craufurd (London: Routledge, 2003).

Pétrement, Simone, *Simone Weil: A Life*, trans. Raymond Rosenthal (New York: Schocken Books, 1976).

Pierce, John R., *Symbols, Signals, and Noise: The Nature and Process of Communication* (London: Hutchinson, 1962).

Pufendorf, Samuel, *De Jure Naturae et Gentium Libri Octo*, trans. C. H. Oldfather and W. A. Oldfather (London: Wiley & Sons, 1964).

Pufendorf, Samuel, *On the Duty of Man and Citizen According to Natural Law*, ed. James Tully, trans. Michael Silverthorne (Cambridge: Cambridge University Press, 1991).

Putnam, Hilary, *Realism with a Human Face*, ed. James Conant (Cambridge, MA: Harvard University Press, 1990).

Raffoul, François, 'Abandonment and the Categorical Imperative of Being', in Benjamin Hutchens (ed.), *Jean-Luc Nancy: Justice, Legality and World* (London: Bloomsbury, 2013), pp. 65–81.

Raffoul, François, 'The Creation of the World', in Peter Gratton and Marie-Eve Morin (eds), *Jean-Luc Nancy and Plural Thinking: Expositions of World, Ontology, Politics, and Sense* (Albany, NY: State University of New York Press, 2012), pp. 13–26.

Rawls, John, 'Kantian Constructivism in Moral Theory', *Journal of Philosophy*, 77: 9 (1980), pp. 515–72.

Rawls, John, *Lectures on the History of Moral Philosophy*, ed. Barbara Herman (Cambridge, MA: Harvard University Press, 2000).

Reinhold, Karl Leonhard, *Briefe über die Kantische Philosophie, Zweyter Band* (Leipzig: Georg Joachim Göschen, 1792).

Ricoeur, Paul, *The Conflict of Interpretations*, ed. Don Ihde (Evanston, IL: Northwestern University Press, 1974).

Saint Leo the Great, *Sermons*, trans. Jane Patricia Freeland and Agnes Josephine Conway (Washington, DC: The Catholic University of America Press, 1996).

Sartre, Jean-Paul, *Essays in Existentialism* (New York: Citadel Press, 1965).

Saussure, Ferdinand de, *Course in General Linguistics*, trans. Roy Harris (Chicago: Open Court, 1986).

Schmidt, James, *Maurice Merleau-Ponty: Between Phenomenology and Structuralism* (Basingstoke: Macmillan, 1985).

Schneewind, Jerome B., *The Invention of Autonomy: A History of Modern Moral Philosophy* (Cambridge: Cambridge University Press, 1998).

Schneewind, Jerome B. (ed.), *Moral Philosophy from Montaigne to Kant* (Cambridge: Cambridge University Press, 2003).

Schopenhauer, Arthur, *On the Basis of Morality*, trans. E. F. J. Payne (Indianapolis: Bobbs-Merrill, 1965).

Schroeder, Mark, 'Cudworth and Normative Explanations', *Journal of Ethics and Social Philosophy*, 1: 3 (2005), pp. 1–27.

Scott, Charles E., *On the Advantages and Disadvantages of Ethics and Politics* (Bloomington: Indiana University Press, 1996).

Scott, Charles E., *The Lives of Things* (Bloomington: Indiana University Press, 2002).

Scott, Charles E., *Living with Indifference* (Bloomington: Indiana University Press, 2007).

Serres, Michel, *Angels: A Modern Myth*, trans. Francis Cowper (Paris: Flammarion, 1995).

Serres, Michel, *Detachment*, trans. Geneviève James and Raymond Federman (Athens, OH: Ohio University Press, 1989).

Serres, Michel, *Genesis*, trans. Geneviève James and James Nielson (Ann Arbor: University of Michigan Press, 1995).

Serres, Michel, *Hermès I: La Communication* (Paris: Éditions de Minuit, 1969).

Serres, Michel, *La Guerre Mondiale* (Paris: Éditions Le Pommier, 2008).

Serres, Michel, *L'Incandescent* (Paris: Éditions Le Pommier, 2003).

Serres, Michel, *Malfeasance: Appropriation Through Pollution?*, trans. Anne-Marie Feenberg-Dibon (Stanford, CA: Stanford University Press, 2011).

Serres, Michel, *The Parasite*, trans. Lawrence R. Schehr (Minneapolis: University of Minnesota Press, 2007).

Serres, Michel, *Rameaux* (Paris: Éditions Le Pommier, 2004).

Serres, Michel, *The Troubadour of Knowledge*, trans. Sheila Faria Glaser with William Paulson (Ann Arbor: University of Michigan Press, 1997).

Shannon, Claude E. and Warren Weaver, *The Mathematical Theory of Communication* (Urbana-Champaign: University of Illinois Press, 1949).

Sidgwick, Henry, *The Methods of Ethics*, 7th edn (Indianapolis: Hackett, 1981).

Silverman, Hugh J., *Inscriptions: Between Phenomenology and Structuralism* (New York: Routledge & Kegan Paul, 1987).

Smart, J. J. C., 'An Outline of a System of Utilitarian Ethics', in J. J. C. Smart and Bernard Williams, *Utilitarianism For and Against* (Cambridge: Cambridge University Press, 1973), pp. 3–74.

Stevenson, Charles L., *Language and Ethics* (New Haven, CT: Yale University Press, 1944).

Stockhausen, Karlheinz, *Hymnen Electronic and Concrete Music*, CD (Kürten: Stockhausen Verlag – Stockhausen 10, 1995).

Suarez, Francisco, *De Legibus, Ac Deo Legislatore*, in *Selections from Three Works*, trans. Gwladys L. Williams, Ammi Brown, and John Waldron (Oxford: Clarendon Press, 1944).

Thibault, Paul J., *Re-reading Saussure: The Dynamics of Signs in Social Life* (London: Routledge, 1996).

Timmermann, Jens, *Kant's* Groundwork of the Metaphysics of Morals*: A Commentary* (Cambridge: Cambridge University Press, 2007).

Waldenfels, Bernhard, *Antwortregister* (Frankfurt am Main: Suhrkamp Verlag, 1994).

Waldenfels, Bernhard, 'Responsive Ethik zwischen Antwort und Verantwortung', *Deutsche Zeitschrift für Philosophie*, 58: 1 (2010), pp. 71–81.

Watkins, John N. W., *Hobbes's System of Ideas: A Study in the Political Significance of Philosophical Theories* (London: Hutchinson, 1973).

Williams, Bernard, 'Morality, the Peculiar Institution', in *Ethics and the Limits of Philosophy* (Cambridge, MA: Harvard University Press, 1985), pp. 174–96.

Wolff, Christian, *Vernünftige Gedanken von der Menschen Thun und Lassen, zu Beförderung ihrer Glückseeligkeit*, in *Gesammelte Werke, Band 4* (Hildesheim: Georg Olms Verlag, 1976).

Index